LIMA-6

LIMA-6

A MARINE COMPANY COMMANDER IN VIETNAM JUNE 1967–JANUARY 1968

Colonel Richard D. Camp, Jr., USMC (Ret)

with Eric Hammel

ATHENEUM   NEW YORK   1989

Atheneum
Macmillan Publishing Company
866 Third Avenue, New York, N.Y. 10022
Collier Macmillan Canada, Inc.

LIBRARY OF CONGRESS CATALOGING-IN-PUBLISHING DATA

Camp, Richard D.
LIMA-6 : a Marine Company commander in Vietnam, June 1967–January 1968 / Richard D. Camp, Jr. with Eric Hammel.
   p.   cm.
Includes index.
ISBN 0–689–12045–1
1. Vietnamese Conflict, 1961–1975—Personal narratives, American. 2. Vietnamese Conflict, 1961–1975—Regimental histories—United States. 3. United States. Marine Corps. Marines, 26th. Battalion, 3rd. Lima Company—History. 4. Camp, Richard D. I. Hammel, Eric M. II. Lima-Six. III. Title.
DS559.5.C35   1989   89–6967
959.704′342—dc20   CIP

Macmillan books are available at special discounts for bulk purchases for sales promotions, premiums, fund-raising, or educational use. For details, contact:

Special Sales Director
Macmillan Publishing Company
866 Third Avenue
New York, N.Y. 10022

Designed by Beth Tondreau Design/Jane Treuhaft
10 9 8 7 6 5 4 3 2 1
Printed in the United States of America

*TO ALL THE MARINES AND CORPSMEN,
LIVING AND DEAD, OF LIMA COMPANY,
3RD BATTALION, 26TH MARINES*

*AND TO MY FAMILY,
MARJORIE, KATHERINE, AND CHIP
MOM, DAD, DONNIE, AND BEVERLY*

C O N T E N T S

I L L U S T R A T I O N S

Lance Corporal Terry Smith

A dozen Lima Company survivors of the September 10 battle south of Con Thien

Between pages 204 and 205

The Lima Company 60mm mortar section undergoing instruction at the Seabee Rock Crusher in mid September 1967

A Lima Company platoon during a prepatrol brief at the Seabee Rock Crusher

Lima Company lived in these Southeast Asia huts at the Rock Crusher

One of the awful bunkers built by the Seabees at the Rock Crusher

A punji pit uncovered by a Lima Company patrol near a hostile village near Camp Evans in early November 1967

Routine sweep through a hostile village

The mine crater on the roadway between the two kneeling Marines is where Lance Corporal Smith was mortally wounded

Sergeant Ric Bender with the CAR-15 carbine

Lima Company Marines inspect the body of one of the NVA officers killed by Lieutenant Nile Buffington's 1st Platoon on January 2, 1968

All five of the dead NVA officers after they were brought in from in front of the Lima Company's lines

Khe Sanh Combat Base from the air, looking north

The Lima Company lines before the siege, in December 1967

The Lima Company CP tent before the siege

Marine sharpshooters stalk NVA from the combat base trenchline

Captain Richard D. Camp, Jr., USMC

GUIDE TO TERMS AND ABBREVIATIONS

A-4   Douglas Skyhawk jet attack bomber
AD   Douglas Skyraider propeller-driven attack bomber
AK-47   Soviet-pattern 7.62mm assault rifle
ALO   air liaison officer
AO   aerial observer
amtrac   amphibious tractor
Arclight   B-52 high-altitude bombing program
arty   artillery
ARVN   Army of the Republic of Vietnam

B-40   Soviet-pattern rocket-propelled grenade
B-52   Boeing Stratofortress jet heavy bomber
BAS   battalion aid station
Bird Dog   artillery/air observation aircraft
boondockers   boots

C4   plastic explosive compound
C-123   Fairchild Provider medium cargo transport
C-130   Lockheed Hercules medium cargo transport
CAC   Marine combined action company
CAP   Marine combined action platoon
CAR-15   U.S. Army 5.56mm carbine
CH-46   Boeing Sea Knight medium cargo helicopter
CH-53   Sikorsky Sea Stallion heavy cargo helicopter
Chicom   Chinese Communist hand grenade
chopper   helicopter
Claymore   U.S. directional antipersonnel mine
CO   commanding officer
COC   combat operations center
corpsman   U.S. Navy medical aidman
cover   hat
CP   command post

DMZ   demilitarized zone
doc   corpsman
duster   U.S. Army tracked dual-40mm antiaircraft gun carrier

E-tool	entrenching tool
exec	executive officer
F-4B	McDonnell Phantom jet fighter-bomber
FAC	forward air controller
fast mover	jet
FDC	fire direction center
Five	executive officer
fixed wing	winged airplane (i.e., not a helicopter)
FO	artillery forward observer
FOB	forward operating base (U.S. Army Special Forces)
G-1	division/corps personnel officer
GP	general purpose (tent)
grunt	infantryman
gunny	gunnery sergeant
H&I	harrassment-and-interdiction
H&S	headquarters-and-service
H-34	Sikorsky Sea Horse medium transport helicopter
helo	helicopter
hooch	living quarters
Howtar	U.S. 107mm towed heavy mortar
HST	helicopter support team
Huey	Bell UH-1E light attack/transport helicopter
illume	illumination
KIA	killed in action
klick	kilometer
LAAW	light antitank assault weapon
LP	listening post
LZ	landing zone
M2	U.S. World War II-vintage .30-caliber carbine
M-14	U.S. 7.62mm rifle
M-16	U.S. 5.56mm rifle
M-26	U.S. hand grenade
M-48	U.S. medium 90mm gun tank
M-60	U.S. 7.62mm medium machine gun
M-79	U.S. 40mm grenade launcher

MACV	Military Assistance Command, Vietnam
medevac	medical evacuation
MIA	missing in action
montagnards	non-Vietnamese tribal peoples living in Vietnam
MP	military police
MSR	main supply route
NCO	non-commissioned officer
noncom	non-commissioned officer
NVA	North Vietnamese Army
Old Man	commanding officer, usually battalion commander
One	adjutant or 1st Platoon commander
Ontos	U.S. tracked 106mm recoilless-rifle carrier
PCV	Provisional Corps, Vietnam
PRU	provisional reconnaisance unit
PT-76	Soviet tracked amphibious reconnaissance vehicle
Phantom	McDonnell F-4B jet fighter-bomber
psy ops	psychological operations (propaganda)
Puff	AC-47 propeller-driven gunship airplane; same as Spooky
punji	sharpened bamboo stake or trap
R&R	rest-and-rehabiltation leave
RPG	Soviet-pattern B-40 rocket-propelled grenade
S-1	battalion/regimental adjutant
S-2	battalion/regimental intelligence officer
S-3	battalion/regimental operations officer
S-3A	battalion/regimental assistant operations officer
S-4	battalion/regimental logistics officer
scuttlebutt	rumor
Seabee	U.S. Navy construction engineer
SEA Hut	Southeast Asia living quarters
Six	commanding officer
skipper	commanding officer; any Marine captain
Skyraider	Douglas AD propeller-driven attack bomber
SKS	Soviet-pattern 7.62mm bolt-action carbine
SOP	standard operating procedure
Spooky	AC-47 propeller-driven gunship airplane; same as Puff
stick	paratroopers in one jump team
survey	discard

TACP	tactical air-control party
tac	tactical
Three	operations officer or 3rd Platoon commander
3-Alpha	assistant operations officer
top	master sergeant, master gunnery sergeant, or first sergeant
UH-1E	Bell Huey light attack/transport helicopter
VC	Viet Cong
WIA	wounded in action
water buffalo	portable water tank
willy-pete	WP (i.e., waterproof or white phosphorous)
zippo	M-48 flame tank

PHONETIC ALPHABET

Alpha	November
Bravo	Oscar
Charlie	Papa
Delta	Quebec
Echo	Romeo
Foxtrot	Sierra
Golf	Tango
Hotel	Uniform
India	Victor
Juliet	Whiskey
Kilo	X-Ray
Lima	Yankee
Mike	Zulu

INTRODUCTION

Dick Camp's narrative is a gift of pure gold for anyone who serves or will serve in the armed services of the world, particularly those whose interest is ground combat. The precision with which the many combat scenes are portrayed has rarely been equaled in my memory.

In the absence of actual experience in war, warriors have no better way to prepare themselves than through study of the experiences of others. Regrettably, too few narratives are written with such detailed descriptions of combat action day in and day out as the author has achieved here.

Study of the actions portrayed in this book should be done in context of the time and place where they occurred. The Vietnam War was in a special phase—the North Vietnamese had totally committed their army to the fray while the United States was still in the process of a slow build up. Our forces were inadequate for the achievement of the victories which would be ours in the years to follow, 1968 and 1969. The withholding of the Ready Reserves along with the limitation placed on funding resulted in a delay of three and a half years, which were required to draft personnel and build from scratch units needed to replace the Ready Reserves—units essential for sustaining our Regular Army and Marine divisions in combat. This slow build up of forces was the main cause for the eventual disaster in Vietnam.

The Lima Company story portrays times in the Vietnam War at their lowest ebb. Instead of attacking the enemy, we were on the defensive; instead of providing security for the countryside, we were "sweeping," doing "search and destroy," trying in various ways to "win hearts and minds." Our overall success in all these was very limited until we finally got the needed forces into the field.

I hated to put this book down.

> Raymond G. Davis
> General
> U.S. Marine Corps, Retired

SOUTHEAST ASIA

(Official USMC Map)

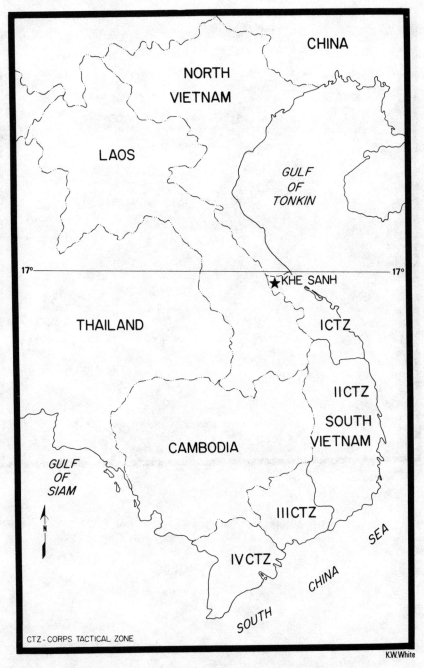

CHINA

NORTH
VIETNAM

LAOS

GULF
OF
TONKIN

17°   17°

★KHE SANH

THAILAND   ICTZ

IICTZ

SOUTH
VIETNAM

CAMBODIA

GULF
OF
SIAM

IIICTZ

N

IVCTZ

SEA

CHINA

SOUTH

CTZ - CORPS TACTICAL ZONE

K.W.White

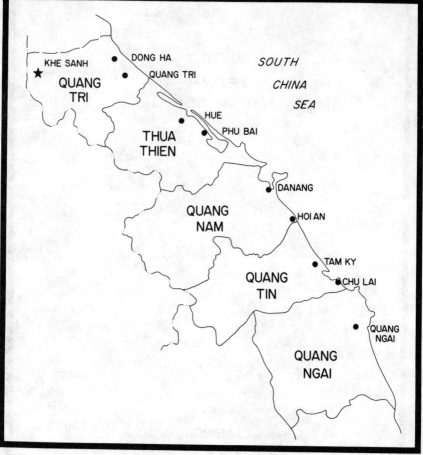

KHE SANH

DONG HA

QUANG TRI

QUANG TRI

SOUTH

CHINA

SEA

HUE

PHU BAI

THUA THIEN

DANANG

QUANG NAM

HOI AN

TAM KY

QUANG TIN

CHU LAI

QUANG NGAI

QUANG NGAI

K.W. White

NORTHERN QUANG TRI PROVINCE

(Official USMC Map)

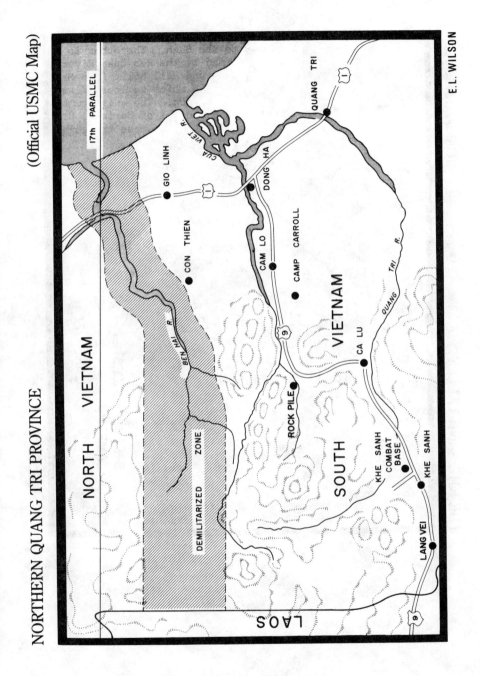

E.L. WILSON

THE KHE SANH VALLEY

(Official USMC Map)

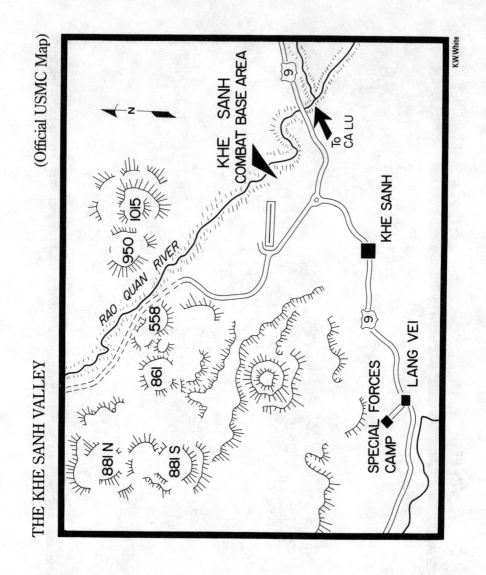

KHE SANH
COMBAT BASE AREA

To
CA LU

9

KHE SANH

9

RAO QUAN RIVER

950 1015

558

861

881 N

881 S

SPECIAL FORCES
CAMP

LANG VEI

N

K.W.White

PART I

THE FIELD

CHAPTER 1

Following a leave at my in-laws' home in Indianapolis, I reported as ordered to Camp Pendleton, California, to attend Reconnaissance Replacement School. At the time—mid 1967—the Reconnaissance Replacement School was designed to familiarize Marine officers and staff noncommissioned officers with current fire-support procedures—artillery, air, and naval gunfire. Though the course was only two weeks in length, being there meant I would be away from home—away from my wife and young daughter—that much longer. But attending the school was the best thing that happened to me professionally. Months later, I had ample reason to think it was a hell of a good school.

I arrived there with Captain Myron Harrington, a friend who had also just left Marine Barracks, Washington, D.C. All the other officers in our course were brand-new second lieutenants, right out of the Basic School, at Quantico. It turned out to be a lot of fun because the lieutenants were enthusiastic and excited and, of course, they looked to Myron and me as being experienced old hands. I got a big lift out of being with them.

We spent the first week at Camp Pendleton reviewing calls for fire and going over artillery procedures. Then we went down to the Landing Forces Training Command, Pacific, at Coronado, in San Diego, which is where the Navy and Marine Corps maintain an indoor naval gunfire target range, a huge computer-driven mechanical trainer designed to allow us to call in nearly authentic naval gunfire missions. Then we ended up back at Camp Pendleton for the aviation portion, in which we coordinated actual air strikes run by fixed-wing jet fighter-bombers whose pilots were no doubt engaged in the air wing's analog to our last-minute infantry training.

The two-week fire- and air-support course got us in the right frame of mind—thinking about fire support—before we even went to Vietnam. I think it was well done as far as it went—big weapons—but it altogether overlooked the importance of familiarizing senior company-grade officers like Myron Harrington and myself with the infantry weapons we would have at our disposal in the companies and battalions to which all infantry officers would eventually be reporting. No doubt, the lieutenants who comprised the bulk of the class had worked with company-level infantry weapons at Quantico, but neither Myron nor I had ever seen an M-16 rifle, nor had I ever seen a 60mm mortar in action. During my last tour in the Fleet Marine Force as a lieutenant, the 60mm mortar sections in my battalion had neither weapons nor the qualified gunners to man them.

After completing the school, most of us traveled up to San Francisco and flew out of nearby Travis Air Force Base. While I was waiting to board the plane, I noticed one lieutenant, a young man, probably five foot eight or five foot nine with very wide shoulders and a squatty body, a very powerful guy. I did not speak with the lieutenant at all on the way to Vietnam, but I noticed him, probably because of his physique.

The flight from Travis Air Force Base to Okinawa was a long one, with just one refueling stop in Alaska. As we got closer to Okinawa, we began getting more excited about the idea of going to war. By then, the trauma of leaving my family had passed; I had been away from Marjorie and Katherine for about three weeks by the time we left California. I was mentally prepared to face what I was going to have to face. I had been a Marine for more than five years and had commanded infantry, reconnaissance, and ceremonial platoons the entire time—two years in the Fleet Marine Force as a rifle platoon commander, a year as a reconnaissance platoon commander, and two years at the Marine Barracks in Washington, D.C., where I was again a platoon commander. I felt really confident of my ability as an officer and as a leader.

The transport plane—a civilian airliner on lease to the Department of Defense—landed in Okinawa and we stayed only long enough to grab a night's sleep and board a C-130 for a straight-in hop to Danang Air Base, in the military sector known as I Corps, the northernmost of the four military regions into which South Vietnam was divided. Danang was a big Marine Corps facility with some Air Force presence.

The first thing that struck me as soon as the crew opened the hatches was the heat. We were all dressed in our heavily starched Stateside utilities, so, as soon as we stepped out into the heat, the starch literally started to melt once the sweat started to get to it. I actually had starch running down my arms and legs. We were immediately identifiable to everybody there as "newbys." Since I was an officer and a captain, I didn't hear many overt comments, but I could *see* the seasoned troops thinking, "Oh boy! I'm glad I don't have as long a time to go over here as he does."

The unbelievable heat and unfamiliar sounds like the incessant, high-pitched whine of jet engines were totally unanticipated. One of the things that really hit me right off the bat, despite my years in the peacetime Marine Corps, was that everybody was carrying *loaded* weapons. That might not sound like much, but it was a shock to me. I had never seen so many Marines carrying loaded weapons, nor so casually.

The arrival scene was a kaleidoscope of different sensations and feelings. I was excited, I was apprehensive, and I was concerned. My mind was racing with unanswerable questions: Am I going to do well? What's going to happen to me? Am I going to get hurt? Will I weather this intact? Will I to make an ass of myself? I was functioning smoothly on the outside, but everything inside was reacting to all the new sights, sounds, and sensations. I kept thinking that I was on new ground, that I was not a bit familiar with the environment, with anything that was going on. I had heard all the stories about the Viet Cong booby-trapping everything. As ready as I had thought myself to be, I honestly did not feel a bit comfortable because I didn't know what the hell was going on.

We were ushered aboard a bus with wire mesh over the windows. That grabbed my attention. It occurred to me right off that the wire was designed to keep hand grenades from being thrown into the bus, and its mere presence just added to my racing thoughts. I kept thinking, "Jesus Christ, you better watch the civilians," but none of us had been issued weapons.

We were driven out to the reception center, a big tin Butler building—prefabricated corrugated steel, and hotter than hell with the sun beating down on it. Inside were stations marked "A," "B," "C," and so forth through the alphabet. We were each told to report in with our orders to a particular station. There was a huge amount of confusion and a lot of yelling: "Is Smith here? Is Jones there? Jones, report here. Smith, report there! Transportation's leaving!"

Most of the men inside were new like me and the few "old salts" working in the center or passing through for one reason or another treated us with superior attitudes—the mindset and body language that told the new arrivals that we were untested. Since I was an officer, the old salts kept their distance, but they still managed to signal their superiority.

All along in the process of getting to Vietnam, there was something in the back of my mind that told me that I was going to go right to an infantry unit. In fact, I just knew that I was going to be an infantry-company commander. I was that confident. The feeling was still with me as I neared the station to which I was called; I was supremely confident.

As I stepped up, the reception clerk said, "Okay, Captain Camp, you're supposed to go to the Third Marine Division, which is located up at Phu Bai."

"That's great!" I had never heard of Phu Bai, so I asked, "Can you tell me where it is?" This was the opening move in a game of Twenty Questions. I was told where Phu Bai was located, but I had to ask how I was supposed to get there. The reception clerk thought the road was closed. How could I find out? He wasn't sure. If the road was open, how could I make arrangements for a ride? I was on my own. Was air transportation available? It might be. If it was, how could I catch a flight? I was on my own. How would the corporal get to Phu Bai if he had orders to report there? He had never flown there; he had no idea. Was there an airfield there? He was not sure if there was a runway or a helicopter pad. Which did he think? He was not sure, but a helo ride was always a safe bet. Where was the nearest helo pad with flights to Phu Bai? There were helo pads right there at Danang and at neighboring Marble Mountain. How do I get there? He pointed out toward the adjacent runway, toward the sound of jet engines and helicopter rotors.

I left the Butler building and started walking toward the nearest helo pad with my seabag on my shoulder, just another sweating, miserable, confused, disoriented, angry captain of Marines in a country, I was sure, full of sweating, miserable captains and passive-aggressive corporals. When I finally reached the flight shack at the helo pad, the staff sergeant manning the desk told me that there were no flights leaving for Phu Bai at least until the next morning.

It was the middle of the afternoon and there was nothing to do. I stepped out of the flight shack and joined up with a large group of officers and Marines standing around in the shade. We were right beside the runway and the noise from the jet engines was unnerving. A few of the Marines, including the powerfully built lieutenant, looked familiar from the flight to Danang, but I didn't know a soul and I was the only captain, so there was no one to talk to beyond exchanging a few observations. Most of the men were dressed in starched utilities, like me, but a few looked broken in—weather-beaten and definitely more at ease. Those old salts were aloof, off to the side, squatting comfortably in the shade while the rest of us stood. I thought of walking off to see what I could see, but I decided to stay where I was in case a flight turned up. Anyway, it was too hot for a walk and there was nowhere to go. I did very little mingling, but I was able to watch the people in the crowd, trying to learn how to react. I saw how the Marines kept their distance from the officers, and vice versa, except for the old salts, who seemed at ease with one another but who continued to display feelings of superiority—uncertainty?—toward the rest of us. I could see that everyone observed me at one time or another, trying to learn what they could without actually speaking to me. There is a certain amount of ceremonial macho attitude associated with such chance minglings. Meanwhile, the little conversation in which I participated had to do with questions and speculations about where we were to sleep or eat.

I noticed that the old salts did not seem to be worried about eating or sleeping so, when they drifted off, I followed them, as did most of the others. They found a mess hall and we all lined up and got served. Then we followed the old salts out to a little tent camp off to the side of the runway. All the tents had sandbags around them, built up to about waist height. That got me to thinking again about an attack. After awhile, I found an empty rack, which I claimed.

It did not seem right to use my rank in that situation so, for the rest of my wait in Danang, I decided, I would play it as one of the boys. I was responsible for no one, and no one was responsible for me. If there was trouble, I only wanted to be around the old salts. I could command them if I had to, but I knew I didn't have their knowledge. I also didn't have a weapon.

The tents were near a major active runway for aircraft going on missions all over the place, and there was a hell of a lot of noise. Even after it got dark, it remained hotter than a bitch. Three June weeks in southern California had by no means acclimated me to the heat and humidity, and the sweat was still pouring off me. I had not had a shower in two days, and I didn't even know whether it was safe to take off my clothes. I had never completely undressed in the field during my years with the Fleet Marine Force, but it had always been okay to remove my boots and shirt. I had no idea what might happen inside an air base that featured buses with meshed windows and sandbagged tents, so I decided to sleep with everything on despite the heat.

I was exhausted. I was still suffering from jet lag and disorientation, and my muscles still ached from the long confinement aboard the airplanes. The heat and sweating were driving me nuts. So were the mosquitoes, which were out in force. The noisy jets took off and landed all night. And my mind wouldn't give in; it just kept cranking out lurid imaginary scenes of a zillion Viet Cong getting ready to overrun the base. I couldn't sleep; I don't think I slept a wink that first night in Vietnam.

I got up the next morning, returned to the mess hall for breakfast, and did all the normal morning things before returning to the flight shack to see about a hop to Phu Bai. They told us that there was nothing going out from the base but that we could catch a bus to another helo pad on the other side of town. On the way, I saw my first Vietnamese plying their business in the busy streets of an utterly alien city. Military vehicles, scooters, bicycles, and uncountable pedestrians created a hubbub I had never experienced in any Stateside city, even New York. After only a short ride, the bus pulled into an enclosed military compound and dropped us off at another helo pad, as advertised.

Helos came and helos went, and the previous day's crowd slowly dwindled as flights were called out for various unheard-of places throughout I Corps. I had not bothered to change into a fresh set of utilities, so the set I had on was soon awash again in sweat and starch. I looked utterly disreputable. I had never felt less squared away, less officerlike. In fact, I felt like shit, pure shit.

At long last, an ancient H-34 cargo helicopter landed on the pad and I stepped forward and shouted at the crew chief the by-then familiar litany, "Phu Bai? Phu Bai!" All of a sudden, the Marine inside the chopper was holding up his thumb, indicating that my ship had come in. I clambered aboard, followed by the five or six other Marines who also were bound for Phu Bai.

It had been several years since my last helicopter ride, which was fine because I never really trusted those birds. The best part—to me, the only good part—was getting up to altitude, where the cooler air overcame the intense morning heat and finally dried off my utilities. I was hoping that Phu Bai was at the end of a long flight, but it was not long enough, given the intense humid heat that greeted my arrival.

As soon as we landed, I used my rank to get directions and a jeep ride straight to the 3rd Marine Division command post. My first assignment out of the Basic School in 1963 had been as a platoon commander in the 1st Marine Brigade's 3rd Battalion, 4th Marines. I wanted to get back in the 4th Marines, which was part of the 3rd Marine Division. I felt comfortable and confident that I was going to be an infantry-company commander, so I was all set to ask for the 4th Marines. Of course, there were no guarantees. My good buddy, Myron Harrington, who had left Travis a few days ahead of me, had been corralled into a logistics job at a rear base despite his exceptionally strong desire to command an infantry company. I didn't know that yet and, frankly, it never entered my head that I would get any job other than command of an infantry company. As far as I was concerned, it was all just a matter of showing up and requesting a company in the 4th Marines.

After learning who my man was, I went right up to the assistant division adjutant in charge of officer assignments, a middle-aged lieutenant who was probably used to telling people what they were going to do and not having any problems. Before he could say anything, I said, "I'm Captain Camp. I'm reporting in. What company have you got open in the Fourth Marines?" The lieutenant looked at me like he was thinking, "Who the hell are you?"

Before he could react, I said, "I was a lieutenant in the Fourth Marines early on in my career and I really want to get back with the regiment." That sort of softened him up a little bit—I no longer sounded like I was a complete smartass—so he looked over his roster and said, "We don't have anything open in the Fourth Marines."

"Lookit," I shot back, "I'll take any infantry company in the Third Division—*any* infantry company."

So he shuffled through a sheaf of papers and finally looked up at me. "Okay, I've got an opening right now in the Third Battalion, Twenty-Sixth Marines." I didn't even know the 26th Marines was in Vietnam at the time—it had been in-country for only six months or so—but I said, "Fine, I'll take it." Then, as he was filling out a form with my orders, I blurted out as a casual aside, "Gee, did the company commander rotate home, or what?"

"No," the old lieutenant responded, just as casually, "the company commander was killed last night."

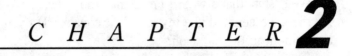

C H A P T E R 2

At the end of June 1967 the main body of the 3rd Battalion, 26th Marines (3/26), was located at Khe Sanh, in the highlands near the Laotian frontier and a little south of the DMZ, the demilitarized zone between the two Vietnams. I knew I would eventually wind up at Khe Sanh, but my immediate objective was the battalion rear echelon at Phu Bai. As with most Marine infantry battalions, the static Battalion Rear took care of forwarding men and supplies to the main body, which was almost always on the move or operating in areas unsuitable for the establishment of a rear supply and administrative base.

There was no immediate transportation to the 3/26 Battalion Rear, so I joined a small group of other officers who seemed to be waiting for rides to various places. A few minutes after I joined the group, I saw the powerfully built lieutenant who had been on my plane from Travis and who, in fact, had ridden up to Phu Bai that morning aboard my helo. I still had not spoken to him, but we had exchanged nods on the helo. When he joined us, I decided to introduce myself and comment on how familiar he was becoming.

"Hey, Lieutenant, I'm Captain Camp. What's your name?"

"John Prince, sir."

"Good to meet you, John. Where you heading for?"

"Third Battalion, Twenty-Sixth Marines, sir."

"Well, shit, that's where I'm going, too. Christ, we'll go together!" By then, he seemed like my long lost cousin. "Do you have a definite assignment in the battalion?"

"Lima Company, sir."

The company I had been assigned to command was Lima Company. "Then I'm your new company commander, John. Welcome aboard!"

After we had been waiting awhile—a chance to get acquainted—someone drove us up to the 3/26 Battalion Rear in a jeep and dropped us off in front of the Lima Company supply tent so we could draw our equipment and weapons.

Word gets around fast. I could see right away that the Marines were watching us, obviously with full knowledge as to who we were and what we would be doing. I also knew what was going on, that I was being sized up and that my troops in the field would have opinions about me before they ever saw me.

I went into Supply to introduce myself and said, "Lookit, I want to draw my gear. I'm going in the field tomorrow." The company supply sergeant said, "Yessir, yessir," showed me a place where I could spend the night, and took me over to the supply area.

The first thing I wanted to do was draw my jungle utilities and get the hell out of those starched stateside ones that were so hot. I also drew all my web gear—canvas belts, ammunition pouches, canteens, pack, and the other stuff I needed to live in the field. As I was in about the middle of drawing gear and trying it on for size, the tent fly flew back and an old pudgy guy came in. He was obviously a senior staff NCO. He wouldn't look directly at me, refused to recognize my rank or my reason for being there. I knew he knew who I was; everyone did! He kind of snorted around, kicked a few things, and snorted out.

"Who the hell was that?" I asked the nearest supplyman.

"That's the company first sergeant, sir, First Sergeant Miller."

I thought, "What the hell is it with this asshole? That was a hell of an introduction!" I found out later that 1st Sergeant Edward Miller's bizarre behavior was a defense mechanism. He had been very close with the company commander who had been killed only two days earlier. When I learned the details later, I realized that I had witnessed a grief reaction. As he saw it, I was a young upstart come to replace his irreplaceable skipper. My sudden arrival apparently brought back some painful memories. He was unable to think in terms of the war goes on, forget about the old guy, and three cheers for the new guy.

As I continued to select my gear, I began getting a feel for the young Marines, developing a rapport, and learning a little about the company, the battalion, and life in Vietnam. After a very brief feeling-out process, I started to feel comfortable, mainly because they were fellow Marines. They answered my questions with the proper work-manlike attitude and even filled in details I had not requested but which I needed to know. Soon, they all appeared at pains to put me at my ease.

After I had drawn all the gear I would need at Supply, I carried it over to the tent I had been shown earlier and began assembling it so I would be all ready to fly up to Khe Sanh in the morning. I had not taken official command of Lima Company, so I had no business nosing around the company rear. I just settled in and did my best to get my gear squared away. I had lunch and supper at the Battalion Rear mess hall with John Prince and the very few other officers and turned in early. Something about the experiences of the day allowed me to rest easy and sleep through the night.

*T*he next morning, June 29, 1967, I boarded another CH-46 helicopter and flew up to Khe Sanh. John Prince was delayed at Phu Bai for some reason, so I flew alone with a load of supplies.

The Khe Sanh Combat Base was up on a high plateau. From the stories I heard, it was supposed to be where the old Emperor of Indochina had hunted tigers and elephants. I had also heard that the Khe Sanh plateau was relatively cool during the day and not too cold at night. It was an absolutely gorgeous place except for the combat base, which surrounded a runway that had been built beside the ruins of an old French fort. The base and several key hills, which had been the center of a major battle in the spring, were manned full time by the 1st Battalion, 26th Marines (1/26), and a 105mm howitzer battery. My battalion, 3/26, which maintained a small forward command post at the combat base, was presently responsible for patrolling and sweeping the heavily wooded hills and valleys centered on the combat base. According to what I heard in Phu Bai, 3/26's four infantry companies— India, Kilo, Lima, and Mike—spent virtually all their time in the field.

The combat base was completely surrounded by triple-canopy jungle, which began between a thousand meters and two thousand meters outside the wire. Nearby was a small town—Khe Sanh—which was the local district headquarters, a sort of county seat. The locals were Bru tribesmen, a gentle, somewhat backward people the lowland Vietnamese disparagingly called montagnards. Besides the lowlanders and a few Bru residing in Khe Sanh ville, the Bru lived mainly in tiny villages spread across the hills and valleys of the region. A Marine Combined Action Company and several U.S. Army detachments lived in and around Khe Sanh ville, and the U.S. Army Special Forces maintained a fortified village at Lang Vei, about eight klicks (kilometers) farther up Route 9, toward the Laotian frontier. In addition to these small detachments, and not counting the Marine battalions at or attached to the combat base, the region was nominally defended by several Vietnamese Civilian Irregular Defense Group, Regional Forces, and Popular Forces companies manned mainly by part-time locals. As far as I know, these Vietnamese units hardly ever left their defended bases and served no observable military function except local patrolling.

National Route 9—little more than a dirt track about as wide as a driveway—wound about fifty miles along a stream from Dong Ha, another major Marine Corps base in the lowlands. In late June 1967, Route 9 was usually open and ambushes were rare, but the best and safest means of travel was in a helicopter.

There were several dominant hills and ridgelines within range of the combat base. One of the most prominent of these was off to the north, the 1015 ridgeline. It was probably three or four miles away, but anybody who was on that ridgeline with powerful binoculars could look right down and see anything that was going on inside the combat base. A defended radio relay tower on the adjacent Hill 950 summit was used to maintain links with bases in the lowlands as well as to eavesdrop on radio communications inside North Vietnam. The so-called Hill Fights of the previous spring had occurred mainly to the northwest, toward Laos, on the 881 ridgeline—Hills 881S and 881N—and out along the 861 ridgeline.

In addition to the runway, the air base consisted of a hardened helicopter pad and facilities for maintaining and refueling helicopters and transport planes. Nearly everything inside the combat base was above the ground, though tents and buildings were sandbagged against artillery or mortar fire. The artillery battery was dug in, but the ammunition supply point that fed it was protected only by a dirt berm just five or six feet high.

Everywhere was the distinctive red clay of the Khe Sanh Plateau. As I later learned, everyone in I Corps could identify members of 1/26 and 3/26 because our boots were invariably caked with red clay and our green jungle utilities had a reddish cast to them.

As soon as I stepped off the helo, I got directions to the 3/26 battalion CP, which was a half mile away, in the northwestern quadrant of the base. As I walked, I was mildly surprised to see the casual nature of the defenses. There was a line of foxholes at what seemed to be the edge of the base, and a single-apron barbed-wire fence. The very few bunkers I saw were above the ground and lacked adequate overhead cover. All the buildings and tents had waist-high sandbag blast walls but no overhead cover. No one I saw was wearing a helmet or flak jacket, and very few men were carrying rifles. The whole place smacked of business as usual. Clearly, I had not yet caught up with the war.

I was unable to see the actual buildings comprising the 26th Marines regimental CP from my route, but I did note the presence of the extensive antenna farm that usually marked the site of a major head-quarters. About the only other civilized appurtenance was the hard-surfaced all-weather road I was treading, a sure sign that there were Seabees in the area. The road was in better shape than the airfield runway, which at that time was only packed earth.

When I reached Battalion Forward, I stuck my head in and was quickly greeted by the battalion executive officer. Right from the start, I could see that Major Carl Mundy was a hell of a fine guy. He was one of those perfectly squared-away Marines who could literally have fallen into a benjo ditch—a sewer—and still come out looking like he just stepped out of a recruiting poster.

At first glance, Mundy looked absolutely immaculate, but I noticed that his shirt and trousers had many tiny rips in them. He looked so squared away, but his clothes had holes in them. I was unable to restrain myself. "Major, what happened to your clothing?" He smiled sheepishly and told me how, two nights earlier, he had hung his freshly laundered clothes to dry inside his tent just before a 122mm rocket attack. He had not been hurt, but every shirt and pair of trousers he owned had been clobbered by shrapnel.

After checking one another out by means of the traditional banter, Major Mundy told me that the entire battalion was in the field, except for the small detachment of communicators and clerks needed to run the CP. It was a typical operation, with the battalion exec "in the rear with the gear."

He took a lot of time to explain things to me. Meantime, when I told him my last duty had been as a ceremonial platoon commander at 8th and Eye, as we called Marine Barracks, Washington, he took special glee in yanking my chain with barbed questions like "Where's your sword, Captain?" or "Did you pack your white trousers?" and "We don't do much parading around here." I was not offended; the major was clearly a man of immense good will and the heckling was inclusive rather than exclusive. The exec also was at pains to introduce me to some of the other officers—the motor transport officer, the supply boss, and the battalion communicator. He started to make me feel at home and to bring me into the battalion.

Naturally, I was anxious to get out to the company because he said it was being run by the executive officer, a complete unknown to me. I heard he was a good man, but, like all unit leaders, I wanted to take charge. However, Major Mundy assured me that there was absolutely nothing going on out in the field and he urged me to delay reporting in until the next morning. With some reluctance, I agreed to spend the night at Khe Sanh.

Khe Sanh was rougher and tougher than Phu Bai had been, closer to the cutting edge. I wondered a little about how casual the troops seemed and how meager the defenses appeared, but I chalked it all up to the elan of combat veterans. I had met a man whose clothes had been ruined in a rocket attack only several nights earlier, and I was hearing the occasional boom of an outgoing round from the artillery battery located at the opposite end of the combat base. In fact, I eventually realized that the sound of the outgoing was the first time I had ever heard shots fired in anger. My company, which I would be joining in the morning, was out in the field, trying to find out where the North Vietnamese set up the rockets that pelted the combat base from time to time, trying to locate North Vietnamese soldiers and kill them.

Though I had slept well at Phu Bai, my mind was reeling again inside Khe Sanh. I kept thinking, "This is it! I'm here!" It felt very natural, and I felt completely at home. This is what I had been working up to for all those years, what I had read in hundreds of books throughout my childhood and teen years and, in fact, was reading still. Now, at last, I was really part of it. It was *my* turn.

*B*right and early the next morning, June 30, they laid on a special helicopter flight for me so I could fly out to the battalion position. I was the only passenger aboard the old H-34 helicopter, with its huge, open side hatches. As the helo flared out to land after only a few minutes in the air, I could see that we were coming down atop a high open hill covered with elephant grass. Foxholes were strewn haphazardly across the crest and helmeted, armed people were walking in the open.

The helo landed and I jumped off into the elephant grass, which was two or three feet high. Looking for the telltale clump of antennas, I began wading through the grass toward the largest group of Marines. It was a really beautiful day, not too hot. I could see Marines in the tree clumps and bushes, obviously manning a defensive perimeter.

As I neared the largest knot of Marines, I saw the antennas of several radios, so I knew I had found the battalion command group. As I neared the group, I began to sense the familiar flavor of the infantry— familiar to me only from scores of training days in the field. I could smell unwashed clothes and unwashed bodies. *Not* typical of Stateside training was the clothing that was ripped and torn or the scraggly beards sported by most of the Marines I could see.

I felt a little down in my confidence as I approached the command group. I was walking into this situation cold; as far as I knew, I had never before met a soul on this hill. I had no idea what to expect. No one was wearing rank insignia, so I didn't even know who was who. I knew the battalion commander was probably a member of the group, but I could not figure out which of the unshaven smelly men he might be.

As I balked at the edge of the group, trying to divine the identity of the battalion commander, an older Marine turned in my direction and came over. I did not know who he was so I throttled an impulse to salute him, which I knew was inappropriate in the field even if he was the battalion commander.

The older man sensed my confusion and said, "I'm the battalion sergeant major. You must be Captain Camp?"

Relieved, I responded in my brightest voice, "Oh, hi there, Sergeant Major." What a great start!

"Sir, the battalion commander's over there," and he pointed toward an older, balding, heavyset man who was standing a little apart from the beehive of activity. Once again sensing my awkward hesitation, the sergeant major added, "He's Colonel Hoch."

That was all I needed. I walked straight over to the battalion commander and came to attention. "Sir, I'm Captain Camp."

First impressions were crucial. I had been assigned to command Lima Company by the division assistant adjutant, but the final say was up to the man I had just addressed in my best parade-ground voice.

Very calmly, the battalion commander looked me over and asked, "What's your first name, Captain?"

"Dick, sir."

"Well, come on over here, Dick. I've got a few minutes and I want to talk with you before you take over your company." He led me away from the bustle of the command group, toward the edge of the perimeter.

As we walked and I took it all in, my eyes must have been the size of silver dollars. The hilltop was covered with beaten-down elephant grass and there were hard-looking Marines manning foxholes. The battalion's 81mm mortars were manned and the gunners looked ready for immediate action. Everyone looked pretty grimy and pretty fierce. Lieutenant Colonel Kurt Hoch, who wore neither helmet nor flak jacket, had on an old green skivvy shirt and had not shaved the stubble from his face for two or three days. All the filth and disorder were pretty difficult for me to take.

My train of discomforting thoughts was broken by the battalion commander's voice. "Dick," he began with a warm informality I had not heard earlier and for which I was totally unprepared, "Lima Company's out that way, on that little hill about three thousand meters up the valley." He pointed up a broad valley, toward a little open hill. It was too far to see if anything was going on out there, but at least I had a sense of the ground. As I concentrated on the terrain, the colonel's gentle voice broke into my thoughts, "Tell me a little bit about yourself."

I immediately launched into a recitation of the things my previous experience made me think a new battalion commander would want to hear about a new company commander who had been sent, sight unseen, by a remote and distant higher headquarters. As I was going on about myself, the leading element of an infantry company, fresh from a trek in the valley below, straggled up the trail on the back side of the hill. What I saw had an immediate and profound effect on me, on my demeanor, on what I was blathering on about to Lieutenant Colo-nel Hoch of the grimy skivvy shirt and stubbly cheeks.

In truth, what I saw brought me to the verge of tears. For there I was, in war-torn Vietnam, watching a Marine combat infantry company walking up a hill. The clothing the troops were wearing was dirty, filthy, ripped, torn, and worn. None of the Marines looked smart or disciplined; I could not even tell the officers from the troops. For all that, though I was still blathering on to my new colonel, my mind kept repeating an awed internal litany: "My God, there they are. That's the bottom line. That's the Marine Corps. That's home."

When I reached the end of my mindless verbal resumé, Colonel Hoch shrugged and said, "Well, Dick, I don't really have anything to tell you other than do your job and do it well. Know that you have support up here."

There was to be no long inquisition; the colonel's attitude seemed to say, "You're on the team, so go over there and do your best." It wasn't inspiring, but it gave me a lot of confidence. We walked back to the command group and a helicopter was ordered up from the combat base to take me over to Lima Company's hill. That was it; that was all there was to it. I was the Lima Company skipper—Lima-6.

CHAPTER 3

As the H-34 got close to the Lima company position, I asked the pilot to circle the lines a couple of times. I'm not sure what made me do that; I just gave in to the impulse to have a look at the company's lines before I landed. As we made a couple of passes, I looked down and thought the positions were too close together. Something didn't look right to me.

As soon as we landed and I climbed out of the H-34, a strapping six-foot-three, blond, blue-eyed man came up and introduced himself as Lieutenant Jaak Aulik, the company executive officer. As I soon learned, Jaak's family had fled Estonia to escape the Russians at the end of World War II. His father had done quite well in the United States and Jaak himself was only three classroom hours away from his doctorate in physics. At the moment of our first meeting, I was impressed with Jaak's physical presence and the warmth of his greeting. Unfortunately, I wasn't so sure about his prowess as a company commander, and I was only moments away from putting my own to its first test.

"Pleased to meet you, Lieutenant," I said as I took Jaak's proffered hand. "I'm Captain Camp, the new company commander."

"Yessir, I know." I could imagine what was going through his mind. He had just lost a company commander he probably had liked and with whom he was familiar. Now he was faced with an unknown quantity who, by the looks of me, probably had just arrived in-country. He had seen my two passes over the company position and so had to be worrying about what was going to happen next. I decided to drop both shoes.

"Lieutenant Aulik, I happened to swing around the lines and I think we need to get the platoon commanders up here and take a look at the positions."

Without batting an eyelash, he said, "Yessir," and turned to the radio operator: "Get the platoon commanders up here." Within a matter of a very few minutes, two lieutenants and a staff sergeant had joined us. I introduced myself and they introduced themselves. Lieutenant Dan Frazer, the 1st Platoon commander, had arrived in Vietnam with Lima Company; Staff Sergeant Marvin Bailey, of the 2nd Platoon, was a Korean War veteran who had joined the battalion the previous winter; and Lieutenant Bill Cowan, of the 3rd Platoon, had joined Lima Company only the day before. Bailey and Cowan had both replaced platoon commanders killed or wounded in the same action that had claimed the life of my predecessor a few days earlier.

As soon as the introductions were out of the way, I said, "Gentlemen, I'd like to take a walk through the lines and check them out with you." As I had hoped, no one responded with anything like even an unspoken, "Well, sir, why don't you get your feet on the ground," or "You just arrived." They all said, "Yessir," as Jaak moved to my side to guide me.

We walked all the way around the company lines. On the way, I had each platoon commander move at least several of his Marines to better positions. I was struck that everything was done in just the manner that I would have expected subordinates in *any* Marine infantry company to react to a superior officer. There was not the slightest bit of hesitation. It was like the company of the 4th Marines in which I had served as a platoon commander three years earlier. I was the skipper and everyone did exactly what I asked. It was just like I had been there all the time, like putting on a new coat that fit me very well without having to be tailored.

As we were walking around the lines, though, I came upon a machine-gun position that troubled me. I looked at the M-60 machine gun and asked the crew, "Where's your tripod?" The gunner responded, "Well, sir, we don't carry tripods out in the field." I said, "Okay." They looked relieved, but I had not bought the story and it would not end there. I had developed the habit of asking a question and saying "Okay" to the answer—not necessarily agreeing with what I heard, just acknowledging that I heard what had been said. I stored the information away and resumed my tour of the lines.

After completing the tour of the outer defenses, I led the exec and the platoon commanders over to the 60mm mortars. This was the first time I had actually seen 60mm mortars. As I had suspected, something was missing. I asked, "Where are the bipods for these mortars?" and the mortar section leader replied, "Well, sir, we're in the field and the gunners are really good. The bipods are just a lot of extra weight, so we fire them free hand." I said, "Okay," and moved on.

So there I was, four days in-country and approaching my first night as a company commander in the field. "Well, Captain," I said to myself, "it's on your shoulders now."

I didn't feel nervous; it all felt comfortable and familiar to me. I had not given much thought to what was going on, but I had given orders that had been carried out by willing officers and Marines who appeared prepared to accept my authority. From what I had seen, my orders were being been carried out energetically. Nobody I had met seemed to imply by word or deed, "Hey, Captain, you're still the new guy on the block." I was feeling comfortable. I felt that I could run an infantry company; I had all the confidence in the world about that.

Late in the afternoon, the company fired in our night defensive fires, which was an invariable ritual in the field. The platoon commanders automatically prepared to set out their listening posts (LPs), another inviolable ritual. When the platoon commanders reported that the LPs were all ready to go, all I had to do was say, "All right, let's see where we're going to put them." The platoon commanders laid it all out for me, and I approved. Next, the artillery forward observer (FO), Tom Biondo, a lieutenant attached to the company from Charlie Battery, 1st Battalion, 13th Marines, came up to me and said, "Sir, where do you want to put out the night defensive fires?" I said, "How about coming up with some recommendations," which Tom immediately did. He was prepared, and I approved the plan. Everything worked just the way it was supposed to work.

My first night in the field with Lima Company was uneventful. The next morning, we got the word we were supposed to move out along the ridgeline to look for NVA rocket sites.

An infantry company, which could be anywhere up to 180 or 190 men, is a big unit to move, especially along a ridgeline. When walking a ridgeline, the company moved in a column that might stretch back as far as a thousand meters between the point and the rearguard. Keeping tabs on everything and everyone is a very big job for the company commander, who generally travels with his radioman and teams who were along to control air, artillery, and 81mm mortars.

Any command post or command group, even down at the company level, shows plenty of antennas because the commander's primary means for communicating is the radio. The artillery FO, usually an artillery lieutenant, travels with his own radioman, as does the 81mm FO, who is usually a corporal or sergeant attached from the battalion 81mm mortar platoon. If an air liaison officer (ALO) or forward air controller (FAC) is attached out at the company level, each travels with his own radiomen, who are typically attached from the tactical air control party (TACP) of the battalion's own communications platoon or the helicopter support team (HST), which is part of the shore party battalion supporting the division. On top of these radio teams, the battalion communications platoon farms out a battalion tactical-net radioman, and the company has its own radiomen to run the company net. If all these people are along, the company command group can be extremely difficult and complex to coordinate, especially if the company is on the move through rough terrain.

I had given a great deal of thought to how I wanted a company under my command to move and function. I held my counsel that first full day in the field with Lima Company because I wanted to see the sort of hand I had been dealt. The officers and men had reacted well to my views and handling during the previous afternoon and evening, but humping the ridges in a combat zone was a matter they knew more about than I did, so I decided to wait and see how good they were or if their techniques were better than my ideas.

The first thing I wanted to do was control the gaggle of bodies in my command group. My idea was to have the various fire-support representatives and radiomen located in specific positions relative to whichever way my body was facing at any given moment. Later, after I got everything worked out and everyone used to my system, for grins and chuckles I sometimes turned around very slowly in a circle just to see my FOs, ALO, FAC, and radiomen move around with me. There was an absolute method to my madness. In the confusion of battle—if we had to hit the deck—I always knew, for example, that on my right rear would be the FAC or on my left rear would be the 81mm FO. It became an inviolable SOP that they all carried out.

I had wanted to take my first sergeant into the field with the company, and I would have ordered him forward when I first went out to Khe Sanh, but I had not been in a position of authority when I passed through Phu Bai, and his little demonstration in the company supply tent had brought me up short of suggesting it. However, my plan was for the first sergeant to control the activities of the headquarters or the command group, to spread them out or kick ass, whatever he had to do to control them. If he wasn't there, then the company gunny would fill in.

Everybody in the company had a mission to fulfill. For example, I had decided to assign one man to monitor casualties of every type, including heat exhaustion or illness. Normally, in Lima Company, that was to be the responsibility of the senior enlisted man in the field. If that was the first sergeant, he carried the company roster, which was simply an alphabetical listing of every man present along with the last four digits of everyone's serial numbers. If the first sergeant wasn't with us, then the company gunny handled the roster. One or the other was to be responsible for casualties and casualty procedures, including evacuation and follow-up. That way, if we were in action, at least one Marine would not overlook getting the wounded treated and on their way to the rear.

I was thinking of these and a lot of other matters and procedures as we saddled up that first morning and stepped off along the ridgeline. However, before I suggested anything more than immediately neces- sary remedies to what I considered a few bad habits by individuals, I kept my mouth shut and my eyes and ears open, taking in how my people reacted and how the company as a whole looked on the move. Of immediate concern were questions like, Are they spread out? How much and what kind of noise are they making? Do the troops seem to be alert? How are the platoon commanders reacting? Are they alert? How are they handling their platoons?

I was pleased. Lima Company was a good company. It clearly had been well led by my departed predecessor. A lot of thought and training had gone into making it a good, cohesive unit. More to the point, these Marines had been in combat, had been shot at. They had taken casualties, but they seemed to operate aggressively; there was no hanging back. The troop leaders seemed to know what they were doing. The troops were responsive.

We got a late start that morning. We moved down the ridgeline—it was about twenty-five hundred meters in length—and wound down into a draw leading to the next hill, which was about five or six thousand meters away. As we were walking, Jaak Aulik told me that the hill toward which we were marching—Hill 689—was the one on which my predecessor had been killed less than a week earlier. I decided to take the plunge and asked Jaak for the whole story. I felt I had to bury the dead man before Lima Company would truly be mine. As it developed, the burial would be tough to accomplish, because Captain Frank Bynum had formed Lima Company back at Camp Pendleton and had been the first and only man to command it in Vietnam. He had been a colorful, well-loved leader whose death had cast a deep shadow across the face of the company.

According to the story I pieced together over the next few weeks, another company in the battalion had been coming off a long sweep and had been approaching the hill, which the entire battalion had been over just a few days previously. For some reason, the company commander had gotten a little disoriented or didn't really recognize where he was. It is unclear if the company was supposed to be on its way over the hill in the first place. In any case, the vanguard took some fire and the point—the Marine leading the whole company—was killed. Immediately, two other Marines from the lead platoon rushed out to rescue the point, and they were both killed. A general firefight developed and Lima Company, which was back at Khe Sanh, was ordered to saddle up and relieve pressure on the embattled sister company.

The company was lifted into the area by helicopters. Frank Bynum, who had been over the hill only a few days earlier, was apparently certain that were weren't any North Vietnamese up there, that the firefight was a phantom. Clearly, he did not have the complete picture when he walked up the hill, encouraging the troops to get up and follow him because there wasn't anybody there. Everybody I spoke with told me that Captain Bynum was a daredevil type who always wore a soft cover, sported a white silk scarf, and carried a walking stick. It was apparently quite a show—right up to the moment he walked smack into the killing zone covered by the NVA bunkers and was stitched by several bullets.

The company's senior corpsman—Hospital Corpsman 3rd Class Larry Bratton—crawled out to rescue him, right through NVA booby traps and literally right beneath the barrels of some of their weapons. As I understand it, Doc Bratton turned over on his back, pulled the captain onto his stomach, and crawled out using only his legs. Unbelievably, both men reached safety.

Meantime, the artillery FO, who had been shot through and through, from one hip to the other, lay in a crater calling in artillery support. The company commander's radio operator, Corporal David Johnson, took the company over because, among others, two platoon commanders were down and the exec was in the rear. He was also the only man in the company who was in a position to let Battalion know what was going on, but it took Lieutenant Colonel Hoch quite a while to arrange for helicopters to lift in more support and drive the NVA out of their bunker complex. By then, Captain Bynum was dead. Either his wounds had been mortal to start with, or he died because there was no way to land a medevac helo until the bunker complex had been reduced. In addition to losing its commander, two platoon commanders, and its artillery FO, Lima company had taken quite a few enlisted casualties.

I had no intention of pushing the company; I just wanted to see how good it was. My objectives for the day were limited. When we got to where I wanted to go, we stopped. The proposed bivouac was a finger or part of a long finger that went on into a hill. It looked like a good place to stop and, besides, the rest of the battalion was nearby, moving along roughly parallel traces, looking for sites from which NVA rockets were bombarding or could bombard the combat base.

We reached the finger about midmorning and stopped after I had consulted with the battalion CP. Starting from scratch, we formed a rough perimeter on the high ground. The area was heavily wooded, but there were no trees on the finger, just the tall elephant grass. After we had set in, I sent Staff Sergeant Bailey's 2nd Platoon down into the jungle, along a stream, to see what it could see. I spent the early afternoon looking the positions over, observing and trying to get a handle on who was who.

Several hours before sunset, around 1600, the roving 2nd Platoon called and said it was coming back in. They had nothing to report.

Next, I called over my artillery FO, Lieutenant Tom Biondo, and asked, "Okay, Tom, where do you recommend that we plot the targets for that night defensive fires?" He made his recommendation and we called them in to the Charlie Battery fire direction center (FDC). When the FDC said it was ready to fire, we got everybody down in their holes just in case there was a short round. We started firing in along all the likely avenues of approach, marking each on our maps with the appropriate numerical target designator furnished by the FDC. This would allow us to get immediate fire on a specific target if we were hit, and adjustments could be made efficiently from any plotted-in base point. Since each reference point was shot in and adjusted with live fire, there was little chance of error.

It was still light when the artillery had been fired in, so I decided to start making a few waves over bad habits I had observed during my first full day in command. The first order of business was setting my lazy 60mm mortarmen and M-60 gunners straight about bringing all their gear to the field.

The M-60 machine gun carried by the company machine-gun section was a 7.62mm fully automatic weapon that could be fired from either the bipod, which is permanently affixed to the weapon, or from a tripod, which is carried by a member of the gun team. Affixing the tripod is simply a matter of throwing it down on the ground and putting the gun on it. Unlike the bipod, the tripod is fitted with a traversing and elevating mechanism valuable in placing fixed fire at a predetermined grazing level. It is especially suited to fixed-zone defensive fires like those the company plotted in every night it spent in the field.

The night before, the gunners had given me some mumbo-jumbo about never taking the tripods into the field. I knew they were a pain in the ass to carry, but they had valuable uses beyond night defensive fires. I had decided at the outset that they were never to be left behind again.

Even more bizarre was the claim by my mortarmen that they never carried their bipods into the field because they were so good they could fire free hand. That was unmitigated bullshit, but I had held my counsel through the first day. However, when Major Mundy called to

tell me to expect Lieutenant Prince to arrive aboard a resupply helicopter near sunset, I asked the battalion exec to send out our mortar
bipods and M-60 tripods. When the major told me the chopper would
be arriving in thirty to forty-five minutes, I ordered the mortar section
to saddle up for a little target practice.

Farther along the ridgeline from where we were set in was a big old
tree sitting out in the open by itself. When the mortarmen arrived, I
told them, "Look, we don't want to take all this ammunition back. Why
don't you guys go ahead and hit that tree. It'll be to a good purpose;
it'll convince me how good you are, give us all a little practice, and,
besides that, get rid of this old ammunition." They thought I had a
great idea; they were going to impress the hell out of their brand-new
company commander. So, they all lined up and anybody else who was
crapped out in the area sat up to watch this tremendous exposition of
Marine fire-support accuracy. Well, they started firing, but I wasn't
sure they could hit anything the size of the whole country of Vietnam.
They never landed one anywhere near that tree.

When everyone was as convinced as I was, I turned around to
the section leader and said, "That's the last goddamn time you
Marines come out here without the bipods." It was a valuable lesson
for the mortarmen and, in fact, the entire company. Everyone now
knew that I was a sneaky son of a bitch, not given to accepting
bullshit answers and not above engineering a little therapeutic public
humiliation.

When I finished with the mortarmen, I let the M-60 gunners know
how I felt about their leaving their tripods behind. But that wasn't all. I
had noticed that the machine gunners were decked out like a gang of
Mexican bandidos. They had taken all their linked M-60 ammunition
out of the ammo cans and had looped it around their flak jackets. It
looked very macho, but bad things happen when you have to hit the
deck and crawl around. Dirt gets into the links and, when the belts are
fed into the machine guns, the guns have a tendency to jam. So, right
then and there, I started clamping down on what the SOPs in Lima
Company were to be. One of the first was that all hands carrying M-60
linked belts were to keep them in waterproof ammo cans with tight
lids. No exceptions.

To make sure everyone got the message about the rules, I next
turned to the matter of carrying hand grenades any way but in grenade
pouches. Most of the troops carried their grenades lopped by the

safety spoons to the suspender straps holding up their web belts. It took no effort at all to work out the safety pin and arm the grenade.

While I was at it, I mentioned that I had counted up all the Communist AK-47 assault rifles my Marines were carrying. I knew that every Marine has a John Wayne streak and that being seen with an AK-47 was good for the image, but there were a few flaws on the practical side. First, the supply of 7.62mm ammunition for the AK-47 was not regular since it could not be requisitioned from our own supply system. More to the point, however, it was important to fire a weapon that differed in *sound* as much as the issue 5.56mm M-16 did from the AK-47. In the utter confusion and panic of a firefight, hearing was often the most important sense. Hereafter, I ordered, Lima Company would carry only issue American weapons. No exceptions.

That ended school that second evening: bipods for the mortars, tripods for the machine guns, ammunition in proper containers, hand grenades in properly designed pouches, and only issue American weapons were acceptable—just the way everyone had once been taught.

Another matter that concerned me was the filth in which my men and I were living. Dirt is a natural enemy of the infantryman, and very little can be done in the field to combat it because there is little or no water available in the field for washing. Usually, arms and hands would be cut by elephant grass and infection would set in. The cuts never healed; they only scabbed over and drained pus. That evening, in fact, I had to order two Marines back to Khe Sanh to have rampant infections treated. They left on the same H-34 that brought out the M-60 tripods, 60mm mortar bipods, and Lieutenant John Prince.

I greeted John when he arrived aboard the resupply bird, told him he was to supersede Staff Sergeant Bailey as the 2nd Platoon commander, and asked him to accompany me and Lieutenants Aulik, Frazer, Cowan, and Biondo for our tour of the company lines. Together, we set in our listening posts after dark and got ready to repel boarders. The night was quiet and uneventful; nothing was going on. My fifth day in Vietnam and my first full day in command of an infantry company had resulted in no fatalities—theirs, ours, or mine.

C H A P T E R 4

We weren't scheduled to do anything on July 2, just stay in place and react if any of the other companies stirred anything up. Nothing happened until around 1900, when I happened to glance out from the finger in time to see four NVA soldiers dressed in green uniforms walking northeast into a treeline. I was so flabbergasted that I had trouble getting the words out. By the time I did, the four men were gone, no doubt as stunned by our presence as I had been by theirs. My 81mm mortar FO got the battalion mortars laid on the treeline, but it was impossible for anyone on the finger to observe results.

After only two days in the field, I became adept at trading food I didn't like for food I did like—actually the result of years of specialized training. My favorite C-ration meal was chopped ham and eggs, pecan cake roll, fruit, and white bread. These items came in two separate meal packs, hence the trading. Cooking began by opening the can with the chocolate powder and crackers, removing the contents, cutting off the top, and cutting three slits on the side so the can could serve as a stove. If the cutting was done imprecisely, the heat tab didn't burn properly and there was big-time trouble breathing. The white-bread can was placed on the stove and two small cuts were made in the top. After the heat tab was lit, three or four drops of water were inserted through the cuts in the top so the bread would soften while it heated. Next was opening the can of ham and eggs (also known as "heavy") in such a way that the top could be bent back to serve as a handle. As the contents were heated, water was added and the heavy was chopped. After the contents of the fruit can had been eaten, water was boiled in it, sugar and powdered cream were dissolved, and the cocoa beverage powder was mixed in. It was food fit for a king—or a very hungry Marine.

Shortly after sunset, B-52 bombers dumped an Arclight mission over the next line of hills. I had never seen such a thing; it was truly awesome. The bombers were in the stratosphere, far beyond our vision. One minute it was a beautiful, starlit night, and the next was filled with an otherworldly hum followed by teeth-clattering detonations that backlit the hills and threw us around in our holes. A minute after that, it was quiet and still again.

On July 3, the entire company patrolled toward Hill 542, but we found nothing and returned to the finger in plenty of time to resume our night defensive position and fire in our artillery.

On July 4, we sent two platoon patrols into the jungle west of the finger. One patrol reported no sightings, but Lieutenant John Prince's 2nd Platoon came across a well-worn log that lay across the stream that ran in front of our finger. Prince—who had already acquired the nickname "Little John"—also reported a possible sighting of one NVA soldier at about the point it had previously located what had appeared to be a footprint. As soon as Little John reported to me, I decided to lead another patrol into the jungle to see for myself. I told him to be ready to shove off at first light.

All of the ridges in the area were covered with elephant grass, but all the draws and valleys were choked and obscured by triple-canopy jungle. It was standard procedure to set up on the high, open ground and patrol the low, covered ground. We had our place and the North Vietnamese had theirs. To get at us, they had to climb up to the open ground; to get at them, we had to drop down into the forested valleys.

I ordered Jaak Aulik to stand fast on the finger with two platoons while I went down into the valley with the 2nd Platoon. It might not have seemed fair to the Marines involved to take out a platoon that had patrolled the previous day, but those were the people who knew what to look for and that was the platoon commander I wanted to see in action. There might have been some bitching and moaning about the unfairness of life—I would have been shocked if Marines had not bitched—but I never heard about it.

So there I was, the veteran of all of a week in-country, going down to find the enemy with only the one platoon to back me up. I was not worried, but I was more alert than I had ever been before. As I was to learn soon enough, I was not nearly as alert as anyone else in that valley.

We were traveling light: no packs, only weapons, helmets, flak jackets, ammunition, grenades, web gear, including as many as four canteens apiece, and some food stuffed into our big cargo pockets. The side of the slope was covered with huge trees and all sorts of low vegetation. Getting through it all was extremely difficult, and the slope was extremely steep—about a hundred feet down over only a quarter mile. Within minutes, the sky was completely blotted out by the triple canopy. I kept thinking, "If going down is so difficult, what's it going to be like going up?" On the positive side, I was pleasantly surprised by how cool it was out of the sun, beneath the triple canopy; I would have expected the growing heat of the day and terrible humidity to have been trapped by the solid overhead growth. As indicated on my map and by the patrol report of the previous afternoon, there was a stream at the bottom of the valley. The streambed, which ran almost dead straight through the jungle, had nearly vertical sides, at least six feet high, but the water was only five or six inches deep. I felt that we were a lot like the pins sitting at the end of a bowling alley, but I also saw that it was absolutely gorgeous down there, and very quiet. I had never thought of Vietnam as being so beautiful and peaceful.

As we moved along the narrow bank right beside the stream, I was probably about the tenth man from the point. In all, there were about forty of us, including my radiomen. We were all being very, very careful, particularly the point and his backup. If anything happened, they would see it or suffer first. It was amazingly quiet; I don't think I even heard anyone breathe. About the only sound was the burbling of the stream. Of course it was quiet; these Marines, who had been on the previous day's patrol, thought they had seen something. I knew that the point and his backup had their M-16s on full automatic, ready to open fire in a heartbeat if they saw or heard anything that might be hostile. Everyone around me was hyperalert. So was I.

For all my years of rigorous training and study, it occurred to me that this was the first time I had ever seen troops really "going tactical." This and a thousand other impressions were reeling through my mind when, all of a sudden, I perceived that the point had stopped dead in his tracks.

I immediately noted that the point had reached a branch in the stream. As I thought about what to do, Little John passed me and walked right up to the point. He hunkered down, whispering, as the Marine pointed to the ground and then down one of the stream branches. I was impressed with Little John's quick, assertive grasp of his duties.

I started forward, but before I took many steps, the lieutenant rose, turned, and motioned me forward. "This is where we think we saw the footprint a few days back," he whispered when I reached him. I stared ahead but saw nothing until he and the point indicated a worn log, six or seven inches in diameter, that bridged the stream. It seemed to have a V-shaped notch in it. The "V" seemed to be pointing toward us and another "V" was pointing toward the embankment. Right at the base of the "V" on the log was a shallow indentation that might have been a footprint. The point whispered that this was also the place at which he thought he had seen the NVA soldier dart through the brush the previous afternoon.

"Which way was he going?" I asked, and the point motioned up the left branch of the stream. I nodded and motioned to tell him to go left, then Little John and I fell back into the moving column. I stepped in about five or six people from the point. That was no place for a company commander to be, most particularly an inexperienced one, but I was excited and curious. I didn't notice it, but Sergeant Albert Peck, the platoon guide, fell in right behind my command group and Little John moved in at about the center of the column, where I should have been.

I was worried because the streambed kept us channelized, with no opportunity to send flankers out. I had practiced this sort of move a hundred times, but this was real and I had to play with what I had been dealt. I craned my neck around several times to see how vigilant the Marines in my immediate vicinity were being. They were scanning high, low, and all around. Everyone looked ready for action. Good enough!

There is such a thing as paying too much attention. I would learn in time to let sights and sounds roll over me, to look for anomalies in the flow rather than try to see and hear everything. But on my first patrol,

I was overeager and underskilled. All of a sudden, for no fathomable reason, I looked up at the point. He was turning to look over his left shoulder, already pulling himself up short and backing up against the high bank of the stream. As I looked on in motionless, frozen astonishment, the Marine brought his rifle up and opened fire. The backup man, right behind, was moving only a beat behind his partner, raising the muzzle of his M-16 and cranking off a burst at something I could not see right in or against the embankment.

"Gooks! Gooks! Gooks!" the point yelled. "Bunkers! Bunkers! Bunkers!"

It was electrifying. I had not even begun to react before two Marines overtook me from behind and shoved me aside—pushed me up against the bank—and thundered by. I vaguely noted that one of the disrespectful cusses was Sergeant Peck, who already had a grenade out.

The point and backup were firing their M-16s as fast as they could, and people behind me were yelling, "Move up! Move up! Get the fucking guns up! Move up!" The next thing I knew, Sergeant Peck reached the point, uncorked the grenade in his hand, and threw the missile *into* the high bank of the stream—right into the wall. There was an explosion, people were shoving me aside from behind and passing me, and more grenades started going off in quick succession around the blind corner. There was so much gunfire that it had taken on the dimensions of a continuous roar. It was mass confusion and pandemonium all rolled into one huge, frightening release.

And then, finally, I found myself running to the front of the line. I had not thought about it; I was simply carried along by excitement and, I suppose, the need to be part of what was going on. The first thing I saw when I turned the corner was a cluster of bunkers beneath the trees, right next to the turn in the stream. Marines were running in all directions, hurling grenades and blowing off rounds right into the firing embrasures of the little camouflaged earthen mounds. As I focused on the scene, I could see a well-defined trail leading back through the jungle canopy, which was about thirty or forty feet off the ground. The line of bunkers was on cleared ground that stretched out on either side of the trail, but there were other bunkers farther back.

My concentration was broken when an M-79 grenadier ran up to me and pointed his little shotgunlike weapon off into the trees. "Skipper, you see that bunker over there?" I saw that he was pointing to a mound about seventy feet away through the trees. "Can I shoot? Can I shoot?"

He was tense, and I was tense. "What the hell, let 'em have it."

The M-79 fired a 40mm grenade with a bursting radius of about ten feet, but the grenade had to be fired a great enough distance to arm itself so it would not injure the grenadier. The kid with the launcher snap-shot, but his aim was fine. Unfortunately, he was aiming at a bunker only *twenty* feet from where we stood. The grenade struck the side of the bunker, but it didn't go off. Just what I needed: a live 40mm grenade in the middle of a platoon of Marines who were running every which way through the NVA camp. "Goddammit, Marine, you go up there and stand right beside the grenade so nobody else sets it off!" He looked really crestfallen—his head was hanging in shame—as he shambled off in response to my order.

By then, things were settling into a rhythm. I was impressed by how well these Marines worked together. After the initial herd reaction, they began looking out for one another, breaking into teams to check out bunkers they had grenaded, advancing cautiously through the encampment, covering every square foot of ground. Fortunately, no one was shooting back.

It was a very good thing that nobody was home. If two or three of those bunkers had been manned, the platoon would have been chewed to bits. It would have been a bitch to clean that place out if we had been contested.

The shooting and grenading went on for five or six minutes, and then Lieutenant Prince and Staff Sergeant Bailey restored order—with a little help from their dazed company commander. I got together with the point and his backup to find out what had set the whole thing off. It turned out that the point had walked past the first concealed bunker, but he had happened to look back over his shoulder from just the right angle to see the firing embrasure. That kid was wound tighter than an eight-day clock, a typical state for any point. What he saw nearly scared him to death, hence the yelling and shooting. It was a reasonable response from a man who had good reason to think he was looking down the barrel of an NVA machine gun.

The platoon quickly—expertly—arrayed itself into a perimeter defense and each squad was given a sector to watch and search. I was concerned that all the yelling and shooting would bring out the local militia, but it was also our job to learn what we could about the setup. So, we started feeling our way deeper into the bunker complex.

The instantaneous mass reaction to the point's discovery and the calmer sweep was my first opportunity to really see Marines in action. Frankly, they impressed me. I was awed to be there and a little embarrassed by my own slow reactions.

The bunker complex was extensive, entirely hidden beneath a low jungle canopy, and extremely well camouflaged. There were nine fighting bunkers, each about four feet square and extremely well constructed and sited. Each fighting bunker could hold four or five men. The overheads were all about three feet thick, constructed of eight-inch-thick logs overlaid crosswise and filled in with packed dirt three or four feet high—thick enough and strong enough to withstand artillery or even bombs. All the structures were concealed with live growth the builders had planted in the raw earth. The builders had thought of everything. For example, we located a four-foot-by-four-foot banana-leaf cooking hut partially dug into a slope about ten feet from the stream; it had a small ditch about eight inches deep by twelve inches wide that ran about twenty meters back into the trees. The ditch was covered with branches and leaves, and at the bunker end was a crude bellows which could blow smoke from the cook fire in such a way that it would dissipate from the ditch through the twigs and leaves. If we had walked alongside the cooking bunker while the fire was going, we probably never would have known there was a fire. All in all, the complex was a tremendous set up. It impressed the hell out of me, which was easy, and it impressed the troops, which was something else again.

While the troops were rooting through the bunkers, I called back to Jaak Aulik and had him dispatch Lieutenant Dan Frazer's 1st Platoon down the hill to join us. Rather than wait, however, I got the 2nd Platoon moving again because I wanted to see if there were more bunkers farther along. I marked the location of the bunker complex on my map so an air strike could be adequately directed, if higher headquarters wanted to go that route.

As we were getting ready to continue our march down the stream, one of the Marines located a trail on the far side of the bunker complex. I decided to follow it. We were all getting pretty antsy. I expected to be hit by at least an ambush; I don't know what the troops were thinking. I figured on going a short distance up the trail before backtracking and meeting the other platoon upstream.

We were about thirty minutes away from the bunker complex when I received a radio call from Dan Frazer, the 1st Platoon commander. He wanted to know where our bunker complex was. "Hey, where the hell are *you*," I asked, and he replied that he must be close to us because his platoon was standing on the edge of a big bunker complex. When I asked him to describe where he was and how he had gotten there, it became obvious that he was somewhere down the other fork of the stream. "No way," I answered, "you aren't even close to us. Check out the bunkers you found and then backtrack to where the stream forks and follow us down the left fork. We'll wait for you." I gave him directions to the trail I was following and signed off.

So, Lima Company had uncovered *two* bunker complexes. The one the 2nd Platoon had found was in very good shape but completely deserted. The 1st Platoon's complex was older, more run-down, and had some old gear strewn around, including several tin dishes with shrapnel holes in them, an NVA steel helmet, and a few rusty 82mm mortar rounds.

Prince's 2nd Platoon proceeded very slowly along the well-made trail until Frazer's 1st Platoon joined up from the rear. Now I had about eight or ninety Marines in tow, a real confidence builder. I felt more secure, but I realized that the trail was leading us between steep embankments, that we were still channelized with no opportunity to deploy flankers.

The trail was very well made, no doubt the effort of a great many hands. As we followed it over the top of the hill right behind the bunker complex, passing covered spider holes every twenty feet or so, I was able to look off five or six hundred meters into the forest, right at the top of another hill. There was a strange, irregular shape on the distant hill—not quite jungle canopy and not quite a cleared area. I snapped my fingers to get the attention of the platoon commanders and, when they turned my way, I motioned toward the far hill. I was in about the center of the 2nd Platoon, and Little John was a little ahead of me. He passed my signal to the Marine in front of him and the Marine passed it on, and so forth until we got the point's attention. He turned, saw me motioning toward the irregularity, found it for himself, and signaled that he would keep an eye on our position relative to it.

I thought about leaving the trail and moving cross country toward the irregularity, but there was every reason to believe—hope—that the trail would lead us to it or closer to it. I hated being on the trail; I wanted to get flankers out because I was convinced that all the noise we had made earlier would draw in any NVA units in the area, if there were any. Our advance directly up their trail was a perfect setup for them. We continued to pass spider holes, each of which was a well-built foxhole whose spoil had been carried off and which were covered by a latticework of leaves, vines, and branches.

My heart was all the way up in my mouth, but I decided to keep the column on the trail. We would get to where we were going that much faster and there was no way the opposition could have failed to have noted our presence if they were in the area. By then, I trusted the point's instincts and the vigilance of the rest of the men. After awhile however, it became obvious that the trail was going to pass the hill on which we had spotted the irregularity, so I once again transmitted a voiceless order to the point to hold up. When he turned to see what I wanted, I motioned him to lead us off the trail, directly up the hill toward the irregularity. As soon as we left the trail, I had both platoons get flankers out. If the irregularity on the hill was what I thought and hoped it was, there was every reason to suppose it would be defended.

As we were nearing the irregularity, which could no longer be seen as such, the point topped a tiny rise, stopped for a moment, pulled back, dropped to his knee, and motioned for Little John to come forward. I caught the signal but stayed where I was. After a few moments, Little John turned and pointed at me, then motioned me forward. I waved to one of my radiomen so he would follow me.

As I hunkered down beside the point and the lieutenant, I asked, "What the hell's going on?"

"Sir," Little John answered, "we found the rocket site."

"Holy shit," I exclaimed, "let me see!"

The point and Little John led the way up the rise. We were all crawling when we reached the top and eased our heads up. About twenty meters in front of us, in a lightly wooded area on the side of the hill we had been approaching, were a dozen or so long black objects, right out in the open. Each was about seven feet long and about fifteen inches in diameter. They were obviously 122mm rocket launchers. Beside each launcher was a line of long stakes with vines wound around them. It was easy to see that the NVA rocketmen could erect the stakes and vines as bipods to support the rocket tubes at angles from which the rockets could strike the Khe Sanh Combat Base, which was directly at our backs, though miles away.

I called Battalion right away to let them know what I had found, and about fifteen minutes later the battalion S-3 (operations officer) called back to tell me that they were sending a helicopter to pick up "a few samples for identification." I was flabbergasted, and rather imprudently blurted into my radio handset, "You gotta be kidding me."

I was content with looking at those things from a distance of about twenty meters, but there was no way I wanted to get up close to them. Talk about sucker bait. I added that I thought the launchers might be booby-trapped, but the S-3 was adamant. "No," he said, "Regiment wants you to load a few in a helicopter and send them out."

"Aw shit," I thought, but I answered, "Okay." As if I had a choice. "Roger. Out.

I gave the handset back to my radioman and thought, "Okay, Captain, your leadership's been challenged. Go ahead and pick two young privates and say, 'You can be Polish minesweepers; go up there and stomp around and see if those things blow up.' " I knew I couldn't ask the troops to do something I wouldn't do in a million years, so I had everyone get down under cover and selected four wide-eyed Marines at random. The five of us made our way straight up the trail to the rocket site, very carefully feeling for trip wires as we inched across the open ground.

We found three 122mm rocket warheads, aiming stakes, fuses, and fuse boxes in among the launchers, each with Chinese markings. It was difficult to tell if the rocket site that ever been used, for we found no telltale burn marks from rocket ignitions. However, bark had been burned from several of the trees, so it was possible that the site had been used. (Battalion later claimed that it was the site from which Khe Sanh had been rocketed on June 28, but I have no idea how that conclusion was reached.)

After placing two of the Marines on lookout, the rest of us began an ardent search for booby traps for long minutes after we reached the nearest fully assembled rocket. All three of us were on our hands and knees, lightly brushing and scratching the ground. There did not seem to be any booby traps, but the general drift of the muttering—mine and theirs—was that we were nuts to press the issue. At last— minutes seemed like hours—I sucked in my breath and said, very softly, "Okay, let's lift it."

We congregated around the deadly metal cylinder, took its weight in our hands, sucked in our breaths, closed our eyes, hunched our heads into our shoulders, thought prayers . . . and heaved it off the ground.

It was dead silent and there was no movement for a very long interval. I looked at the others and they looked at me. One of them shrugged and the other broke into a grin. If they were alive, then I was alive. The overbearing *whomp, whomp, whomp* of the H-34 arriving overhead confirmed our analysis that we were still alive, still in Vietnam. One of us—maybe it was me—said, "Whew," and we started pulling the rocket out to the clear patch of ground on which the helo was settling.

The helo crew yanked the first rocket into the cargo bay and sat rock still while we quickly selected and lifted the second specimen. After we had heaved the third rocket, two additional launchers, and all the fuses and fuse cases aboard the H-34, the crew chief handed us a bunch of demolition packs. I could not hear what the man was saying, but it was obvious that we were expected to demolish any remaining rockets and launchers we could find.

The helo left and the rest of my Marines arrived. I sent fire teams in all directions to guard the site and then I had a look around. First, I checked my map and noted that the launchers were indeed oriented toward the combat base. This must have been the site from which the base was regularly rocketed—one of them, anyway. So, chalk one up for Lima Company. Of course, new launchers would be brought in and set up elsewhere, but this day's work would provide a little respite. The setup was crude but effective. The launchers were manufactured, of course, but they were stabilized on bipods constructed of wooden poles cut in the forest, pounded into the ground, and tied off with jungle vines. Neat!

We uncovered a total of twenty-two launchers, including the five we had sent back. As soon as the remaining launchers were blown, I had the platoon commanders reform their troops so we could continue down the trail, which led over the back side of the hill. The leader of the fire team that had been guarding the trail said that he had been about seventy-five meters out, that the trail was in even better shape than it had been to that point, and that there were even wide steps cut into the side of the hill, leading down into the next draw.

We were by then quite far from Khe Sanh, and getting farther away with every step. We crossed over the hill the rocket launchers had been on, descended on steps into the next draw, and climbed more steps up the side of the next hill. The string of spider holes never gave out, leading me to believe that they were less fighting positions than covered shelters in which NVA soldiers could avoid being seen by our aircraft.

After we crossed the next hill behind the rocket hill, we walked along a ridgeline until we came to a sort of graduated slope. Off to the left I could see plainly a small bunker complex. We checked it out and found that it was a small medical facility. Bloody waste bandages were strewn throughout the site, as were many broken glass medicine vials. Obviously, some of our counterbattery or harassment-and-interdiction (H&I) fire had drawn blood, though it was impossible to tell how long before our arrival that had been—days or even weeks. Probably the latter, for there was no smell of death.

I grew increasingly apprehensive as we plodded farther up the trail. I could not accept the evidence that nobody was home, that this extensive network of trails and fighting, living, and even medical bunkers had been abandoned or painstakingly built up for no apparent reason. In one sense, *we* were the reason for building up the defenses. So, here we were. Where were they?

We were somewhere deep in the jungle, with no terrain features except an unmapped enemy trail to guide us. I could not see any of the hills or other prominent terrain features that showed on my map that would have told me where the winding road was taking us. Even scarier was the realization we had probably walked beyond the edge of the artillery fan from the combat base. We probably would have to duke it out without artillery support if we did run into the local tenants.

The point had been bitten by the same bug. Progress had slowed to a series of stops and starts as he literally tested the wind for smells and noises only senses supercharged with fear could ever pick up. After awhile, though the view ahead up the trail was clear, he was stopping every few steps to sniff the air and listen. Every time he stopped, the backup man stopped to do the same and the lead fire team spread out with their weapons pointed outboard and their eyes scanning the overhead canopy and on out to the edge of their vision.

I was running all this through my mind when the point suddenly dropped to his belly. I looked right at him as he pointed up around a bend and motioned for Little John. Shortly, Little John motioned me forward. When I got there, the point pointed and I peeked around the bend. I saw that the foot trail we had been following suddenly widened out to about the width of a truck. I motioned the point forward and followed him with Little John and our radiomen in tow. Sure enough, the trail had become a road, complete with tire tracks from heavy trucks. That certainly got my attention. As near as I could tell, we were in the middle of nowhere with no previous information about a truck road anywhere nearby.

We eased on down the road about a hundred meters, testing the air every few steps but perceiving no overt danger. Then I called Battalion to report my estimated location and to tell them what we had found. This, along with all the other news we had reported, put Battalion into a dither. The order I soon received borders on the classic: "Hey, get your buns back here. We're pulling the whole battalion back out of the field." They wanted me to return to the company base on the finger for a helo flight back to the combat base.

In a way, I was relieved, but I couldn't believe what I was hearing, so I told them again what we had found, reinforced my estimate of the situation, and suggested that we do something about it. I wanted to ambush the truck trail. What a setup!

The S-3 told me that, regardless of the apparent correctness of my plan, I was to work my way back to the finger to be picked up. He added that the entire company was to be there within ninety minutes or two hours. If we were going to do it, we had to leave immediately and really hump our way out of there. So, I acknowledged and set the platoons in motion. Truth to tell, I was ready to go back anyway; the presence of the truck road seemed to support my surmise that we were outside the range of our artillery support. As I collected the fragments of my disappointment, I realized that I needed to start getting concerned about my attitude; I might have allowed my enthusiasm to lead us all into a situation in which we would have needed help. The thwarting of my impulsive enthusiasm proved to be a valuable early lesson, for I soon realized that the same sort of emotional response probably had killed my predecessor and, no doubt, countless others.

So, we reversed the column and moved a hell of a lot faster going back than we had come. We remained careful and vigilant—we assumed the NVA had moved in behind us—but we knew what to expect from the trail and where all the apparent danger points were. We arrived atop the finger, exhausted and emotionally wrung out, but without incident, as the first flight of helos was descending.

We were in the Khe Sanh in plenty of time for a hot supper.

CHAPTER 5

Calling Khe Sanh a combat base was a misnomer in the summer of 1967. Everything was above the ground and there were no defensive positions per se. If an infantry battalion or company was back in the base, it went into position on the perimeter line, but the place was really defended full time by its tenant units. These included a battery or two of 105mm howitzers, a few 107mm towed mortars (Howtars), part of a reconnaissance company, a company or so from 1/26, and various headquarters and support units belonging or attached to the 26th Marines headquarters. All the combat base's fighting positions had been dug by hand; there were no trenchlines and no fortified bunkers except for a few old concrete bunkers the French had built in the 1950s. Of these, one had been taken over by the regimental headquarters and at least one other was in the hands of a supply unit. As far as I know, none of the French bunkers were on the so-called defensive perimeter. All in all, in my estimation, Khe Sanh was less a combat base than an open encampment partly surrounded by crude, minimal defenses.

My first view of the combat base had been at the end of my helicopter flight from Phu Bai, the last part of which had followed Route 9 straight up from Dong Ha. Route 9, over which any relief force would have to advance, was a long, winding road barely wide enough to allow two jeeps to pass. It took a drastic turn at Ca Lu, crossed the Rao Quan River, and followed the twisting watercourse up the escarpment to Khe Sanh. Most of our supplies and heavy building materials climbed that long, narrow, vulnerable dirt road. There were plans to lengthen and hardtop the runway, but most of the stuff that flew in came on helicopters and the occasional Air Force C-123 cargo plane. The strip was also used for light planes, including artillery spotters. A few Huey gunships were more or less permanently stationed at the helo pad, but that was about it for close air support unless fast movers—jets—were available from Danang or the other lowland air bases.

The combat base was on the largest expanse of flat ground on the plateau because of the runway. In every direction, Khe Sanh was dominated by high ridges, from many of which mortar fire could reach the runway. Two of the hills that had figured prominently in the Hill Fights—861, to the northwest, and 881S, farther to the west—were permanently occupied by companies of 1/26, and Hill 950, with its radio tower, was permanently guarded by a reinforced rifle platoon from 1/26. All the other hills were regularly visited by patrols from the reconnaissance company, one of the remaining companies of 1/26, or all or parts of 3/26, which had more or less been assigned as the regional maneuver element for the duration of a long-running sweep program called Operation Crockett. The U.S. Army Special Forces people at Lang Vei also ran patrols, no doubt into Laos, and the Marine combined action company (CAC Oscar) at Khe Sanh ville regularly visited all the villages in the area and patrolled the countryside.

In addition to the platoon of Howtars and one or two batteries of six 105mm howitzers apiece, Khe Sanh could be reached by long-range Army 175mm self-propelled guns located at Camp Carroll and the Rockpile, both to the east. A platoon of 4.2-inch baseplate mortars was also working out of the combat base and had guns set up on Hill 861 and Hill 881S. There was also a platoon each of M-48 tanks (five tanks, each with a 90mm gun) and Ontos (five light tracked vehicles, each mounting six exposed 106mm recoilless rifles), but that was it, except for the infantry battalions' organic 106mm recoilless-rifle and 81mm mortar platoons.

There was no question about the presence of NVA units out there, but contacts had been fairly light since the conclusion of the Hill Fights, in the spring. The big fear was that the NVA could cross the Khe Sanh plateau and mount a massive attack into the lowland portion of Quang Tri Province. Our being there made it harder for them to get organized without running into trouble. Though the NVA generally stayed out of the Marines' way, they occasionally rocketed the combat base, mortared our large sweeping units, and ambushed smaller patrols. We drew blood and they drew blood, but neither side accomplished much. The officers who were with the battalion when I joined didn't think we were getting much done.

*B*ecause 3/26 was operating out of Khe Sanh temporarily, as part of a special operation, our battalion rear echelon remained in Phu Bai. Since we might be called upon to move anywhere at any time, it was felt that we needed the flexibility of the centrally located base camp. However, because the main body was expected to operate out of Khe Sanh for several months, the battalion rear echelon had been stripped of some assets, which, under Major Carl Mundy, had established a hybrid battalion rear CP at Khe Sanh. Like all the other units residing or rotating through the combat base, Major Mundy's battalion rear CP group lived in hard-backed GP tents, which were large enough to house twenty or thirty people apiece. Whenever one or more of the letter companies rotated back to the combat base, everyone lived in the GP tents, few of which had sandbag blast walls and none of which provided a lick of overhead protection. No one I spoke with was concerned about that; the June 28 rocket attack that had ruined Major Mundy's utilities was the first such attack on the base during 3/26's tour.

The S-3 worked in the battalion combat operations center (COC) with his assistants and their clerks and all their radios. Generally, the CO also manned the COC if there was some action going on, but Lieutenant Colonel Hoch liked to work in the field, so the S-3 and a large part of his COC watch team were often with him. When that happened, Major Mundy oversaw the cut-down rear COC. (Normally, the battalion exec would have been living with the battalion rear echelon at Phu Bai, but the unusual circumstances of Operation Crockett justified his presence at Khe Sanh.)

The 3/26 encampment at Khe Sanh was located in the northwest corner of the combat base. Because the ground inside the combat base took a gradual slope toward the northwest, we could actually look down onto the runway area. At its closest, our area came within about

150 meters of the runway. We manned no fixed lines. Every time a company came in, it manned a little bubble around the CP area. If two companies came in, they manned two bubbles, and so forth.

Each company had its own CP tent, which was shared by the company commander, exec, first sergeant (if he was forward), and company gunnery sergeant. In Lima company's case, Lieutenant Tom Biondo, our artillery FO, also squeezed in. The company command radiomen and the company senior corpsman lived outside the CP tent in lean-tos they built from their poncho liners. The Lima Company command group usually amounted to eight or nine men. We all had to stand radio watches in rotation, but it was often impractical to include me in the rotation because I was frequently away at meetings at Battalion or attending to other business.

Each rifle platoon manned a fixed portion of the company bubble, and the weapons platoon divided up its M-60 machine guns and set up its 60mm mortars, all assets belonging to the company commander and deployed at his pleasure. Each platoon commander and platoon sergeant was obliged to sleep somewhere close behind his own platoon's position, along with the platoon radiomen and corpsmen.

The company had one or more listening posts out every night, and even while in base there were always a few patrols to be run. Basically, however, being back at the combat base was a paid vacation, intentionally easy so the officers and men could get some rest, good food, and new gear before going out again. We also used our time in the rear to do all the little things we couldn't do in the field. In addition to eating a lot, we showered, read and wrote letters, took care of medical problems, cleaned our weapons and gear, and, in my case, tried to accomplish all the little administrative chores that I was not able to do out in the bush.

As soon as Lima Company got back to the combat base at about 1700, July 5, we began eating regular A rations. The battalion had several mess tents erected—one for officers and staff NCOs and the others for sergeants and below. Even if the whole battalion was in town, we could all go inside and sit down at tables.

Prior to dusk, at around 1800, the battalion commander regularly conducted a meeting with his senior staff and any company commanders who happened to be in. When I arrived for my first staff meeting shortly after flying the company back into the base, I met the S-3, face to face for the first time. I also met the Mike Company commander,

Captain Andy DeBona, a former sergeant, about thirty years old, who had been directly commissioned from the ranks.

Andy DeBona was impressive. He had been the supply officer (S-4) when 3/26 arrived in Vietnam, but he had been given Mike Company several months prior to my arrival. He had a good reputation as a fearless leader and was rumored to be extremely well liked by his men despite the rather onerous sobriquet his company had acquired— Medevac Mike, in honor of all the casualties resulting from Andy's unquenchable urge to close with the enemy.

Major Carl Mundy, the thoroughly professional but thoroughly likable exec, was a great jokester, always ready for a laugh. He had pranged me a few times during our time together on my way out to Lima Company, and he and Andy started right in as soon as I arrived, unshaven and unwashed, that first night in the rear. By the time Lieutenant Colonel Hoch arrived, Mundy, DeBona, Camp, the S-3, and a handful of staff officers were rolling in the aisles with tears streaming down our cheeks. I had to believe that this was a fairly common occurrence around the 3/26 CP, but the CO had the look of an adult who was mystified with the behavior of children. I think he might have been upset because he was being left out.

The humor was stinging, and it went in all directions. At one noon meal after the entire battalion had been in town for a few days, Major Mundy arrived a few minutes late, greeted the tableful of captains, and headed for the chow line. Of course, we had dreamed up a little stunt before he arrived, based on the jocular untruth that the whip-thin exec was a chowhound of the first order. As soon as Mundy reached the line, I had two of my young Marines stand on either side of him, holding meal trays. After a few moments, the exec bit in. "Hey, Marines, this is the officers' line. The enlisted line is in the next tent." The two Lima Company men turned to him and, as we had coached them, said "Well, Major, we're just here to help you carry your food." The major caught on right away and turned to find us all bent over in laughter.

*I*t wasn't all fun and games. The battalion had been alerted for possible involvement in a new operation, dubbed Buffalo. Apparently, the Marine base at Dong Ha was getting hit hard by NVA mortars and rockets, and an all-out NVA attack was expected. On July 7, when

Dong Ha reportedly took nine hundred rounds in a twenty-four-hour period, we were placed on twenty-hour-hour standby to proceed off the plateau by helicopter and truck on direct order by the 3rd Marine Division commander. We hung around Khe Sanh all day on July 8 and 9, getting ourselves and our gear into shape.

Early on July 10, Lima Company was ordered out on a search-and-destroy operation in the area southeast of Khe Sanh ville and Mike Company was sent on a similar mission toward nearby Hill 832. We were to land by helicopter on a little flat area on a long razorback ridge.

We quickly worked out the plan by which we were going to land in the tiny zone right on the ridgeline. Tom Biondo, our artillery FO, developed a fire plan to prep the landing zone, and it was approved on the run. The fog on the hills was so thick that day that it was nearly noon before we finally were able to begin. We broke the company down into helicopter loads and left the Khe Sanh helo pad to mount the assault. I was aboard the third of eight twin-rotor CH-46 transport choppers assigned to carry out the lift.

The arty prep started on time and we launched the eight helos, circled while the 105mm shells landed, and then followed the leader toward the ridgeline. Someone blew it. Somehow or other, we went into the wrong zone or the arty had prepped the wrong zone; something was screwed up. When my helo was flaring out to land, I saw that we were circling an obscure point that was covered with high elephant grass—not a landing zone at all! It was absolutely obvious to me that no artillery rounds had landed there. I was sure that someone in the lead bird—the flight commander, maybe?—would figure out that we weren't supposed to be going into an unprepped grass-choked zone when all the maps showed a cleared area.

Well, the first aircraft went in and we quickly followed. The elephant grass was ten or twelve feet high and the helicopter pilots wouldn't actually land because they didn't know what they were getting into; they hovered and the troops had to jump off the back ramp. This was insane! All the Marines were carrying forty- or fifty-pound packs on their backs, plus all their other equipment—helmet, rifle, flak jacket, canteens, ammunition, probably a few mortar rounds or M-60 ammo cans—and the pilots were asking us to go jumping into elephant grass so high we didn't exactly know where the ground was. There could have been logs, rocks, or pits down there. Punji stakes? Anything!

When it became completely obvious that the helos weren't going to touch down, my Marines started jumping, albeit with immense trepidation.

The first two aircraft unloaded and then my turn came. I jumped and landed okay, but I couldn't bull my way through the elephant grass to make room for the rest of my "stick." Now we had thirty or forty men on the ground in an area only thirty meters by thirty meters, none of us was making much progress to the edge of the zone, and there were still five helos loaded with Marines hovering overhead.

It took an immensely long time to get the lead platoon and my command group off the minuscule "drop zone" so the next platoon could try its luck in this free-fall, airborne cluster fuck. After the sixth helo dumped its load, I called to shut the whole thing off.

We had two reinforced platoons on the ground, which was about all we could handle right then. I told the rear platoon commander, who was still airborne, to take the day off. If there was trouble, the remaining platoon could be dropped in to aid us or clear and protect the zone.

With my command group between the two footborne rifle platoons, we started moving along with the spine of the ridge, which was narrow and fell steeply away about a hundred feet into narrow draws on either side. We were on a very distinct trail going right along the top of the ridge. It was heavy jungle all the way, with sixty- and seventy-foot trees blotting out most of the sunlight. We had no idea what was ahead on the ridge, and we had made a lot of noise jumping in, so we were very careful about moving along. I was extremely concerned because we were channelized along the trail, moving in a column, literally one Marine behind another one. I could not put out flankers because of the steep drops only a foot or two from the trail.

At about 1400, the point penetrated into an old Marine position, undoubtedly left over from the Hill Fights. It was very distinctly a Marine position, with our distinctive type of foxholes and littered with parts of Marine uniforms and equipment. Among other American gear, we found two M-14 bayonets, a burned M-14 rifle stock, and two bandoleers of rusty M-14 ammunition. There were also a number of jackets, poncho liners, helmet liners, even a jungle boot, and a few cases of C rations.

When I reported our findings, Battalion said they were sending up a helicopter to pick up all the debris in case it related to any Marines who were posted as missing in action. That made it time for a break, so I set out fire teams ahead and behind on the trail and gave the order to stand easy without removing packs or web gear.

I was looking around, watching what was going on, when I happened to look over toward my company radioman, Corporal David Johnson. There were big blotches all over the legs of his trousers. I thought, "What the hell?" and called out, "Hey, John, what the hell you got on your trousers?'" He looked at them and said, "Jesus, I don't know." He stood up and dropped his trousers and we discovered that we had run into leeches. The blotches were where his trouser legs had squashed some of the bloodsuckers. The beasts were about two inches long and fatly engorged with his blood. That gave me the slimiest, creepiest feeling I had ever had. Johnson kept muttering "Oh, Jesus Christ!" as we squirted the leeches with lighter fluid and insect repellent so they would drop off. Fortunately, the docs knew better than to pull them off because their heads would stay in and the wounds would become infected.

After Doc Bratton, the company senior corpsman, finished working on Corporal Johnson, we looked around at the grass and trees and, sure as hell, I could see armies of little leeches, each as big as a pencil head, each one sniffing the air, trying to find out where we were. When I ordered everyone to check their bodies for leeches, we found out that a lot of people had them. As soon as the debris had been loaded aboard the helo from the combat base, I gave the order to move out, to get as far from the leeches as we could.

As we headed up the trail, we encountered the usual stop-and-start delays as the point checked out every square inch of ground out ahead. Suddenly, during one delay, I saw the Marine right in front look up, look again, and then look again. He turned slowly toward me and pointed so I could see what he had seen. After a moment of staring, I saw a tiny movement in the tree by his shoulder. We stared and stared until we drew a little crowd, and finally someone said that it was a bamboo viper. I had heard of them; if bitten, you get about three screams and you're a goner. Lovely!

We continued to shuffle along, stopping and starting, stopping and starting. At length, we stopped but never started again. I couldn't figure out what the hell was going on, so I called up the 3rd Platoon point to find out what the holdup was. The platoon commander, Lieutenant Bill Cowan, said, "Come forward." Corporal Johnson and I went forward and found the point sitting on the ground, shaking like a leaf. I looked at him in utter disbelief and finally asked, "What the hell's the matter with him?" No one answered, so I leaned over the point and asked, "What's the matter, Marine?"

The story finally emerged. A good point is a vigilance machine, a human sound and movement detector. He has his weapon on full automatic and constantly screens the ground in front of him, looking for ambushes and booby traps. Being that way is how a point stays alive and keeps everyone else alive. It is a very, very dangerous position to be in, an incredibly intense experience. So, there was our point, out ahead of his backup man and the vanguard fire team, his attention riveted on the ground. (The backup man searches high.) What he didn't see was a pair of rock apes as they swung through the trees, literally right beside him. When the Marine looked up in response to a noise and saw those black, hairy beasts swinging through the trees, it just literally scared the shit out of him. He had to sit down for a long time to get his nerve back up.

By that time, the day was getting on, so I decided to hold up there. Setting in a night defense is a snap on a razorback ridgeline with a distinct trail; all we had to do was set in a machine gun at either end of our bivouac. No fuss.

We spent an uneventful night, but when we awoke we found ourselves on the brink of a terrible tragedy. One of the Marines slept with his mouth open and a leech had fallen off a leaf into his throat. The leech had swelled up before the Marine realized it and the poor guy woke up gagging. He almost smothered to death in his own vomit before Doc Bratton got the goddamn thing out of there.

My initial understanding was that we would be in the hills for a week, but evidently we had done whatever Battalion or Regiment had wanted us to do. As soon as we checked in by radio on the morning of July 11, the COC told us to come on back. We turned around and hiked back the way we had come—another uneventful walk in the sun in which I saw nothing of interest. We reached our former drop zone, cut the grass down, and prepared to be extracted. The helos arrived, landed, and lifted us out without incident, all in one flight. I have no idea what the whole trip was about.

C H A P T E R 6

W e remanned our company bubble as soon as we returned to the combat base on the afternoon of July 11. Unfortunately, one of the artillery batteries was set up right behind our company position and, since they fired H&I missions at odd intervals throughout the night, we got very little of the rest we craved and were supposed to be getting.

As soon as I dropped my gear on the deck of my part of the company CP tent, I decided to head for the communal shower to wash off the grime. As I walked across the battalion area, a friendly battalion staff officer called me over and said, "Hey, come on over to my bunker."

"Shit," I replied, "I didn't know there was a bunker around here."

"Yeah," he nodded as he led the way, "we've got a bunker over here."

It was a hell of a deal. A small cabal of battalion officers had gotten somebody—probably the Seabees—to dig a deep pit, which they had covered over after lowering in some packing crates. It reminded me of a World War I movie. We had to walk down about ten stairs and there was even a door. When I passed through the door, I found myself in a little room, about ten feet by ten feet. Nice, but I wanted a shower. "No sweat," the officer claimed as he went over to the far wall and—opened it up! Behind the false wall was a shower! He showed me where they had buried a 55-gallon drum and installed a pipe with a spigot head. The whole thing ran on gravity. There was even a drain! He told me that the water tank was completely buried except for the camouflaged filler hole.

Of course, nobody was supposed to have a personal shower, but this baby was a well-kept secret and its proud owners were very discreet. The mere fact that I had been offered knowledge was a sure sign of my acceptance by my fellow officers, an honor of the first magnitude.

We maintained the shower secret—or thought we did—for a few more weeks after my initiation. However, one day, one of the crew unknowingly emerged from the bunker with a rather lurid yellow cast to his skin. It turned out to be marker dye from a smoke grenade. We never found out for sure who the trickster was, but it was noted by many that Lieutenant Colonel Hoch—who was not a member of the shower club—had a smirk on his face every time he saw one of us.

We had a weird experience several hours after we got back into the combat base on July 11. Scuttlebutt had it that the NVA had used gas during an attack on Con Thien—which was under siege at that time—so Regiment sent word that all the troops were to be issued gas masks and taught how to use them. Lima Company was just turning out for a gas drill when two planes happened to fly over the base. Someone in one of the tanks guarding the perimeter saw the planes and then saw a horde of Marines wearing gas masks. He jumped to a logical but incorrect conclusion and snapped off a warning to the regimental CP that the base was undergoing an aerial gas attack. Regiment had no idea what was going on, so they called down to Chu Lai and got two fast movers scrambled to look for the attackers. Meantime, the entire base was put on Red Alert until we got the whole screwup straightened out. Then, everything fell in on my head and I was sure I was going to be sent home in irons. However, everyone was laughing so hard that the matter was discreetly dropped.

On July 12, Lima Company detached one platoon to assist Kilo and India companies in a sweep along the 758 ridgeline. The rest of the company was on standby to fly out if the sweep produced any results, but nothing turned up. That night, I planned to accompany an ambush patrol through the wire to set in astride a possible NVA reconnaissance route. At the last minute, I decided to remain in camp. That might have been because they served a steak dinner that evening, the first really good meal I had heard about since my arrival in-country.

We ate like pigs, but who was watching? I turned in after the usual evening bull session, but I was awakened at about midnight by a stomach ache. No big deal, I thought, and I went back to sleep. However, at about 0400, a sharp pain in my lower right side sat me straight up in my rack. I was in a cold sweat.

I had had this same type of pain years and years earlier, as a youngster. It had happened on a Christmas Eve and, because it was Christmas Eve, the family doctor decided he wouldn't take my appendix out and just dosed me up with penicillin. The appendix went down and they didn't have to operate.

So there I was, a company commander in the front lines at Khe Sanh and I realized with a start that I was having another appendicitis attack. I thought I could hold on to it, but the longer I laid there, the worse it hurt. After awhile, I knew that I had to get down to the sickbay. My exec, Jaak Aulik, heard me stirring around and moaning and he called softly through the canvas partition, "What's the matter?"

"I think I'm having an appendicitis attack."

"Oh shit."

"I think I've gotta go to the rear."

"Well," Jaak offered as he came up off his rack, "let me get a couple of troops to go with you."

"No, I'll go by myself." But, when I stood, I nearly passed out from the pain. Jaak rousted Doc Bratton, who agreed with me that I probably had appendicitis. Doc offered to accompany me to the Battalion Aid Station (BAS), but I told him to go back to sleep. He didn't want to let me loose on my own, but I made it an order.

Now I had to make it back through the company area and on into the battalion area. I was challenged about every ten steps, but I was too sick to play the game; besides, the password had been driven from my mind. "Who's there," a sentry would challenge, and I would reply, "It's me." To which would follow, "Who's 'me'?" I would tell the sentry, "This is the Six," and then he would recognize my voice. I must have had that exchange a half-dozen times just getting through the company area. I have no idea how I negotiated the battalion area because I was delirious from the pain and exertion by then. It was pitch dark and I couldn't see a thing; I was feeling my way across the ground with my feet.

Somehow, I worked my way about a hundred meters to the BAS and woke up a pair of corpsmen. They were upset about having to get up, even when I said, "Lookit, I'm having an appendicitis attack." They asked me to describe the pain and, when I told them, they woke up the battalion surgeon. The corpsmen had me laid out on a cot by the time the surgeon arrived.

"Where's it hurt?"

"It's in the right side of my abdomen."

Instead of taking my word for it, the son of a bitch pushed his fingers down right into my side. God, that hurt! It hurt so bad that I threw up all over the BAS. And, dammit, I missed the doctor, who observed in that haughty-doctor way, "Yep, I think you've got appendicitis, all right."

"Okay," I croaked, "what do I do?"

"Well, there's nothing we can do tonight. You'll just have to gut it out till morning."

I was so new in-country that I didn't realize that I was an emergency medevac—a guy who was in danger of losing life or limb, which is about what an appendicitis attack amounts to. I was supposed to be evacuated for hospital treatment right away because the damn thing might burst at any moment. But either the doctor was new or he didn't give a damn, and I didn't know any better, so I said "Okay, all right, doc."

By then, thank goodness, Doc Bratton had had second thoughts about sending me to the BAS on my own and had come down to see how I was getting on. "Skipper," he exclaimed as he entered the BAS, "what's the matter?"

"Well, the doctor agrees that I've got an appendicitis attack."

"Oh shit," he responded, "what are we going to do?"

"The doctor says I've gotta wait till morning."

"Well, hell, I'll help you back to the company area."

I got up off the rack, but I couldn't straighten up because of the pain. We worked our way back through the lines and finally reached my tent. By then, everybody was concerned about what was going on, which made me feel good despite the unbearable pain.

With Doc Bratton in attendance, I drowsed in my rack until first light and then Doc helped me back down to the BAS. As soon as we arrived, they tagged me for a flight to the rear. Battalion was notified that the exec had taken over the company.

I was all set to go, but they told me I was going to have to wait until they found a helicopter for me. So, like a complete numbnuts, I walked out and waited beside the runway. I had no idea when the helicopter was going to get there and I was doubled over from the pain. No one from the BAS took the trouble to see how I was doing.

Finally a CH-46 came in. I got to my feet and staggered out to see if they would give me a ride. When the crew chief saw my evacuation tag and how bent over and white I looked, he helped me up the ramp and ran forward to speak with the pilot. The bullshit ended right there. We took off as soon as they could get the blades revved up.

We got up in the air and, of course, the damned helicopter was shaking my guts. By then I was moaning uncontrollably and had shakes of my own. It was only a twenty-minute flight down to Phu Bai. We landed and, fortunately, as soon as I shuffled off, all bent over, I spotted a meat wagon that happened to be parked at the edge of the helo pad, only about twenty feet from the helicopter. I struggled over and asked the driver, "Hey, can you give me a ride to the med battalion? I'm hurting." The corpsman said, "Yeah, I can see you are," and drove straight over to the 3rd Medical Battalion. I got out of the ambulance and shuffled over toward the reception tent. As I walked in, everybody looked up at me. From the expressions on their faces, I could tell they knew I was hurting.

Before I really knew what happened, they had my clothes off, asked me what was the matter, and started to go through the diagnostic procedures. I don't remember much except that I ended up in an air-conditioned hut, freezing to death because I was buck naked. Someone said, "Hey, Captain, take a shower and we'll be right with you." The last thing I wanted to do was take a shower because I was freezing to death—and really, truly hurting—but I managed to do what I was told.

I managed to walk back out and, the next thing I knew, I was on a gurney, being wheeled down the passageway. That's the last thing I remember until I woke up hours later. The pain was gone and I felt a mound of gauze bandages covering what I imagined to be a great big scar over where my appendix used to be.

Coming out of the anesthesia, I found that I was lying on my right side—at least my head was rolled to the right—and I opened my eyes to see a Marine whose jeep had hit a land mine and had suffered a traumatic amputation of one of his legs. The whole leg was off and there was no bandage on the stump, which was literally right in my face. That made me feel terrible.

The med battalion's intensive care unit was air conditioned. I had worked in a meat market as a teenager and was immediately reminded of the smell of cool meat. As I came awake, the smell sort of gagged me.

There were all sorts of injuries. Two beds up from me was a Vietnamese interpreter who had taken mortar fragments in his abdomen. All of his intestines were sitting on his chest, just covered with a kind of cheese cloth. Periodically, someone had to go over and tell him to cough—I guess to keep pneumonia from setting in. I could not imagine the terrible agony that man had to face every time he had to cough while his stomach was split wide open.

I was probably the only nonbattle casualty in there. Late in the day—whatever time it was—some senior officer showed up a load of Purple Hearts and, when he got to me he asked, "Jeez, Captain, where were you wounded?" And I replied, "Aw shucks, I just had appendicitis. Don't leave a Purple Heart for me." He didn't, either.

Well, like everybody who is crazy, I tried to get out of there as soon as possible. Fortunately, there was an ironclad rule about the recuperative period in Vietnam because of the terrible heat and dirt. They told me right off that if I got out too soon my abdomen could become infected and I could get peritonitis, which was often fatal.

There was a Lieutenant Commander Price working at the med battalion—a Navy psychiatrist who called himself "Major" Price because he was working with Marines. He stood about six foot five and had shaved his head completely bald except for a tremendous handlebar mustache, which must have extended six inches away from his face on either side. He was an extremely funny man, but, since he was a psychiatrist, no one knew if he had a terrific sense of humor or if he was just crazy himself.

There was a story making its way through the ward that Price had found out that the MPs had seized some skin flicks that somebody had brought back from R&R and had been showing to the troops. As the story went, Major Price was trying to find some way to raise the morale of the wounded troops and happened to hear about the films. He went over the MPs and told them that it appeared that the purveyors of the filth were going to go be court-martialed and that, as a psychiatrist, he had to preview the films to see if there was something that might be psychologically wrong with the prisoners. The MPs bought it hook, line, and sinker. As soon as Price got the films, he brought them over to the med battalion and started showing them to the wounded men, which raised morale tremendously.

I got hold of a book the day after surgery, a story about the military and some highjinks. It was funnier than hell and got me laughing out loud. The only problem was that every time I started laughing I got a huge pain in my side. I was afraid I was going to bust my stitches, but the humor was a tremendous relief and I couldn't stop reading.

The med battalion was a weird place, full of bad omens. The helicopters never stopped flying in the wounded and dead from forward areas. There were big conex boxes—steel shipping containers about ten or twelve feet long, six or eight feet wide, and about six feet high—in which they stacked all the gear the casualties had on when they were flown in. At least one of the conex boxes was full of every type of weapon imaginable—machine guns, rifles, pistols, the whole shooting match. They just sat there until, periodically, the field logistics support group people would come out with empties and take the full ones back to their camp so they could repair or survey the weapons, utilities, and other gear.

Early one evening about a week after I had arrived at the med battalion, I heard a lot of commotion out in the front part of the hospital so, since I was by then ambulatory, I went out into Triage, a section of the hospital where the casualties were first brought in and evaluated and categorized by type and severity. Triage is also the place where they weed out the people who are dead on arrival and where they strip off the clothing and gear the dead and wounded are wearing. When I got out there, I saw that six or eight litters were propped up about chest high, each with a casualty on it. Off to the side were fifteen or twenty ambulatory wounded, crowded in along the wall. One of the litter patients was swearing a blue streak. I went over to see what the matter was and noted that he had a great big wound where he had been shot right through the fleshy part of his thigh. The bone did not appear to be damaged and it looked like he was going to be okay. I'm sure the wound was painful as hell, but he looked okay. I pegged him as a lieutenant and said, "What the hell's the matter, Lieutenant?"

"This is my whole goddamn platoon here," and he explained that they had been caught in an ambush and the whole platoon—twenty-seven men—had been wounded. He didn't think he had any men killed, but the whole platoon was there. The lieutenant was just madder than hell.

I have never gotten the hang of just sitting around, and ten days in the sickbay was as much as I could handle. On the morning of July 23, I got some clean utilities—no doubt a set recycled from the med battalion conex boxes—and discharged myself in time to grab a flight back up to Khe Sanh. When I reported back in at the battalion CP, good old Lieutenant Colonel Hoch got a look of deep concern on his face and dropped whatever he was doing to rush to my side. "Goddammit, Dick, what the hell are you doing here?"

"Well, sir, I'm coming back in. I'm in great shape."

"That's a bunch of crap, Captain. My brother had appendicitis and he was out for two or three weeks and *still* managed to get peritonitis. I want you to take it easy."

When I insisted that I was ready to take over the company again, he gave me a dubious look but nodded his head and clapped me on the shoulder. "Just take it easy, Dick. Okay?"

CHAPTER 7

When I returned to the company area and resumed command from Jaak Aulik, I learned that the day before Lima and Mike companies had been assigned to provide reaction forces to truck convoys using Route 9 between Khe Sanh and Dong Ha. Our designation was Sparrow Hawk and the convoys were known as Rough Riders. The duty obliged us to have a reaction force of up to the entire company ready to go with only thirty minutes notice.

Nothing had happened on July 22, the first day of the assignment, and nothing happened on July 23, my first day back. On July 24, while Lima Company sat on its thumbs, most of Mike Company was sent out onto Route 9 to sweep for mines. Frankly, I was just as happy to be sitting on my thumbs.

Our first call for Rough Rider duty came on July 25. We were flown down to Dong Ha, which is where Route 9 merged with National Route 1, a true highway. When I checked in with the convoy commander, I found out that the preceding convoy had been ambushed on the road. That made me really uptight so, being the ace tactician I knew myself to be, I decided that we were going to go tactically. We spent a lot of time getting sandbags, filling them, and placing them on the empty beds of the trucks so the troops could sit on them. We broke the company down into tactical units and spread them out so, if any particular part of the convoy got hit, we would have infantry right on hand. I also had the platoon commanders and squad leaders work out some immediate-action drills. I thought we did a pretty good job in the absence of directives.

I happened to write my mother that day that we had pulled out of Khe Sanh and that we were escorting trucks. A few weeks later, I got a letter from her that said, "I'm so thankful that you're okay and that you're just having to load trucks." That struck me as funny because there we were, armed to the teeth, alert for anything, the first unit to go through after a big ambush, ready to engage in instantaneous action. My mother got the letter and all she saw was trucks. She didn't understand what we were doing.

We commenced the run from Dong Ha late in the morning and ran west straight up Route 9, paralleling the Cam Lo River through Cam Lo, a Vietnamese village and Marine outpost, to Camp Carroll, a hilltop artillery base that had been named for a Marine captain who had been killed taking the hill. The highway then edged southwest for about five klicks to another artillery position known as the Rockpile—literally a pile of huge boulders. There, the road turned sharply south for five or six klicks to Ca Lu, where it again turned sharply west to follow the meandering Quang Tri River valley for about ten klicks up the steep escarpment to Khe Sanh.

The steep stretch between Ca Lu and Khe Sanh was real Indian country. All the way, the jungle grows down to the edge of the road. If anything was going to happen, that was the place. Beginning three or four klicks west of Ca Lu, the road verges were covered with spent casings from 40mm rounds fired by Army dusters—tracked dual-40mm antiaircraft gun carriers—and .50-caliber cartridges from Army quad-.50 antiaircraft vehicles. It looked to be the habit of the Army convoy escorts to simply fire randomly into the trees to keep the opposition's heads down. The trail of spent brass was four or five klicks long, really impressive. I later learned that this was just above the area in which the preceding convoy had been ambushed. According to the scuttle-butt, the Army had been moving several self-propelled 175mm guns through the area and they had been ambushed. All the 175s had been saved and the NVA had been defeated. In the few days between the ambush and the passage of our convoy, the Army air-defense battalion working in the area had been running recon-by-fire missions along the road, hence the spent brass.

I spent the whole trip in an open jeep riding with both legs outside the vehicle and my rifle across my lap. My radiomen, Sergeant Donald Vogt and Corporal David Johnson, were sitting back to back in the rear of the jeep, all set to jump out. A Bird Dog—a light single-prop artillery-observation spotter plane—was overhead, screening the roadway ahead and the verges. All my troops were locked and cocked; I don't think any of them put their weapons down for a second. It was very, very tense all the way up through there because we were expecting to get hit any minute.

We were just below Khe Sanh when we spotted green-clad men on the road. The tension rose until we could see that the men were Marines. At last, I could see that Andy DeBona was standing beside the roadway while his Mike Company Marines were sweeping for mines. I pulled out of the convoy to chat with Andy and learned that Mike Company had swept all the way down from the combat base, a distance of three or four miles.

As my troops passed Medevac Mike, Andy's troops shouted insults such as "Look at the candy-assed Marines riding." My guys yelled back stuff like, "We appreciate your support."

We were back in our company bubble by 1530. It had been a tense day that thankfully came to nothing. At the battalion commander's brief that evening, Lieutenant Colonel Hoch told me that Lima Company had done such a wonderful job that he was assigning us to escort the empty trucks back to Dong Ha and the very next convoy from Dong Ha back to Khe Sanh.

We got up long before sunrise the next morning, July 26, and found that it was raining like the dickens. When I checked in with the battalion CP, the S-3, told me that the Rough Rider mission had been scrubbed—literally—until the rain ended and the slippery roadway dried. Meantime, 3/26 had been designated as the 3rd Marine Division reserve and was on two-hour standby to support an attack by the 9th Marines into the DMZ.

We were rained out again on July 27, but the weather broke and the road dried, and we left Khe Sanh with the return convoy at 0940, July 28. Before we left, Andy DeBona led Mike Company back down the road and swept it for mines and booby traps to a distance of about three miles. When I passed Andy on the way out, I asked him if there was anything I could get him in Dong Ha. He told me he had smoked his last stogie and was nearly out of snuff; a year's supply ought to do it. I was so happy with the road-clearing job that I bought a week's supply for him.

The weather got crummy again before we could return to Khe Sanh and we wound up sitting around in Dong Ha like a bunch of orphans until the next big convoy formed and left on August 1, 1967. We got back up to the plateau well before noon and rode straight out to the Lang Vei Special Forces Camp, to which most of the trucks were carrying building materials (great stuff like concrete and milled lumber that the Marine Corps would never think of sending to Khe Sanh). We stopped in at the 3/26 area in Khe Sanh to grab fresh clothes and pick up our mail, and then we headed straight back to Dong Ha.

August 2 was a repeat of August 1. We escorted another immensely long convoy of trucks filled with heavy-duty construction materials to Lang Vei and arrived just before noon. Then we drove straight back to Dong Ha. We returned directly to Khe Sanh with another convoy on August 3, arrived at 1645, and were given the night off in our own tents.

That stopover provided the only incident of note for the entire period. I was dying of thirst and could not find a handy water buffalo, so I drank about a quart of water from a shower drum before I read the sign that warned it was nonpotable. I made the entire run down to Dong Ha the next day with my ass hanging outboard from my jeep. That was great fun for the troops at my expense, a little comic relief provided by the skipper for the benefit of company morale. That proved to be our last round trip of the period. We were back home in plenty of time for supper on August 5.

Nothing at all happened to us for the entire week following our relief from Rough Rider duty. Kilo and India companies ran daily patrols and sweeps in the hills around the base—took fire, captured or destroyed enemy weapons and gear, and even killed a few NVA. Later in the week, Mike Company also sent out several platoon-size sweeps, but we stayed in the combat base, providing security. Somewhere along in there, I realized that I had been an infantry company commander for over a month and had yet to experience—or even hear—an enemy weapon fired in my direction.

The respite provided the backdrop for a painful dilemma. Little spurts of action had stripped India Company of every one of its commissioned platoon commanders. Since all three of Lima Company's rifle platoons were commanded by lieutenants, I was ordered to send one officer to India Company. It was a given that I was not going to dispatch Little John because we shared a common arrival date in-country, so I had to decide between Bill Cowan and Dan Frazer. I thought long and hard and finally settled on Bill. I had nothing against him and no good reason to pick him—he was a very bright, extremely resourceful Annapolis graduate and a really fine field Marine—but I had to pick *someone*.

As soon as Bill was gone, I had to fill the 3rd Platoon command billet. I thought of letting the platoon sergeant take over, but he was a relatively junior sergeant. A better solution was moving the company gunny, Gunnery Sergeant Juan Almanza, up to the 3rd Platoon command slot and replacing him with the company's only other staff NCO, Little John's platoon sergeant, Staff Sergeant Marvin Bailey. The big advantage to all this was getting Gunny Almanza into a command billet. He was quite simply one of the finest Marine noncoms I ever worked with—before or since—and I knew that he would serve as the perfect role model for Lieutenants Frazer and Prince. Gunny Almanza was such a good company gunny that I hated to lose him there, but you can't have everything.

Among the many administrative chores that had been awaiting a break in the Rough Rider grind was the overdue promotion of several of our enlisted Marines. I decided to hold a company formation and promote them in style. It is traditional for the Marine who is promoted to have his new stripe "tacked on," an ordeal that entails bearing up to a punch on the arm by every man in the company of equal or greater rank. To appease tradition, we lined the company up in two lines and had the newly promoted Marines walk the gauntlet. The result of this rite of passage at the hands of fun-loving colleagues was a bunch of badly bruised upper arms. I actually found myself feeling sorry after seeing the results, but I knew that, in true Marine fashion, payback would eventually end the matter, even steven.

Late that week, we learned that the 26th Marines was going to have a change of command. The old CO, Colonel John Padley, was up for routine reassignment and they were bringing in Colonel David Lownds.

Regiment decided to give Colonel Padley a real send-off and Colonel Lownds a real welcome in the form of a ceremonial parade. I can imagine the conversation that revealed that a recent ceremonial platoon commander from 8th and Eye was sitting on his thumbs out in the 3/26 bubble. Naturally, Lima Company was given the task of providing the honor guard for the change-of-command ceremony.

I wasn't all that hot on the idea because I wanted to go out in the field. I didn't want to whip Lima Company into shape for a parade and I definitely didn't want to bear the humiliation if I wasn't able to do so.

Nothing is ever taken for granted in the Marine Corps, so we practiced and practiced for a week. All we really had to do was stand in ranks. The Marine Corps being the Marine Corps, we were called upon to shine our boots and clean everything spic and span. The troops were just overjoyed. Then we had to run inspections, do more cleaning and polishing, more inspections, and so forth. By about the third day, the troops were *begging* me to take them back into the field.

The ceremony went off without a hitch. What's to go wrong when you're standing at attention? I did a little marching and saluting as I passed the regimental colors between the colonels, and the troops got their pictures taken. It was a good change of command and everyone involved wound up feeling good.

*T*he sometimes bewildering variety of jobs, the on-again-off alerts, and the amazing lack of sustained operations in the field in pursuit of the enemy seemed strange to me, an avid reader of books about World War II and Korean War combat. I wondered where the war was during the whole of my first six seeks in command of Lima Company, most of which were spent in halfhearted, static vigilence on the Khe Sanh perimeter. But after awhile I stopped noticing all the things that were *not* taking place and concentrated on the work at hand, however unexciting and unrewarding. We all did. It was the way things were.

An infantry company is an unbelievably destructive component in a modern military force. It is designed and equipped to be self-contained and independent. A company commander has at his disposal his own organic supporting arms—60mm mortars and M-60 machine guns— and he can reasonably expect support from artillery and air units of virtually any strength. As such, an infantry company and its com- mander wield enormous destructive power.

A captain commanding an infantry company is the highest-ranking officer who lives with and like the grunts he commands. He has everything to do with policy execution but almost nothing to do with policy formation. Though often out of sight of his superiors, he is almost never out of radio contact with them or other higher headquarters.

Much has been made of the search-and-destroy strategy developed for the Vietnam War by General William Westmoreland, the overall commander of all U.S. forces in Vietnam. The objective of the strategy was to locate an elusive enemy, pin him, and destroy him. To do the job in its area of responsibility, the Marine Corps deployed twenty-one infantry battalions—which we called maneuver battalions—in Vietnam through the middle of 1967. Numerous bases were developed to provide the maneuver battalions with logistical, artillery, and air support. Those twenty-one battalions should have had an easy time controlling the countryside in South Vietnam's four northernmost provinces—I Corps—but the hard fact I was learning was that very few of the twenty-one maneuver battalions—eighty-four infantry companies—spent the majority of their time maneuvering in the field, finding, fixing, and destroying enemy units. Most companies of most maneuver battalions spent most of their time guarding the vulnerable bases from which the maneuvers were supposed to be supported.

While Lima Company was spending most of its time guarding Khe Sanh or escorting convoys bringing supplies and building materials up to Khe Sanh and Lang Vei, the senior Marine command in I Corps—III Marine Amphibious Force, a corps headquarters located in Danang—was turning our de facto lack of maneuverability into a virtue by developing something it eventually called the set-piece strategy. Since we could not get enough battalions into the field because we had to guard bases and supply routes, we were going to try to get the enemy to attack our bases—draw him into range of our guns and bombers and fighter-bombers so he could be destroyed. My company and all of 3/26 was about to be drawn briefly into the first set-piece battle, which had been shaping up at Con Thien all summer. Eventually, we also would be drawn into the best known set-piece battle, the siege of Khe Sanh.

But that was in the unknowable future. By mid August, I had stopped wondering where the war was or whether I would get into it. I went where I was sent and I did what I was told when I got there. It was the way things were.

Almost as soon as we completed the change-of-command ceremony at Khe Sanh, word came down that part of the battalion—Kilo and Lima companies and the Alpha command element—were to be detached to the control of the 9th Marines to assist the 2nd Battalion, 9th Marines (2/9) in a sweep operation into Leatherneck Square, an area just below the Ben Hai River, bounded at the corners by Con

Thien to the northwest, Gio Linh to the northeast, Dong Ha to the southeast, and Cam Lo to the southwest. Except for Rough Rider duty, this was to be Lima Company's first time away from the battalion since I had joined in late June. However, it was typical of the war the Marines were running in northern I Corps in 1967. In fact, we were lucky that half the battalion was going; often, individual companies would be detached from their parent units and would belong to some other battalion, often for weeks at a time. A lot of the time, battalions wouldn't belong to their parent regiments for months. (For example, at that time, 2/26 had *never* yet served under the direct control of the 26th Marines commander.)

A little after noon, August 13—as soon as we saddled up and joined Kilo Company and the Alpha command group—we were flown down to Dong Ha in helicopters. Facing us was a morning ride in waiting trucks.

Leatherneck Square was a fairly large cultivated area, about eight kilometers square. There were a lot of rice paddies interspersed with abandoned war-torn villages and scrub growth that sometimes grew to a height of ten or twelve feet. Except for two or three good roads, it was a very difficult area to get through.

The factor that made Leatherneck Square so important—and dangerous—was that it was located immediately south of the DMZ. It was fairly flat, but the high scrub proved to be excellent concealment for North Vietnamese Army units moving farther south into Quang Tri and neighboring Thua Thien provinces. Because III Marine Amphibious Force didn't have a lot of maneuver forces it could send out on sweeps, Leatherneck Square and neighboring areas were imperfectly and infrequently swept whenever troops could be spared.

With Echo Company, 2/9, in the lead and part of Alpha Company, 3rd Tank Battalion, interspersed through the column, our half of 3/26 left Dong Ha in a vehicle convoy at 0700, August 14. I felt very uncomfortable as we moved straight up the road into the market-garden area. Echo Company, 2/9, which had been working this area for months, seemed to have acquired a roadbound mentality. They led us straight out along the road without posting any flankers. My experiences humping the jungle around Khe Sanh had made me a believer in the rule regarding flankers—get them out at every opportunity because, if you walk into an ambush in a column formation, the enemy can chew you to pieces before you can get enough fire going forward.

Nothing happened. We drove west along Highway 9 from Dong Ha to Cam Lo and then turned north on a Marine-built roadway leading to Con Thien. After passing an artillery fire base known as C-2, we stopped in the middle of nowhere and disembarked. The trucks left as soon as we hopped off. The next and succeeding days would be spent on our feet, humping through the blisteringly hot, unbelievably humid lowlands east of the main supply route (MSR) linking C-2 with Con Thien.

In the morning, August 15, Kilo Company was bolstered by three tanks and Lima Company got two tanks. Each company was assigned a separate objective to sweep toward. Our objective was about a klick east of our night bivouac and our route of march was straight through the bush just to the north of an east-west trail.

Right off, we had a hell of a time with heat casualties. The troops, who had become acclimated to the cooler highlands, were dropping like flies. We even had a few heat-prostration cases, and there was every danger that one of them might die if the docs couldn't bring their temperatures down. Fortunately, we kept the sickest men alive long enough to get them medevaced by helicopters, but that process added to my woes because the helos clearly marked our position for any NVA or VC artillery or mortar forward observers who might be tracking our progress.

The tanks were a mixed blessing. It was nice to have their 90mm guns along, but every time I looked back along the spread-out company column, I saw a huge, distinctive dust cloud rising from beneath their treads. Every once in awhile, one or the other of the tanks sort of spun out. That made the loose dusty dirt pile up and usually led to a thrown tread. We had to stop each time and set out a defensive perimeter while the tank crew replaced the tread. Progress was agonizingly slow. When we reached our objective, I called Battalion and received orders to proceed east another two klicks and set in for the night.

It was more of the same—the same heat, the same dust, the same progress-impeding screwups. By the time we started toward the second objective, we were running out of water. Then we really started having problems. The heat casualties were piling up, but we couldn't get helos to respond to our calls. I couldn't just sit out on the road with the company, so I began putting the heat cases on the backs of the tanks. Of course, the tanks' engine housings were hot, so the heat cases got hotter. That wasn't doing them any good.

We couldn't get the heat casualties flown out and we couldn't get any water lifted in. I pulled out my map and located a little blue pencil point about two klicks from us; it was probably a little pond.

I shot an azimuth toward the blue spot and we moved out to find it. We did hit the pond even though it was not more than ten meters wide. In fact, we bisected it. I was so proud of that piece of land navigation; I couldn't believe it.

The only hitch was that the pond was covered with scum. But that didn't deter the troops, who were spitting dust by then. It was harder than hell to keep them from running right into the water, scooping it up, drinking it as is, and coming down with some loathsome disease, such as amebic dysentery. It took a major effort by the officers and troop leaders to make sure everyone put halizone tablets in their canteens and waited the prescribed fifteen minutes before they drank it. I wasn't so naive as to think that many of the thirsty troops didn't sneak sips before the halizone took effect, but we tried.

The thing that really pissed me off was learning that the tanks had been carrying five-gallon cans of water the whole time and the tank crews didn't let us know. I had no sooner learned this from one of my troops, who saw the tankers drinking from their water cans, than one of the tankers jumped into the middle of the pond, stark naked with a bar of soap, and started washing himself. I was so mad I was going to shoot the rascal. I mean, here we were, dying of thirst, and all he could think about was getting the dust off his body. He got out of there real quick when I found my voice.

As soon as we finished drinking and had restored ourselves and our canteens, I ordered the company to backtrack to our assigned objective. When we got there, I reported in and Battalion told us to set in for the night.

The whole day had been so tremendously draining that I formed the company in a beautiful rice paddy with dikes around it and told the men to set in. The paddy was a natural defensive position, requiring little additional excavation. I settled the men down—they were totally drained—put the listening post out, and organized one ambush team. I told the ambush Marines that I wanted them to curve off a faint trail leading to the rice paddy and set up on the side of a little hill so they could cover the trail and the paddy.

In the field, we always maintained at least a 50 percent alert at night—one man in every two-man foxhole was awake in rotation throughout the night. The tanks, 60mm mortars, and M-60 machine guns were manned by scratch crews, the platoon commanders and platoon sergeants traded shifts monitoring their platoon radios, and the company radios were manned in rotation by one in every four members of my command group. Typically, each man worked two hours on and two hours off through the night.

I was sound asleep when, all of a sudden, I came immediately awake. Whatever woke me up brought me instantaneously alert and I jumped to my feet. I knew something was wrong. It was a little after midnight, and deathly quiet. My two radiomen were asleep; everyone in my company command group was asleep. I ran out to the platoon positions. All the platoon commanders were asleep. The entire company, because of the tremendous physical struggle in the heat, was sound asleep. Instinct alone had awakened me.

About the time I finished yelling, "Wake up," I heard a burst of fire from out in front of us. I yelled, "What the hell is going on?" Then I ran back to Corporal Johnson and said, "What the hell is going on?" Johnson told me that the ambush team had just shot at something. Then Battalion called to ask, "What the hell is going on?"

"I think our ambush has sprung something," I replied.

I had Johnson order the ambush team in. It should have taken it several minutes to return, but only a few moments passed before we heard American voices outside the perimeter yelling, "Hey, we're ambush. Coming in! Coming in!"

As soon as the ambush team came in, I grabbed the team leader and asked, "What the hell is going on?"

"Well, sir, we . . . uh, the machine gunner saw something. *He* saw something. He, uh, fired at it." I tried to get details, but the Marine was incoherent from fright. They all were.

As the story developed, I found out that, instead of going to where I told them to set in, the ambush team had set up in a little dry gulch because "it looked like a good position." As soon as they got there, they all crapped out—just like the rest of company. Somehow or other, the machine gunner happened to wake up just in time to see a shadowy form not more than five or six feet from him. Fortunately, he had the presence of mind to pull the trigger of his M-60. He got off about ten rounds before his night vision went and all hell broke loose. Then the whole ambush team just picked up and ran.

We went out the next morning and found an AK-47 assault rifle and a camouflaged NVA helmet lying about ten feet from where the M-60 gunner said he had been lying. The AK-47 was smeared with blood and had five bullet holes in it. We figured, if the NVA soldier had been carrying the AK-47 at port arms, he took about five rounds right in the chest and upper body.

As we pieced it together, some sort of NVA patrol had come through a treeline that ended about thirty feet from the dry gulch in which the ambush team was sleeping. One of the NVA, probably a scout, had run across the open space and the machine gunner had opened his eyes just in time to see him coming. If he hadn't, the NVA scout would have run right over him.

We were very lucky. For me, it all added up to an important lesson about taking extra special precautions when there was physically debilitating stress on my troops. I learned a valuable but painless lesson on that one.

After we had checked around the ambush site and reported, Battalion ordered Lima Company to scour a fairly wide area out to a point about five hundred meters to the southwest. It was another walk in the sun, through more low scrub interspersed with bald dusty stretches. Water discipline was better, but we all suffered from the heat and dust. We found nothing at our objective, which we reached at 1245, and Battalion told us to dig in there, a relief of the first magnitude. We found another suitable rice paddy and dug in along the dike. That evening, I made sure everyone knew how important it was to stay awake while on watch. Not surprisingly, we had no repeat of the previous night's near disaster.

Next morning, August 17, as we stood to awaiting an ammunition and ration drop from helicopters, Battalion ordered Lima Company to attack a small rise on the far side of the rice paddy adjacent to our night defensive position.

I ordered both tanks to move up to a dry wash on our flank, but they couldn't get across so I ordered them to give us overhead cover as we assaulted across the rice paddy. As we got the company to the edge of the rice paddy and spread in attack positions, I ordered the 60mm mortar crews to set up so they could throw some rounds into the ridgeline. Then I busied myself with the rifle platoons for a few minutes. When I happened to look back, I saw that one of the mortars was set up right in front of one of the tanks. I walked back and told the mortar crew, "Okay, I want you to move about twenty feet to the right." They were all set up, so there was a lot of grumbling but no movement. "Just goddamn do it!" So they moved.

I moved back up to the paddy dike, where several of the troops greeted me with news that they thought they could see buildings on the objective. I got out my binoculars so I could have a close look at the ridgeline, but I wasn't sure about what I could see. As I was looking, to be on the safe side, I said to Corporal Johnson, "Have the tanks open fire on the objective."

The first tank opened fire and *BOOM*—there was an instantaneous detonation right behind me. I was on the ground. Everybody was on the ground. We were all wondering what the hell had happened.

I looked back and saw that there had been a tree limb right in front of the first tank. The first round had impacted on the tree limb and exploded. Right where the mortar crew had been, it looked like somebody had raked the ground. If I hadn't moved that mortar crew, we'd have lost it. I couldn't believe it. I was so goddamn mad; I was really steaming because I couldn't understand how that stupid tanker could do something like that.

As I was stalking back there, the tank commander saw me coming. He ducked into the turret and pulled the hatch shut. When I had finished yelling and screaming at the silent tank, I had worked up a real sweat, so I stopped on my way back to the paddy dike for a drink. I pulled out one of my canteens and started drinking, but the water ran down my chest. I couldn't figure out what was going on. Then I realized that the troops were laughing—at me! I looked up as someone yelled, "Skipper, look at your canteen." A piece of sharpnel from the tank round had gone right through the canteen, which had been on my right hip. The shrapnel missed hitting me by less than an inch. As I fought to control the shakes, someone else yelled, "Hey, Skipper, look at your flak jacket." I had three chunks of shrapnel in my flak jacket.

Except for the danger imposed by our own tank, the attack was walk-through. We found five bunkers, each six feet by three feet and covered with a foot of dirt and foliage. Before blowing the NVA fighting positions, we retrieved a large container of raw rice, three Chicom grenades, a magazine from an SKS carbine, another magazine from an American grease gun, six American radio batteries, and a stack of typewritten materials none of us could read. My understanding is that similar assaults by Kilo and Echo companies turned up a few other bunkers and similar junk, but no VC or NVA.

It was hotter than it had been so far as we scoured the open hill. We were on the verge of running out of water, so I called Battalion to request a resupply, but they told me to "bring 'em on back in." They gave me no details, but it was clear that they wanted Lima Company to report in as soon as we could hump down to the CP area.

I found out some months later that Special Intelligence thought all along that the next hill to the right of the one we assaulted had an NVA battalion command post on it. Apparently, the higher-ups didn't want to let us know because they thought the NVA might be able to figure out that somehow or other we had broken a code. I have no idea why we bothered assaulting the wrong hill.

We reached the battalion CP position without difficulty, though we were parched. Food and water awaited us. Also some good news: after Hotel Company, 2/9 joined us the next morning, Lima Company would remain with the battalion CP and serve as a blocking force while Kilo, Echo, and Hotel companies swept an area reputedly occupied by a full NVA battalion.

The attack jumped off late in the morning of August 18 and Hotel and Kilo companies flushed several NVA soldiers, killing most of them. However, the NVA battalion, if there was one, evaded our sweeping force into the afternoon. A light plane broadcast psy-ops messages asking the enemy to surrender, then a bombing mission was launched, following which our companies jumped off again. The rest of the day went like that—minor contacts resulting in major use of bombs and even flame tanks and Army dual-40mm dusters. A few NVA were killed, but no NVA battalion rose to meet us. The only casualty our side sustained was a Marine from Hotel Company who was killed that evening by one of our own 81mm mortar missions.

We returned to Dong Ha the next afternoon, August 19. The 3/26 Alpha command group and Kilo Company were flown back to Khe Sanh, but Lima Company was left behind under the operational control of 2/9.

*I*t was late in the afternoon, August 20, and 2/9 was moving along a trail in the area immediately north of the sector in which our half of 3/26 had been operating the week before. I was starting to get anxious because I didn't know the people from 2/9 and I didn't like the way they operated.

As we moved along the trail and were pulling up over a hill, there was a terrific explosion behind me. The whole column stopped as I thought, "Oh shit. I wonder what the hell's happened this time." I worked my way back in the column to discover that an Ontos we had with us was blown all to shit.

An Ontos was an ungainly tracked fighting vehicle mounting six external 106mm recoilless rifles. It was not armored at all. In fact, a .50-caliber round could go right through it. As far as I was concerned, bad things always happened to Ontos and the men around them.

It looked like our Ontos had been the victim of a command-detonated mine, which usually amounted to a dud 500-pound bomb dropped by our side and salvaged by the other side for use against tanks, Ontos, and amtracs. This mine—thankfully something lighter than a 500-pound bomb—had gone off beneath the Ontos and sheared the track, driving wheels, and all three recoilless rifles off one side. When I arrived, the two crewmen were sitting on the ground beside the trail, dazed but unhurt. Everyone else was just standing around.

It was staring to get dark and we were still on the road. I was getting concerned and the troops were, too. Finally, as we moved up and over the hill, the battalion CP told me to move in on the right side of the road and form a perimeter. As we got in, I saw that there was a large open area right behind us.

Fortunately, I had an SOP worked out so we could form a perimeter in the order of march. The lead platoon moved first, straight into the nearest designated position, followed to the right by the middle platoon, and then by the rear platoon. As soon as we got the word from Battalion, I called the platoon commanders back and verbally sketched it in for them. They each said, "Right," and we literally started running the troops in so we could dig in before the sun set.

I checked in with the platoon commanders, each of whom escorted me as fast as we could walk around his platoon's section of the line. As we went, I checked the position of each fighting hole and particularly the field of fire of every M-60 machine gun. I tightened up here and there, but the platoon commanders had known me from my first day with Lima Company, and they had trained their troops in my ways. It took only a few minutes to check the entire company and make sure we were tied in with the companies on our left and right flanks.

After dark, as my troops were settling in, without telling me, Battalion sent its 81mm mortar platoon right into our company position. It was full dark by then, but the mortar platoon walked in on us with flashlights on and portable radios blaring. I was really upset, so I walked back to the 81mm platoon commander and said, "If you don't knock that bullshit off, I'm going to shoot you myself."

I hated being with 2/9. I had not been favorably impressed from the first day we had operated with their Echo Company a week earlier, I was not impressed with the battalion commander, I was not impressed with how late we had started setting in for the night, and I definitely was not impressed with the 81mm platoon's sense of noise and light discipline. Fortunately, and despite sleepless hours of concern, we spent an uneventful night. Nothing happened.

At stand-to the next morning, August 21, the battalion CP gave me the word that Lima Company was going to move out on an independent company-size sweep. I didn't want to be around 2/9 and I was used to operating on my own. I couldn't have been happier.

Bright and early, Lima Company found itself moving along a ridgeline through a dense bamboo thicket that channelized us on the only trail. The bamboo was so thick that we had to stay on the trail to get through it. Unbeknownst to me as we moved along the little ridge—it was only fourteen or fifteen feet high—the point bent around a little bit too far to the right and started down off the ridgeline toward an open area, a complex of rice paddies.

As the first four or five men of the lead element approached the nearest rice paddy, they took several sniper rounds. As soon as I heard the *pop* of the sniper rounds, I got on the radio to the lead platoon commander, the 3rd Platoon's Gunnery Sergeant Almanza. "Okay, Gunny, what's going on, what's going on?" I knew that he was already trying to find out from his vanguard squad, but I wanted news as soon as possible.

We had all of four or five scattered sniper rounds, but that was good enough. They stopped the point and the point stopped the whole column on the ridgeline inside the bamboo. The main body of the company never got out in the open, probably had not been seen.

When Gunny Almanza confirmed that the point had been fired on, I said, "Okay, hold your position. I'll come forward." I worked my way through the troops angling down the slope. As I neared the point, I saw the rice paddies for the first time. Beyond them, directly across from us, was another low hill. Another low hill was to our rear.

I called the rear platoon and told Little John, "Move back along the trail, hook a left, and see what you can see along the ridgeline to our rear. We'll look around down here."

Little John's 2nd Platoon backtracked, as ordered, and Little John eventually came up on the net with his report. He had worked to the left and had located a bunker complex. That made me extremely nervous. The main body of the company was on the side of a hill. To our right rear was another ridgeline with a bunker complex. Out ahead was an open area of rice paddies. There were snipers out there, probably on the ridge beyond the open area. Lima Company was in a box. There was no way out.

Normally, Lima Company would have rated a forward air controller (FAC), a fully qualified naval aviator, a pilot ranked lieutenant or even captain. This time out, however, we had no FAC. There weren't enough in 2/9 to go around. What we had was a tactical air-control party (TACP) operator, Private First Class Terry Smith, who was trained primarily to guide resupply and medevac helicopters. As I pondered my options, Terry came up beside me and said in a very calm, collected voice, "Skipper, how'd you like some air?" I said, "Shit, I'd love some air." I didn't know it then, but Terry had never actually run a tactical air strike. He had been cross-trained to call in jets, but he had never really done so.

Terry got on the tac-air frequency and called for any aviator to respond. Fortunately, there was a Bird Dog in the area, and he responded to Terry's first call. He said he was right over us and that he had some fast movers—jets—standing by. Terry told him that we had received some scattered sniper fire from our front and gave him an azimuth. I switched over to the tac-air frequency and added, "I'll fire my mortar section on the rice paddy if you'll make sure the ridges are fairly well clear."

The aerial observer (AO) flew around our flanks and reported that he could not see anything on the hills. Meantime, I ordered the mortar section to deploy and gave the section leader, Corporal Patrick McBride, an azimuth to fire on. After McBride eyeballed the range and said the guns were ready, I told him I would spot for him.

We threw several rounds into the far edge of the open area and the AO came right up on the air in a jubilant voice, "My God, you just blew a couple of them into the trees!" I immediately shouted back to McBride, "Let 'em have it. You just blew some NVA into a tree!" That was all those gunners needed to hear. They went into automatic overdrive. They were throwing mortar rounds down the tubes as fast as they could. They were really going through their supply of mortar rounds, no doubt encouraged by the ammo humpers' desire to lighten loads.

The AO kept reporting, "My God, you're right on target. I can see them running. They look like they're ants scurrying from a broken nest. You just blew a couple more of 'em into the trees." Then he added, "I'm gonna get some air on this."

Not five minutes after the AO called for fast movers, Lima Company had ringside seats for the greatest air show any of us probably had ever seen. The AO was bringing in flight after flight of fixed wing. They were using napalm and 500-pounders. They really dusted off that hill. They worked it over for twenty or thirty minutes without letup.

During the whole thing, I kept updating Battalion. The CO was really into it, but when I said, "I want to go up on the hill," he replied, "No, no, no! Wait a little while longer. Bring in some artillery." So we waited a little while longer and called in some artillery. When I reported that the artillery had really dusted the hill off again, the CO said, "Okay. "I'm sending up two tanks. Wait for them, then go take the hill."

The tanks worked their way up to us and, as soon as they arrived, I started Lima Company moving out to the edge of the near rice paddy and on toward the hill, which was to our right front as we walked, about 250 meters away. The company was in the open, well spread out, but we didn't take any fire. As we started up the hill, we entered the bamboo again. It was so thick we had to stop and wait for the tanks to knock down a pair of trails we could walk along. I didn't like having the company forming up in two columns behind the tanks, but there was no other way for us to plow through that really thick vegetation. Talk about tunnel vision: Except for what we could see ahead, past the tanks, we were completely hemmed in by the bamboo.

Suddenly, the tank that I was following fired its 90mm main gun. I was instantly on the intercom phone attached to the tank's rear fender, yelling to hear myself over the ringing in my ears, "What the hell did you do that for? What are you doing?" The tank commander told me that the tank had just broken through onto an unseen trail when the gunner had spotted a North Vietnamese RPG team just in time to push the firing button on the 90mm. After I acknowledged, the tank commander added with considerable glee, "We just dusted them off. There's just a spray of blood and guts where those guys were."

The tank started up again and we followed it the rest of the way up the hill, which had really been blasted. Napalm had burned off most of the growth and there were deep bomb craters everywhere. We couldn't find anything but we could smell death. We couldn't find a sign of any NVA or their positions. I had no idea what the AO had seen, but I could smell death.

As the platoons set in and continued to search the hill, my company radioman, Corporal Johnson, sat down at the edge of a huge bomb crater and took off his radio. I went over to join him, but as I approached I smelled something terrible. "Goddamn John, there's something dead around here somewhere." He said, "I know, sir, I can smell it, I can smell it." He stood up and looked around. Right where he had been sitting was a big chunk of meat that had obviously come from a body of a North Vietnamese soldier. Johnson had been sitting right on it. Grease from that chunk of meat had penetrated into his trousers and he smelled to high heaven.

As soon as I realized what had happened, I said, "Get away! Just get the hell away!" And he was muttering, "Oh, my God! Oh shit! My utilities!"

Little John's 2nd Platoon started moving off the top of the hill, toward a little shoulder to the left of our former line of march. Down the back side of the hill, the Marines started hitting ground that hadn't been burned off or bombed. A Marine suddenly yelled, "Hey, I got some bunkers over here." And a few other people said the same thing. One of the Marines, Private First Class David Francis, stuttered every time he got excited. As the other Marines were yelling about the bunkers, I heard Francis yell even louder, "I-I-I-I s-s-s-see th-th-th-them! I s-s-s-s-see th-th-them!" He no sooner got that out than a terrific burst of fire came in on us. It sounded like on the rifle range, when everybody shoots at his target at once. Everybody went to ground—except me.

There I was, kneeling on the ground beside the command radio. I was just kneeling there like a dumb shit when it dawned on me: This was the very first time I had ever been shot at. The troops—even the green ones—were a little smarter than me. They were all on their bellies by the time my little pea brain was thinking, "Hey, they're shooting at me." Like a broken record, my mind was stopped on that one central fact, "They're shooting at me. They're shooting at _me!_" Leaves and twigs knocked loose from a tree were falling down on my head.

As I realized what was going on, I started getting lower and lower. Finally, I was down on my stomach. By then, if I could have cut the buttons off my shirt to get any lower, I would have.

My two radiomen, Johnson and Vogt, were in the bomb crater behind me. They had been yelling from the moment the first shots were fired, but it took awhile for me to realize that they were yelling at me: "Skipper, come here, come here. Get in this bomb crater." I crawled backward and jumped into the bomb crater beside them. As I focused on wider vistas, I heard how much shooting was going on, how much yelling and screaming there was. Machine guns were going off, and dozens of rifles. It was mass confusion. As I recomposed myself and tried to figure out how to respond, I realized that I could not begin to decipher all the sounds and voices.

I jumped into the bottom of the bomb crater. As soon as I did, a bullet plunked in beside me. Obviously, it had come from somewhere up in the treetops. As I was articulating the thought in my mind, an M-60 gunner crawled up to the edge of the crater, got up on one knee, looked in, and announced, "There's a fucking gook in that tree."

With that, the M-60 gunner stood up on both knees, put the weapon into his shoulder, and started firing. From my place at the bottom of the crater, I could see chunks flying off of a palm tree about fifty or sixty meters away. The M-60 gunner sprayed forty or fifty rounds into the palm tree and then stopped. He looked down, right at me, and said, "I think I still see the fucker." Then he blasted the tree again with another fifty rounds. I called up, "Jesus Christ, if that goddamn NVA is still alive after that, don't shoot at him again. You're just gonna piss him off." The M-60 gunner looked down at me again and said, "Oh, yessir." Then he crawled off.

I was still trying to get a handle on the situation when, above the sound of many M-16s and a few M-60s, I heard someone nearby yelling threats. I climbed back up to the lip of the crater and saw our senior corpsman, Doc Bratton, beating a Marine on the chest, swearing as loud as he could, "Goddammit, you're not gonna die! Dammit, you son of a bitch, breathe! Breathe!"

As the firing died down—it was all ours by then—I found another Marine lying on his rifle in another bomb crater. He was sort of kneeling at the edge of the crater, with his arms and hands in a firing position on his rifle, but his head was leaning against the rifle on the ground. I said, "Are you all right, Marine?" I took him by the shoulder and pulled him back. It was Private First Class Francis, the stutterer. His eyes and mouth were wide open, but a second look revealed that he had been hit right in the back of the head. He was dead. He was the first dead Marine I had ever seen.

I called one of the corpsmen over to take care of Francis and then I went over to see how Doc Bratton was doing with the wounded man. Doc was beating on the man's chest to try to keep his heart going. I saw that the Marine was one of my best squad leaders, Corporal Pat Cochran, formerly a semiprofessional football player, a handsome six-foot Texan with enormous, wide shoulders. Cochran had taken a round in the initial burst of enemy fire that sort of creased his scalp. Lance Corporal Anthony Benedetto was kneeling right next to him when Cochran turned to him and said, "I'm hit." Benedetto said,

"Right," and reached around to get a bandage. By the time Benedetto turned back, Cochran had been hit again—right in the head. The second round had penetrated Cochran's skull and gone right into his brain. He was brain dead, but his body functions were still going on, so Doc Bratton was trying to keep him alive.

Though the firing was dying off, Lima Company was still beset by enormous confusion. Staff Sergeant Marvin Bailey, the company gunny, was yelling for stretcher bearers and Sergeant Vogt was starting to call casualty information to the battalion CP. The CP said it was trying to lay on a helicopter for emergency medevac. Then the NVA started shooting again and all the Marines on one side of the hill returned the fire. There was an enormous amount of confusion. The battalion commander kept calling, trying to figure out what the hell was going on. I was trying to get reports from the platoon commanders, but I couldn't quite make sense of the confusion, so I couldn't relate much to the CO.

Suddenly, I realized that we were the only ones shooting. So did a bunch of other people. I yelled, "Cease fire! Cease fire!" and, pretty soon, everyone was yelling, "Cease fire! Cease fire!"

As the last rounds were fired, Little John came up to me to report. There were tears rolling right down his face. I said, "What's the matter, John? What's the matter?" He told me he had been advancing toward the sound of the original gunfire, his radioman in tow, when an NVA soldier had jumped right up in front of him and shot the radioman. Little John had had a clear shot at the NVA, but his rifle had jammed. He still was so angry that tears were rolling uncontrollably out of his eyes.

The helicopters started coming in for the casualties, who were being staged beside the big burned-out area on top of the hill. The litter teams Gunny Bailey had organized were really sweating. It takes six or seven men to lift a makeshift poncho litter. We got the two serious WIAs on the first helo and Cochran and Francis waited for the second. Two other Marines who were lightly wounded opted to stay with the company.

I looked up briefly from a conversation with a platoon commander and spotted the 2/9 CO just as he was walking up. He must have come out on one of the medevac helos. "Hey, Captain," he said as he arrived at my side, "what's going on?" I tried to explain what I knew, which apparently satisfied him because, after hearing me out, he ordered, "Okay, I want you to continue on in this general direction." I acknowledged the order and he left the hill aboard the second helo.

By the time we reorganized the company and got going again, it was the middle of the afternoon. I was getting worried about having to set in again after dark, but the battalion commander's order to track down the fleeing NVA had been firm. However, just as the point pushed off the hilltop and started along the ridgeline bordering another rice paddy to our right, the battalion CO ordered us to come back because it was getting too late in the day to be pushing our way across hostile territory. He got no argument from me.

As I was ordering the point to fall back, we heard one of the tanks fire a round. I checked with the senior tank commander by radio and learned that several of my Marines had spotted a pair of North Vietnamese moving behind a paddy dike, trying to sneak away. The grunts had talked the tank's gunner into firing a 90mm round, which, the tank commander said, produced a big red spray where it exploded.

Next, I learned that four of my Marines had gotten out into the middle of the rice paddy, which had a stream running through it. I was angry with the men who had ventured out without orders, so I stalked down the hill to collect them myself.

As I approached the rice paddy, one of the miscreants called out, "Hey Skipper, I see a mine in that stream." I thought, "Jesus, what now? What the hell is a mine doing in that stream?" Then I called to the four Marines, "Okay, let's take a look at it now." So there we were, the company commander and four Marines going out in the middle of the open, exposed rice paddy.

I looked back up the hill to see if anyone was covering us. By then, the company, which had been turning itself around when I left, was crapped out. About twenty men under Sergeant Blackman were visible, lying on the forward slope of the hill, "Blackie," I called, "give us a little cover here. Cover us. We're going out there." He sort of waved at me.

The five of us walked out into the middle of the rice paddy. One of the men had a grappling hook, so I told him to hook the mine and then we would crawl back a ways and pull the rope. We got back about twenty feet, hunkered down, and pulled. The object we yanked up was a weird-shaped log. I looked at the guy who had reported it as being a mine and said, "Jesus, you need glasses."

The Marine I was addressing was standing to my right front, looking right past me. I could see he wasn't looking at me and I was about to get angry when he pointed past my shoulder and asked, "Skipper, are those two guys Marines?" I looked over my shoulder at two men walking upright thirty or forty meters away. The Marine certainly did need glasses.

The two men were definitely North Vietnamese soldiers, complete with camouflage hanging all over them. They were right out in the middle of the rice paddy. I am sure they needed glasses, too. Obviously, they had mistaken us for their comrades. I guess they had arrived too late to hear all the shooting.

"Holy shit!" I raised my rifle and tried to zero in. Talk about a guy with buck fever: I couldn't put the front sight on either of those two NVA.

Finally, I fired one round. Then my rifle jammed. Those two North Vietnamese sort of turned toward us when they heard the rifle go off. I could see their mouths drop open, as if to say the Vietnamese equivalent of "Holy shit!"

By then, Sergeant Blackman's Marines on the hill, who were supposed to be covering, were yelling, "Gooks! Gooks!" and started shooting. The two North Vietnamese just jumped behind one of the paddy dikes, which were about waist high. They had about thirty Marines shooting at them, but they were safe; we weren't going to be able to hit them as long as they stayed put behind the dike. The only Marines who had any chance of getting the NVA soldiers were me and the fire team with me.

It was a textbook setup. We had an ample base of fire up on the hill and a maneuver element down beside the rice paddy. It was a classic fire-and-maneuver solution.

"Okay," I hollered above the din of the firing as I pointed to two of my riflemen, "you two Marines go up about five or six yards and cover us. Then we'll go up, and so on. We'll leapfrog up on 'em." We advanced to within about twenty meters of the NVA. It never occurred to me that we might take them prisoners. All I saw in my mind's eye were two NVA soldiers, armed to the teeth, certain to resist.

For all my years in the Marine Corps and all my weeks in command of Lima Company, this was all a new experience for me. As we all stopped for a breath at the twenty-meter line, I remembered the classic Basic School solution: If you can't shoot them, throw a hand grenade on them.

I always carried at least two fragmentation grenades in a standard Marine Corps grenade pouch I had on my belt and tied to my leg. I had been humping those grenades for weeks; it was time to put them to use. I reached down to the pouch, but I could not get the snap off. I pulled and pulled; I almost pulled my leg right off my body. Finally, I got the snap open, pulled the first fragmentation grenade out, and pulled the pin. The whole detonator came out in my hand. I could just imagine what the troops were thinking: "My God, who is this Keystone Kop?"

So, there we were, all five of us leaning against the paddy dike while I screwed the fuse back into the body of the grenade. Once I got it in there, I pulled the pin, flipped the spoon, and lobbed the grenade over onto the North Vietnamese. The floor of the rice paddy was so dry and hard the grenade bounced away from them before it went off. "Okay," I said half aloud, "one more time."

I pulled the pin on the second grenade, flipped the spoon, and tossed it underhand. It went in just right and detonated. We waited and waited. The Marines on the hill stopped firing, so we stood up and started moving in very cautiously. As I eased forward across the dike, I could see the bodies of the two North Vietnamese. As we got to within about ten feet, one of them settled. The Marine off my left shoulder opened fire at full automatic. I thought he had blown my whole side away, he was that close. I could feel the air from the rounds as they went by me. "Jesus Christ," I screamed at him, "who are you shooting here?" That stopped him.

The North Vietnamese were obviously dead. One had taken a load of shrapnel in the head and part of his skull was blown away. I don't particularly care for bodies, but I looked at those two guys, the first dead North Vietnamese I had ever seen. I could see right inside the one man's head. It was the first time I had ever seen brains.

By then, a whole squad of Marines was standing around, so I ordered them to spread out and look around for more NVA, dead or alive. The two dead men were armed with AK-47s. They had large NVA packs and full rice bags that looked like old blanket rolls around their shoulders. In their packs were American C rations and a few maps, which had more detail than our maps. The maps led me to believe that they were part of a forward-observer team. There was no radio, but I couldn't imagine what NVA grunts would be doing with maps as good as the ones we found.

I started thinking to myself that we had had two men killed and four wounded and we had nothing except those two bodies to show for our trouble. Obviously, we had engineered the destruction of many NVA in the bombing, and we had almost certainly killed others in the firefight on top of the hill. But these were the only dead NVA we had. I decided on the spot to take them back to the 2/9 CP with us. If nothing else, I thought, all the troops in Lima Company deserved a look. It sounds gruesome, but men who have seen combat deserve to see the tangible results.

The four Marines who had helped me score the kill were standing beside me, so I pointed to two of them and said, "Hey, you two Marines, go get some bamboo." Of course, they both looked around as if to say, "Who? Me?" So I said, "You guys get some bamboo poles, shove them through their clothes, and we'll haul these guys back to where the company is."

It just happened that one of the Marines was about six foot four and the other was about five foot two. As luck would have it, the big guy got on the feet end of the guy with the cracked skull, and the little guy got on the head end. When they lifted, they tilted the NVA soldier and his brains fell all over the short Marine who was carrying the head end. The look on the short Marine's face was terrible as the brain matter fell all over his hands and onto his utilities. I almost threw up. "Screw it," I said. "Leave them there, we're not going to . . . Ah, to hell with it."

They dropped him then and there and the short Marine started to clean himself off. I felt terrible.

That was when one of my sergeants came up beside me and said, "Sir, let's mutilate them." I couldn't believe what I was hearing. I looked at the man and thought, "What the hell do you mean 'mutilate them'? This guy's head's all blown away. They're both shot to pieces." I couldn't believe what he was asking of me. "Okay," I said, "I'll tell you what, Sergeant. Let's mutilate them. I'll tell you what we'll do. You see that hill over there?" The hill was about a thousand meters away. "You stay here. As the last man of the company goes over that hill, you mutilate them all you want and then join us." The sergeant was a good soul, but he obviously was susceptible to bad advice. He caught on real fast that I wasn't big on his idea, so he backed away and returned to the troops on the hill.

We left the bodies where they had fallen and moved back up the hill. Then we hiked back to the 2/9 battalion position.

When we got in that afternoon, the 2/9 battalion commander told me that, next morning, Lima Company was going to go back out to the same location and assault across the rice paddy to take the other hill. I said, "Aye, aye, sir," and returned to the company area to discuss it with the platoon commanders and Gunny Bailey. "We're gonna have to go across that goddamn stream. I don't know how deep it is, so we'd better get some bamboo that we can throw across it just in case we can't jump it." The word went out that I wanted the men to cut bamboo poles. However, I didn't realize that the part about needing the poles *to get across the stream* had failed to get out to the troops. They thought they were cutting the poles because we expected to have heavy casualties and that we were going to get use them to fashion litters. Instantly, the company's morale dropped off below zero. As soon as the officers found out what was wrong, we got the whole word out. The troops brightened up a bit, but they remained unhappy about returning to the area.

Meanwhile, we started experimenting with the rice bags the two dead NVA had been carrying. We were so sick of C rations that we were willing to try anything to brighten up our supper. Someone in the command group had a spare helmet that had belonged to one of the casualties. We built a fire, put what we thought was a decent amount of water in the helmet, and dumped in what we thought was a decent amount of rice. After awhile, the whole mess started bubbling and boiling and the rice started floating over the side of the helmet. It looked like the creature that grabbed New York. While the rice was boiling, someone said we couldn't just eat rice alone, so we dumped in all kinds of C rations. Then somebody dumped in some Tabasco. The concoction bubbled and boiled for over an hour, until it smelled about done. By then, everyone was saying, "Jesus, we're going to have a hell of a meal." We scooped it out and gave everybody a chance to eat some. It was the lousiest shit I've ever had in my life. Almost everybody threw his share away.

Before sunup the next day, August 22, we moved back to the rice paddy below the bamboo-covered hill and scouted the objective. After I reported that the attack would have to be made across open ground and a stream entirely dominated by the objective, Battalion told me to delay the assault until it could arrange a preassault artillery preparation and on-call artillery support.

The paddy dike that was our jump-off position—the same one at which I had killed the two NVA with a hand grenade—was wide enough for only one platoon at a time, so I decided to leapfrog onto the objective in columns of platoons—a classic infantry assault technique involving absolutely standard fire-and-move tactics known to everyone in the company.

After we heard that the artillery support had been arranged, as soon as the rifle platoons were ready to jump off, Lieutenant Tom Biondo, my artillery FO, quickly mapped out a fire plan with the exec of the supporting 105mm artillery battery. As the first artillery rounds impacted well ahead of us, I thought, "I can't just send the lead platoon across, I've got to be with them." So, there we were, the company commander and Corporal Johnson, up with the lead assault platoon. I was lying behind the paddy dike, looking at my watch, waiting for the last artillery round to fall, per schedule. As the seconds ticked away, I looked up. The whole thing reminded me of the old World War I films, when zero hour approaches. Everybody glancing around at everybody else. They were all crouched down, ready to go. We had even fixed bayonets. All I lacked was a whistle with which to signal the start of the attack.

I kept looking at my watch, silently counting down the last seconds. Just as the last artillery round fell in, I yelled, "Okay, let's go." Everybody went up and over the paddy dike. It was *exactly* like an old World War I movie.

We moved across the paddy dike as fast as we could. Everyone was assault firing from the hip and shoulder while moving steadily forward. When we reached the stream, the Marines carrying the poles we had cut hastily threw the lumber in from bank to bank. Almost without missing stride, everyone crossed in good order and started up onto the hill itself. As we mounted the slope, the squads and fire teams instinctively began the complex ballet of fire-and-move tactics that are the hallmark of a savvy, experienced combat infantry unit. Behind the lead platoon and beneath the suppressive curtain put out by the rear platoon's base of fire, the middle platoon launched itself over the paddy dike, crossed the stream, mounted the hill, and attacked through the lead platoon. As the former lead platoon stopped to establish a base of fire, the rear platoon advanced from the paddy dike and followed the middle platoon to the top of the hill. At last, as the middle and rear platoons attacked right, left, and straight ahead at the top of the rise, the former lead platoon joined them, ready to spring into action as needed.

The assault was letter perfect. Unfortunately—if you choose to view it that way—there was no one home. In fact, there was no sign up there that anyone had ever been home. It was a completely dry hole. We returned to the 2/9 battalion position.

At about 0100 the next morning, August 23, some joker from the battalion CP woke me to tell me that the entire force would begin pulling back to Cam Lo at 0530. I have no idea why someone hadn't told me that before I went to sleep. It was pitch dark out there and we had to send runners out to try and locate the platoon commanders. Then the runners and the platoon commanders had to work their way back to my CP. They all literally had to *feel* their way in, it was so dark. When I had them all together, I gave them the word. Then the platoon commanders had to feel their way back to their platoons so they could tell their squad leaders we were moving out at 0530. By the time the squad leaders got the word, it was about 0230, and no one could get back to sleep.

At the stroke of 0530, Lima Company was ready to go. Nobody had had nearly enough rest, but when I said "Move them out" we were moving. The unfortunate thing is that the rest of the battalion wasn't ready to go. They told me to stop. I was so angry I started muttering imprecations that, in a rare lapse of judgment, Sergeant Vogt, my battalion-net radioman, repeated verbatim on the air. The furor this raised resulted in a few piquant exchanges with the 2/9 staffers and ended with an apology from me that was something less than heartfelt. It wasn't until 0900 that the CP group and the other companies were ready to go. By then, I was fit to be tied, but I kept my big mouth shut.

Later that morning, Kilo Company, 3/26 arrived to relieve us. We returned to the control of 3/26, whose Alpha Command element was at Dong Ha. When I reported to the 3/26 Forward CP, I learned that Lieutenant Colonel Kurt Hoch had been rotated to a job at the 3rd Marine Division command post on August 20. Our new Old Man was Lieutenant Colonel Harry Alderman, who had just arrived in-country.

C H A P T E R **10**

Dong Ha was where the 3rd Marine Division Forward CP was located. It was a an extremely large combat base in which upward of ten thousand Marines lived. In addition to Division Forward, the headquarters of the divisional artillery regiment, the 12th Marines, was also located at Dong Ha, as was the headquarters of the first-rate 2nd ARVN (Army of the Republic of Vietnam) Regiment.

The bivouac Lima Company moved into was up on a high spot on which Division maintained a number of GP tents for the infantry units that rotated through Dong Ha. There were just old smelly cots in the tents, and the area was dusty and littered with the trash of the previous tenants. There was a constant wind blowing through Dong Ha, and there was always dust and dirt in the air. It was also within artillery range of the DMZ so, periodically, the North Vietnamese fired a few rounds down toward the combat base in the hopes of blindly hitting something. For all that, Dong Ha was heaven compared to living in the field.

Within a day or two of our return from Leatherneck Square, I got the word that Lima Company was going to operate independently as part of the County Fair program, in which tiny Marine combined action platoons (CAPs) waged a unique war in the villages. Our job was to support the CAP based at Co Bi-Thanh Tan, in the rugged area northwest of Dong Ha called the Street Without Joy. As I learned from the old hands, 3/26 had been baptized in blood around Co Bi-Thanh Tan shortly after its arrival in Vietnam, almost exactly a year earlier. According to the old hands, citizens of the Street Without Joy had waged an unremitting war against the French in the 1950s, and they were waging one against us and the ARVNs more than a decade later.

Battalion told us to take rations for five days and proceed to Co Bi-Thanh Tan up Highway 1 by truck the next morning, August 29. I was to report in to CAP Papa-2 to help them carry out the 9th Marines' directives for an operation called Liberty. Essentially, we were to patrol around Co Bi-Thanh Tan while CAP Papa-2 won hearts and minds in the ville.

Here, we faced new and, to me, troubling rules of engagement. This was my first time out in a densely populated area, and we were cautioned that we would be dealing with large numbers of Vietnamese civilians as well as various arms of the ARVN, including second- and third-rate Regional Forces and Popular Forces companies conscripted from the local villages. I listened to the briefing and took notes, but I kept thinking about the order to take rations for five days. We usually ate two meals a day, so that meant that each man had to carry ten rations plus all his water, ammunition, and other gear. That added up to a tremendous load for each man.

We drove down Highway 1 without incident and pulled into the CAP compound, which was in the nice grove of trees in a a sandy area. It was a lovely place. We disembarked and set in for the first night. The big problem in my mind was the populated village just 250 meters to the west of us, and the open area around us to a distance of about a hundred meters. On one side of the CAP compound was a raised right of way supporting the tracks of the defunct state railway. Moreover, with the local Regional Forces company in residence, it was very crowded in the compound, and everyone for miles around—good guys and bad guys alike—knew exactly where we were.

I sent out a patrol that first night. As it walked along the paddy dikes, we could hear the village dogs barking, marking its progress. I was nervous and upset, but the first night passed without incident.

In the morning, we left the CAP compound to patrol up a side road. I think the CAP Marines were as happy to see us go as I was to leave.

As we humped down the dirt road toward the back country in extended column, six or seven Vietnamese women came walking by us. I found it odd that they glanced at us without really appearing to do so. I thought they didn't want to appear too obvious or forward. However, right after the women disappeared from sight, we started receiving scattered sniper fire which fortunately did not hurt anybody. That got our attention right off the bat. We were playing by new rules, ours and theirs.

We continued to move down the road toward a large mountain. On either side of the road and dead ahead were high knolls. Though the terrain was fairly open, the knolls severely restricted visibility. It was dangerous terrain, so I kept the company well spread out, maintained flankers out as far as the knolls, and cautioned the point and rearguard to be extra vigilant.

As we came over one knoll, I looked up and saw the vanguard, which was about a hundred meters ahead of me, just as it was engulfed in an explosion right on the edge of the roadway. Someone had tripped a booby trap. My first thought, as I ran forward with my command group, was "Oh shit—how many did we lose? How bad was it?"

As the company stopped and deployed on either side of the roadway, I worked my way up to the point and found one Marine lying on the ground. His trousers, which were in tatters, had been pulled down around his ankles. He was on his stomach with his head propped up on his elbows. The platoon corpsman had gotten the Marine's legs spread apart and was swabbing the inside of his thighs and calves with merthiolate. There were big scratches all up and down the Marine's legs. I asked my usual question, "What the hell happened?"

One of Marines standing nearby answered, "Skipper, a booby trap went off right between this Marine's legs. It must've been a Chicom grenade because sometimes they pulverize and don't really give a shrapnel effect. I think that's what happened. It went off right between his legs." I looked down and noticed a fine, gritty powder spread around the Marine, on the roadway, and on his trousers. All the grenade had done was shred the point's trousers and scratch the inside of his legs.

I kneeled down beside the injured Marine and asked, "Are you okay?"

The kid looked at me like nothing had happened and said, "Skipper, I'm okay." That was then. About five minutes later, the shock set in and he started shaking so badly we had call in a medevac. He was

THE FIELD · 95

totally in shock. He rejoined us several days later, after he had calmed down, but he never ran point again; he was too nervous.

While we were waiting for a helo to take the hysterical point out, I sent a squad up a nearby knoll. They had no sooner walked out of sight than we heard another explosion. Three more Marines were wounded. One was hurt quite seriously, but the other two were only slightly injured. I had all three flown out on the medevac helo with the point.

We continued on, working our way into the first row of high hills or little mountains. Before it started getting dark, I decided to pull back out of the high area for the night. We were not molested.

Before leaving Dong Ha, I had visited with the battalion intelligence officer to get the latest dope on the area around Co Bi-Thanh Tan. He had told me that there were supposed to be elements of an NVA regiment working in the area. I asked him how large the NVA "elements" were, but he replied that he wasn't sure. Based on that and the rolling, broken terrain, I decided to keep the entire company together for at least a few days rather than dispatching platoon and squad patrols. I wanted to get a feel for the land and for the size of the local VC and NVA forces, and a sense of how the war was fought out there.

As we moved out on September 1, I became really upset with the lead platoon because it didn't seem to be moving fast enough. I kept pushing them and pushing them. I kept calling the platoon commander, Lieutenant Dan Frazer, who, by that time was about a month shy of rotating home. Dan was a good platoon commander, but he was really upsetting me that morning because I couldn't seem to get his 1st Platoon to move it out fast enough.

I kept calling to rag Dan with orders to "Push it out, push it out." As I was calling, I kept getting closer and closer to the point. All of a sudden, I spotted Dan's lead elements and saw Dan and his radioman standing in the middle of an open area, about thirty meters by thirty meters. What Dan was doing was strictly taboo; we never wanted an NVA observer or sniper to be able single out the unit leader because he had a radioman in tow or because he simply looked like he was in authority.

I crossed a little intervening stream with my radiomen, FO, FAC, and other members of my command group. Then I walked right up to

Dan, who was concentrating so hard on something that he didn't hear or see us coming. I playfully hit Dan on the shoulder and bellowed, "Goddammit, Dan, you know better than to stand in an open area." I took a step away. No sooner done than about thirty rounds were fired right at us. I am sure it was just one NVA who fired one AK-47 magazine and disappeared.

As I ducked away, out of the corner of my eye I saw Frazer and his radioman, Private First Class Francis DeGrazia, drop to the ground. As I hit the ground, I saw my radiomen as they had been when the burst of fire went off. Johnson and Vogt had stopped beside the stream to scoop cooling water over their heads with their helmets. The water was still pouring down on their heads when I looked up, but they were halfway to the ground. They laughed about it later because, they said, for the first time in my short combat career, I was able to beat them to the ground. They also told me they could see rounds going between my legs and dust puffs all around me where the bullets impacted.

Before the echo of the last round died away, I heard myself yelling, "Get the platoon sergeant up here. Where's Sergeant Mullins?" I knew before I realized it that Dan Frazer had been hit. My first coherent thought was centered on the need to push the lead elements of 1st Platoon up to uncover the sniper and maybe get him. We had to operate fast. I kept yelling for Mullins as I made my way back along the company. There was no more fire and, within the minute, Sergeant Wendell Mullins had pushed a squad into the thicket to try to get the sniper.

After convincing myself that the company was ready to repel an attack, I went back to the clearing to see about Dan Frazer and anyone else who might have been hit. As I feared, Dan was down, and so was his radioman. DeGrazia had taken a round just beside the edge of his flak jacket, on his right shoulder. The bullet had just opened up the flesh of his arm without breaking any bones. He was lying on the ground with one of the docs working over him. His flak jacket was off and set up to keep the sun off his face. One of the rubberneckers pulled out a camera and asked, "Hey, DeGrazia, is it okay if we take a picture of you?" DeGrazia was a little out of it, but he mumbled "Yeah, go ahead."

Lieutenant Frazer had taken a round right through the wrist and he was in a lot of pain. As I kneeled beside him and the platoon doc, I asked, "Goddammit, Dan, are you okay? Are you okay?"

"Yeah, I think I'm all right." But I could see he wasn't. I left to check on the squad that was trying to track the sniper. By then, Gunny Bailey already had a report in to Battalion and medevac choppers were on the way. The last time I saw Dan Frazer was when they were pushing him onto the chopper. I never got a chance to say good-bye. I found out later on that there was some nerve damage in his hand because of the wound in his wrist. He never made it back to us and I am sure he was surveyed out of the Marine Corps.

We never did find the sniper. We just took two men wounded and got nothing out of it. Next day, we were pulled off the County Fair operation and reassigned to Rough Rider duty.

During the first week of September, immediately following our County Fair experience around Co Bi-Thanh Tan, Lima Company escorted a truck convoy to Khe Sanh and another down to Hue. The contrast was almost too hard to handle.

Hue, the former imperial capital, located on the coast in Thua Thien Province, was fascinating, the real "big city" for us highland country boys. It was a fairly densely built-up city, a very pretty place with a distinct French or European influence. There were wide, broad boulevards and lots and lots of trees. It was, for an Asian city, extremely well maintained and seemed to me to be very cosmopolitan. Hue's most prominent feature was the old imperial citadel, which completely surrounded the old imperial compound and dominated vistas from many of the newer neighborhoods.

We arrived in Hue as convoy guards. As soon as we hit town, the trucks were obliged to crawl through city traffic toward the logistics center on the inappropriately named Perfume River. There were thousands of Vietnamese civilians—and hundreds of Vietnamese soldiers—going about their daily business as if there was not a war raging only a few klicks from the edge of town. Long used to seeing rough country women in concealing black pajamas, it was something of a shock to see the gorgeous city ladies dressed in traditional tight *ao dai* dresses with slits up the sides. It was also surprising to see how many Vietnamese were dressed in Western clothes, though there were scores of pajama-clad peasants interspersed through the crowds. The wheeled transportation was interesting. There were uncountable motorbikes, peddle-driven rickshaws called cyclos, and relatively few cars. Vietnamese soldiers and American Marines presumably on official business careened hither and yon in the typical range of military vehicles. All in all it was extremely reminiscent of a major American city, yet with the unique attractiveness of a place in which East and West clearly intermingled with a comfortable ease. I was surprised that there was such a place.

During one long delay, I hopped out of my jeep and passed orders up and down the column that all the men were to stand fast—stay at their posts. Before long, of course, the local vendors were streaming toward us to sell everything but the kitchen sink to the troops. I found myself staring down at a loaves of fresh French bread. We had not had fresh bread in I couldn't remember how long. It looked too good to be true, so my radiomen and I bought several loaves and dug right in, hand to mouth. It was like eating candy, it tasted so good. As I was eating, I had to break it open to tear bite-size pieces off. I saw all these little brown specks in it. At first, I didn't think anything of it. Then curiosity got the better of me and I picked out a few of the brown specks, thinking they were sesame seeds or some exotic Asian spice. They were flies and bugs, but that realization sure as hell didn't stop anybody from eating.

Some of the troops were unstoppable in another respect. We probably weren't halted longer than fifteen or twenty minutes. Days later, at the end of the normal incubation period, two of the troops showed signs of having been infected with one sort of venereal disease or another.

PART II

THE AMBUSH

CHAPTER 11

While Lima Company was detached on County Fair and Rough Rider duty, Mike and India companies continued to operate out of Khe Sanh under the direction of Major Carl Mundy's rear command group and Kilo Company and the battalion Alpha command group remained in Leatherneck Square under the 9th Marines.

The big idea sweeping through III Marine Amphibious Force that summer was to prevent the NVA from infiltrating large units across the DMZ and Ben Hai River by monitoring their progress around Con Thien and hitting them in Leatherneck Square. Marine engineers had bulldozed something called the Trace, a quarter-mile-wide no-man's land along the Ben Hai. This was part of the McNamara Wall, named for the systems-oriented Secretary of Defense, Robert McNamara. In and around the Trace was no end of electronic surveillance gear deployed to find the moving NVA troops no matter how dark or rainy a day or night. A huge investment in barbed wire and mines—not to mention the manpower to deploy them—was more than matched by the number of Marine battalions sucked in to scour and defend the area.

It was all a pipe dream. There was no way it was going to work. But the amount of treasure and sweat and blood that went into bulldozing the Trace under constant artillery fire sacrificed many Marines. I can't to this day figure out why we did it. In fact, as it later came out, the

Trace *was* a pipe dream, literally. One of the 3rd Marine Division assistant division operations officers, a very busy major, was briefed on McNamara's concept and ordered by his boss to come up with a route for the Trace. When the major asked if the secretary was serious, the colonel told him that it was all busywork and would quickly be forgotten. Overwhelmed by urgent pressing business, the major simply and thoughtlessly drew a line across a map and sent the map up through channels. Unbelievably, the major's line was accepted without modification as the route for the Trace.

The focal point of the barrier became Con Thien, a little high place next to the DMZ that overlooked much of the Trace in that region. Somewhere in the signals-crossed drama, the higher ups decided that Con Thien was such a good lookout that it had to be defended at all costs. Adding immeasurably to the delusion was the NVA's decision to try out some new siege tactics and to test our reaction. Everything came together at Con Thien. The fools on our side decided to hold Con Thien at all costs against the trial siege campaign the fools on the other side decided to launch.

Artillery bases were emplaced to support Con Thien and other fortified observation points along the Trace. Of course, the NVA dug their artillery in north of the DMZ, in similar artillery fire bases. (The big difference between their setup and ours was that we could hit theirs with air but not with infantry—which was not allowed north of the DMZ—and they could hit ours with infantry but not air—which dared not fly when our fighters were around.) Of course, the high ground at Con Thien was as vulnerable as it was conducive to observation. Our guys could see them, but they could see our guys.

There is an old line reputedly uttered by the legendary Chesty Puller when his battalion was surrounded on Guadalcanal—"Boys, they got us just where we want them." Or maybe it was, "Boys, we got them just where they want us." Either way, they both work when describing the situation along the Trace, particularly around Con Thien.

Con Thien was on the western end of the Trace. On the eastern end, on old Highway 1, was Gio Linh. It was also subjected to a great deal of interdiction by artillery fire. I never got inside Gio Linh, but I was told that, with field glasses, you could look at what they called the Peace Bridge, the bridge across the Ben Hai between North Vietnam and South Vietnam that looked like an ordinary border crossing, complete North Vietnamese flag at one end and South Vietnamese flag at the other. The far-western anchor of the McNamara Wall, well beyond the Trace, was Khe Sanh.

Behind Artillery Fire Base C-2, which had a battery of 105mm howitzers covering Con Thien, was Dong Ha, which had more artillery capable of reaching C-2 and Con Thien. Gio Linh was backed by the artillery fire base known as C-1. Heavy artillery—Army long-range 175mm self-propelled guns—were at the Rockpile and Camp Carroll, both within reach of Khe Sanh, Con Thien, Gio Linh, C-1, and C-2.

Con Thien was really tough, really rugged. There were no concrete emplacements built, but Con Thien had been built up over several years from sandbag barriers that steadily became thicker and higher and endowed with more and more layers of overhead cover. The constant artillery fire had cleared all the vegetation for hundreds of meters all around the hill, resulting in perfect fields of fire for the many, many automatic weapons that had been staged into the front-line bunkers and pillboxes. By the summer of 1967, everyone at Con Thien lived, ate, slept, crapped, and played underground. Life was miserable, so infantry battalions rotated in and out every thirty days or so. Every rotation resulted in casualties from incoming artillery fire, but the alternative would have been hundreds of armed Marine mental cases. All in all, Con Thien was just a terrible meat grinder.

Gio Linh was another story. Except for Marine artillery forward observers and FACs and a naval gunfire control team, the place was completely in the hands of ARVN troops. As I heard it, Gio Linh was even more terrible than Con Thien, mainly because the ARVN troopers did very little work fortifying the place. The bunkers were unsafe to live in _between_ artillery attacks. During the rainy season, the unlined, unsupported, hand-dug trenches all but disappeared. Gio Linh was a terrible place to be on a _quiet_ day.

Things started heating up in earnest around Con Thien at about the time Lima Company was engaged in County Fair duty following our service with 2/9. It looked as if the NVA was going to launch a major assault to overwhelm Con Thien any day. Among numerous other battalions, the emergency sucked in the rest of 3/26.

_L_ima Company happened to arrive at Doug Ha with a supply convoy on the afternoon of September 7, around 1700. After escorting the convoy inside the base gate, we made our way straight to a newly established Battalion Rear encampment to engage in the usual ritual of showering, getting clean clothes, and catching up with our mail from home. As I jumped from my jeep in front of my tent, I yelled across to Gunny Bailey, "Okay, get 'em billeted and let's see if we can't get some chow." Normally, the mess-hall hours were not that long and they might not have been expecting us, so I wanted to get the troops fed before we did anything else.

And as the gunny was getting the troops down to chow, I went over to the battalion rear CP, which was set up in a big GP tent. When I got inside, I could tell right off that there was some action going on; there was quite a flurry of activity, unusual in that the main body of the battalion was in the field, up near Con Thien.

I asked the first young lieutenant I collared what was going on. "Jesus, sir, the battalion's in action."

"Well, what the hell's going on, Lieutenant?"

"Well, sir, we don't know. It's kind of confusing out there, but we do know that we got a lot of casualties and they're coming into the Delta-Med, down by the runway." As I was chomping that tidbit, I heard the lieutenant say in a very distinct voice, "Yeah, India-6 has been wounded. He was hit in the head. They got a lot of casualties down there, sir."

"Jesus," I exploded, "what's going to happen?"

"Well, sir, we don't have any word, but it looks like you're going to go out in the morning."

Without waiting around to get more information from the busy staff, I ran down to the mess hall and located Gunny Bailey and called a meeting of the platoon commanders and the key staff. It was a motley crew because the only officer besides me was Little John. Dan Frazer, who had been wounded on September 1, had not been replaced by another officer, so the 1st Platoon was commanded by Sergeant Wendell Mullins. Gunnery Sergeant Almanza was still the 3rd Platoon commander; I didn't want an officer to replace him. Jaak Aulik was still the exec, but he was on R&R and not due back for several days. I never had had an officer commanding Weapons Platoon. So, the meeting consisted of me, Little John, 1st Sergeant Miller, Gunny Almanza, Gunny Bailey, Sergeant Mullins, several other sergeants, and even a few corporals.

"Okay," I said after telling them about the battalion's fight, "it looks like we're going to go out in the morning. Make sure that we get an ammunition resupply and that all the troops are well fed. Be prepared to move out at first light."

Next, I trotted back over to the battalion rear CP and said to the senior officer present, the assistant S-3, "Give me more scoop. Where the hell is the battalion?" The 3-Alpha couldn't tell me exactly where the battalion was, except that it was somewhere northwest of C-2, out toward Con Thien. He told me that the battalion had gone out the preceding afternoon to relieve a two-company element from 1/9. Apparently, one or two of our companies had spent most of the morning and afternoon of September 7 patrolling the area around the little destroyed village at which the battalion had set in. The news after that was vague. Clearly, India Company, whose skipper had been wounded and evacuated, had been hit hard and had taken numerous casualties. Beyond that, there was no hard information. As the evening wore on, repeated trips to the CP produced vague reports that mainly sounded like "Things are not going well out there," or "It's not looking good." It was obvious that the battalion was getting hit harder and harder, without letup. By the late evening, the entire battalion was up to its ears in NVA, who were attacking in the dark in an effort to overrun the battalion perimeter. It appeared that all or part of India Company was fighting a separate, isolated battle for its life somewhere beyond the battalion main perimeter. The outpouring of disjointed, incoherent bad news got me to the point where I found myself thinking in terms of taking Lima Company out there to *rescue* the rest of the battalion, that we would be the cavalry going to the rescue.

I told Top Miller and Gunny Bailey to round up every swinging dick they could find, and Bailey later reported that they had scouted the battalion area and had come up with a list of about thirty men who had come out of the field because they each had less than six days left to do in-country. At the time, there was a policy that if a Marine had about a week left in Vietnam he would be pulled into a rear area to turn in his gear and get himself ready to go home. A week might not seem like a big deal, but I knew that it was a very big deal to men who had put in thirteen months less a week in Vietnam. I felt extremely bad popping the question, but thirty combat-experienced Marines represented a significant group of reinforcements, virtually a platoon.

I stalked through the battalion area, list in hand, and discussed the situation with each of the short-timers. I did not feel right ordering any of them back into the field, but I made sure each man knew how important his personal presence might be to the outcome. I told them that the battalion was getting hit hard and that it looked like we were going out the next morning. I said the battalion needed help and I needed volunteers.

Most of them volunteered to go back out, so I sent them down to Supply to redraw their gear, which had already been turned in. I had always felt that being a Marine carried with it certain obligations, but the performance I witnessed on the afternoon and evening of September 7, 1967, was something special. A few of those Marines had been counting on leaving for Danang and the Big Bird home with our scheduled return convoy in the morning. They didn't have to go, but they did.

Before I went to work on the short-timers, I had directed Gunny Bailey to round up every cook, baker, and bottlewasher he could find and get them saddled up so we could take them with us. In this case, I was empowered to issue orders, and I did. We also dragged in about two dozen men who had just arrived in-country and who had not been assigned out to the companies. Gunny Bailey had to see that they drew combat gear and Top Miller saw that the S-1 accounted for their arrivals and quick departure.

The cooks we were leaving behind kept the mess hall open so we could grab coffee and chow as we worked into the night to get Lima Company up to snuff and the reinforcements squared away. I kept making passes through the CP tent to follow the battalion's progress, which, if anything, appeared more serious with each new report. The main body appeared to be fighting for its life and had suffered heavy casualties.

I managed to get a few hours sleep, but I was up well before sunrise, at least an hour before the relief force was to form on the road beside the rear CP area. As I was checking in with the operations duty officer to get the latest dope on the battalion—nothing new—I was waylaid by the operations chief, Master Gunnery Sergeant Thomas McHugh.

Top McHugh was Old Corps. By the time he joined 3/26 I suppose he had had twenty-six years in the Corps. He had served in the Pacific in World War II and, no doubt, in Korea. He was one of those old-time senior enlisted Marines who rarely condescended to speak with somebody who wasn't a field-grade officer, a major or above, except on official business. As I was leaving the CP tent, Top McHugh glanced sideways at me and said, "Hey, Skipper, you got a minute?"

"Sure, Master Guns, what do you need?" I was really surprised that he had initiated the conversation, but I was bowled over by how friendly he sounded.

"Come on over to the tent, sir. I want to talk to you."

I thought, "Jesus, what the hell could he want?" I followed him over to his tent and he sat down, looked at me, and said, "Well, you know, sir, it's going to be tough out there."

"Yeah, I imagine it is, Master Guns."

"Well," he said, "I want to wish you the best of luck."

I thought, "Jesus!" and said, "Thanks, Master Guns, I appreciate that." I turned to leave.

"Hey wait a minute, sir." He held up his hand. "Here's something I want you to take with you." He handed me a canteen.

"Thanks, Top. What's in it?" I had a pretty good idea, after the big build up.

"There's something in it, Captain, that you may need. It's just a little medicinal alcohol, but if it really gets tough, I mean, you can have this and maybe it'll help you out."

I thought, "My God, I have *arrived*!" I mean, here was a master gunnery sergeant who had not only condescended to speak with me off the record but who had given me his best go-win-one-for-the-Gipper speech. I was authentically touched by the depth of feeling behind this normally reticent man's heartfelt display. I thanked him, literally from the bottom of my heart, and went off to complete arrangements to leave Dong Ha.

C H A P T E R **12**

Bright and early on the morning of September 8, I ordered Gunny Bailey to get Lima Company fed and on the road. It was SOP to put about twenty Marines on each truck, so a 130- or 140-man company needed seven trucks. When I went out to take charge of the company that morning, I counted about six supply trucks for the battalion and the seven troop trucks for Lima Company. However, there must have been 270 Marines standing on the roadway, geared up and ready to go.

It was the biggest formation of Marines I had ever taken over. I was dumbstruck. Sure, we had told many of these men, "Get your ass in formation; you're going out with us," but the majority of the extras were volunteers, many of whom up had turned up on their own, without any appeal from me or my sergeants. A tremendous feeling of pride came over me as I gave "Right face" and 270 men responded with nearly parade-ground precision. It was very emotional.

The drive down Highway 9 to Cam Lo was uneventful. From there, we turned north and then ran the short distance into C-2, the artillery fire base supporting Con Thien. The main body of 3/26 was somewhere out beyond C-2. When we arrived at the artillery position, I halted the column and stepped down to try to get directions from someone in the base CP. I still didn't know where the battalion was. The fire-base commander wasn't sure either, so I radioed the battalion CP and spoke with Lieutenant Colonel Alderman, the new CO. He told me to follow the road out from C-2 about 750 meters and that he would send an officer back to guide me in.

I had given the troops a break, so it took several minutes and the usual amount of yelling to get them back aboard the trucks. While I was waiting, I ran into an old friend, Captain Bob Johnston, who told me that his battalion, 3/9, which also stopped at C-2, was on its way to relieve the Marine battalion holding Con Thien. As soon as Bob told me where he was going, I blurted out, "That's too bad." Then, catching myself, I laughed and asked, "Hey, Bob, can I have your watch?"—reassuring banter like that. Then I found myself repeating, "Jeez, Bob, good luck," over and over, as if to say good-bye to him for the last time. Bob was very calm, very stoic. He kept saying, "Oh, it's going to be okay."

We left C-2 as soon as everyone was back aboard the trucks and proceeded up the Con Thien road, which was nothing more than an all-weather dirt lane that probably wouldn't have shown up on most local road maps in the United States. As narrow and crude as the road was, it was the combat base's MSR and, as such, heavily used by jeeps, tanks, amtracs, and trucks. My convoy of about twenty trucks, including resupply vehicles, moved out into the traffic and ground forward less than a thousand meters, to the spot at which I was to meet the officer from the battalion main body. We pulled over as far as we could to give other traffic sufficient clearance, but we created quite a bottleneck because the roadway was so narrow. Bottlenecks are targets, so I immediately ordered the troop leaders to "get the troops off the trucks" and "spread 'em out."

There was no end of confusion. We had nearly 270 men on and around the roadway, the trucks, and all the vehicles trying to pass in both directions. Confusion? It was sheer chaos.

The more I looked around, the less I liked where we were. There were shallow drainage ditches on both sides of the roadway, maybe eight or ten inches deep, and the brush had been bulldozed clear to a distance of a few hundred meters on both sides, to lessen the likelihood of ambushes. The place we had stopped was on a little knoll, with a clear view in every direction—and which could be observed from cover extending virtually in every direction. I didn't like what I was seeing, so I got on everybody's case about spreading the troops out, getting them off the roadway, away from the traffic jam.

I was standing tall on the roadway with my command group, waiting to find out what was going on, when I spotted a line of troops coming through the scrub growth. I could see that they had four tanks with them. I figured it was the group the CO had said would come back to guide me to the battalion main body. I pointed it out to the others and we rubbernecked as they got closer. The word spread among the troops, who, on their own, started getting ready to move out, they were that motivated to help their comrades.

As the column closed on us, I could see that it was most of a company accompanied by the tanks—something a great deal more than the expected officer guide the battalion CO had spoken of. As the tanks got closer still, I could make out bundles on their rear decks, and the bundles slowly resolved themselves into bodies. The tanks were covered with Marines who had been killed and wounded in the previous night's battle royal. There were a lot of them. The effect of those bodies on my troops was mixed; they wanted revenge, but they were sobered.

The company—it was two platoons from Kilo—pulled right up onto the MSR and, without a word, some of the infantrymen started pulling the KIAs and WIAs off the tanks to put them on our trucks. Also without a word, some of my Lima Company Marines pitched in to help. It was downright eerie, particularly as the normal traffic flowed past us in both directions.

As I was standing there, with my mouth agape, my good friend, Captain Tom Early, the battalion communicator, walked right up to me. Obviously, he was the officer guide. As Tom approached, his eyes got real wide and he glanced around at my troops. Then he kept repeating, "Spread 'em out, Dick, spread 'em out!" Tom was usually very calm, very collected, but he was nearly hysterical when he reached me. By then, he was yelling—"Spread 'em out, Dick, spread 'em out! They're gonna get you."

I was flustered, but I managed to say, "Hey, Tom, take it easy. Jesus, we're all right. What the hell's going on here?"

As I was trying to get Tom under control, I happened to glance over at the nearest tank. There, I focused on a dead Marine whose body was frozen in a grotesque attitude of death. This kid's whole face was just blown out. His head was there, but his face was gone. As I watched, the men were trying to get him off the tank and onto one of the trucks, but things kept falling out of his head. It was a real mess. "Holy shit," I said to Tom, "What the hell is going on here?"

It took some doing, but we were finally ready to move out. Just as I was about to pass the word, I heard the distinctive *swoosh-swoosh-swoosh* of rockets being fired from a distance. Just what I needed! "Incoming! Incoming," I screamed, a cry that was taken up before it actually left my mouth. I just dropped, right into the drainage ditch beside the roadway, which was all of about eight inches deep and two feet wide. I heard more and more rockets being fired as I went into overdrive, trying to pull my helmet right around my ankles, trying to dig deeper with the buttons on my shirt. I thought the first rocket was going to hit me right in the back. I cringed. The adrenalin was coursing through me as—*boom-boom-BOOM-BOOM-BOOM*—the rockets started impacting around me. The noise of the detonations was overlapping and continuous. I quickly lost count and I damn near lost control of my bodily functions as the ground heaved and buckled beneath my body. Close, very close. Too close.

There was a little break in the roar of the detonations, so I chanced a quick peek over the lip of the drainage ditch. As I had been falling flat seconds earlier, I had noticed that Tom Early had jumped underneath the nearest tank, which was sitting in the middle of the roadway. As I lay cringing during the first salvo, I found myself wishing that I had been as sane as Tom, that I had thought of it first. Well, when I looked up, the tank was long gone. Its driver was even saner; he was racing to get clear of the large gaggle of people that was attracting the incoming. What I saw was Tom, alone and exposed, out in the middle of the roadway, a human version of an ostrich, with his head approximately invisible and the rest of him trying to crawl into his helmet. It would have been as funny then as it seems now if I had been watching from a klick or two away.

A second salvo arrested all thoughts about the future. Then there was dead silence for several long beats of my heart.

I found myself lying head-to-head with my company radioman, Corporal Johnson, who was yelling, "God, I'm hit, I'm hit!" He was writhing, so I said, "John, take it easy. You're all right, you're all right. Stay down, just stay down." But he kept writhing and yelling, "I'm hit, I'm hit!" I wasn't ready yet to get up and take a look, so I kept repeating, "Just take it easy, John. Take it easy."

When I was sure the barrage was over, I got up on my knees and checked Johnson over. I found a gigantic jagged piece of shrapnel—probably eight or ten inches long by three inches wide—resting on his leg. It had just fallen on him, obviously with some force, but it had not penetrated. It bruised his leg and was so hot it had burned right through his utility trousers. He had felt a terrific thump and terrible burning. No wonder he thought he was hit.

I knocked the shrapnel off him and told him what it was, adding, "Jesus Christ, John, now how about taking it easy." We started kidding about it, but the humor was flat. It had been a close one; we both knew how close.

The NVA rocketmen were very good, very smart. They fired and then hid out because we were bound to call in air to comb the scrub looking for the clearing from which they had fired. I was sure they had been on us with the first round, without adjusting. They must have had that knoll zeroed in, the fire was so accurate. Altogether, they fired thirty-five 140mm rockets at us.

As soon as I finished getting Corporal Johnson back on track, I jumped up to resume command of the company. By then, dozens of Marines were jumping up and running around, counting up the number of men who had been hit and helping to treat them. I ran over to a young Marine I found lying out on the roadway. He had a grisly arm wound. I was sure the doctors would never be able to save his arm. I didn't recognize him, but he had definitely come out with Lima Company because the Kilo people were well off to the side, in their own area. I felt dumb asking, but I had to know who he was. "Marine," I said in his ear, "Who are you? Who are you with?" He was in a lot of pain and going into shock, but he managed to tell me that he was a brand-new Marine, had just arrived in-country, and that he hadn't even been assigned to a unit yet. The S-1 had sent him out to pick up any company that could use him. It was very sad. He hadn't been in-country a week yet and there he was, severely wounded, probably going to lose his arm. All that training, all that personal pain, all the good and bad dreams—for nothing. I held his good hand and promised, "Okay, Marine, we're gonna get you out of here. You did a good job." But it was bullshit. I just felt so damn sorry for the kid.

After the new man was carried off, I came across another casualty, a Lima Company man who had been lying on the deck when one of the rockets landed right in front of him. The force of the blast had cut his helmet right across the top and forced the jagged edges into his scalp. He had a pretty nasty scalp wound, a deep gash from ear to ear. When I found him, he was just standing there, off beside the road, holding the top of his head while blood cascaded down his face. He looked terrible, like he was going to keel over and die any second. I was shocked when I saw him. "My God," I blurted out, "sit down, sit down." I thought he was going to die right there. I grabbed a corpsman and he immediately wrapped a bandage around the Marine's head. The bandage was dripping blood almost as soon as the doc tied it off. In the end, not only did the Marine survive, he rejoined Lima Company within a month, complete with a great big scar that ran from ear to ear across the top of his head.

We had twenty-eight Marines wounded and one killed. As we gathered them in, my sergeants were stopping jeeps and trucks trying to pass us on the MSR—who could blame the drivers for not stopping? The troop leaders were commandeering the vehicles to rush our WIAs to C-2. Most of the WIAs were thrown aboard any passing vehicle without even getting any first aid; anything to get them off the exposed roadway and into the artillery fire base, which had a medical bunker. Gunny Bailey was moving like a madman, trying to get the names of the WIAs so he could keep the company roster up to date and have the radiomen report names and probable destinations to Battalion Rear. It was pandemonium. Meantime, we didn't know if the NVA were finished clobbering us, so everyone had an ear cocked to detect more incoming. All the motion, emotion, responsibility, and concentration kept the adrenalin flowing until I nearly keeled over.

We finally got the KIA and the last of the WIAs evacuated and finished sorting ourselves out. Kilo Company formed up ahead of us and we started humping our tired bodies and all the fresh ammunition and supplies cross country, out toward the battalion area.

The remainder of our journey was blessedly uneventful. The battalion had moved about a klick south, closer to C-2, from the destroyed village at which it had been attacked during the night. It turned out that the move had been programmed in advance as part of the battalion's mission, which was to try to flush out the headquarters of the regiment that was reputedly operating in the area south of Con Thien. When we reached the new battalion area, Mike and India companies and the battalion CP were still digging in. Lieutenant Colonel Alderman greeted me and showed me where he wanted Lima Company to deploy along the perimeter line. I passed the word to my troop leaders and they instantly shook out their Marines and got down to business. Meantime, Gunny Bailey went to work feeding the few replacements and volunteers we rated into the company.

About an hour before dark, a runner arrived to escort me to the battalion CP for a command meeting. As I approached the CP, which was all dug in and below ground, I nearly ran into a huge mound of equipment—packs, rifles, helmets, field gear, boots, parts of uniforms—that was sitting on the ground. The mound was maybe six feet high and about twelve feet around. It was all castoffs from the casualties the battalion had suffered the night before. I looked at it, trying to evaluate it in terms my mind could comprehend, but all I could think was "Holy shit, they really got hit hard!" I figured there was enough gear in there to equip seventy or eighty combat Marines. My mouth dropped open as the extent of what had happened the previous day and night started hitting me.

I had just been hit by rockets, my company had lost men without getting a chance to shoot back, and my battalion had been hit harder than I ever thought possible. Everybody attending the command meeting was nervous—not outwardly, but I could feel it. We were listening to what was being said, but our attention was directed outward. Our antennae were up and we were extremely alert. As the battalion commander was droning on, one of the tanks cranked up its engine. There was the familiar initial whiny crank-up noise, but for some reason it sounded a little like the start of incoming rounds. Without anybody saying anything, without missing a beat, everybody was suddenly lying on the deck. One second we were standing there, listening to Lieutenant Colonel Alderman, and a half second later, everybody was on the deck. Then, typical of Marine officers, we all started restoring our individual macho images. Suddenly we were all on our feet again. To a man, we were flicking dust off of our utilities, saying dumb things like, "Aw, I tripped," or whatever nonsense came to mind.

The meeting ended and we all split up to return to our troops or other duties. As I left the CP, which was just a bunch of holes in the ground, I started feeling sick. I got sicker with every step. I was really sick, sick to my stomach. Then I was throwing up. I became incapacitated. I was so sick, I hurt so bad, that I was bent over. I didn't know what hit me, but I'm sure now it was the result of everything that had happened that day. It might have been some bad water, but I'm sure it was from the strain. I finally turned to Little John, my only officer, and said, "You've got it. I can't do anything. I'm just going to curl up in my poncho liner. You got the helm tonight."

I was shivering and shaking, sick as a dog, but I finally fell asleep. Sometime later, I thought I heard Little John saying, "Goddammit, they just hit India Company. They killed a Marine." In the background, on an open radio channel, someone was cursing up a storm. I later learned that somebody had taken down the wrong coordinates and India had gotten hit by one round of our own artillery—a 175mm air burst. Other than that, it was an uneventful night, for which I an eternally thankful because I would have been too sick to defend myself. Next morning, I woke up and there was nothing wrong with me. I had had a great night's sleep and I felt great; there was nothing wrong.

CHAPTER *13*

September 9 was a pretty nothing day. Lima and India companies sent out security patrols, but they turned up nothing, and the battalion began moving to a new location at about 1600. As the day progressed, I slowly picked up details of the continuous series of fights the battalion had weathered on September 7 and on into the wee hours of September 8.

It all began when the battalion, minus Lima Company, had been ordered up to relieve two companies of another Marine battalion which were holding a defensive position near a destroyed and abandoned village called Nha Tho An Hoa, one of a cluster of wrecked villes in a big formerly cultivated area south of Con Thien. By dumb luck, we figured out later, our troops were delayed by a rainstorm and did not complete the relief until after sunset. Thus, as near as we could tell, any NVA who had been observing the previous tenants assumed that Nha Tho An Hoa was still held by two companies—not three, supported by the battalion's 81mm mortars and a platoon of three M-48 gun tanks and one M-48 flame tank.

Next morning, September 7, Lieutenant Colonel Alderman had ordered Mike and India companies to send out patrols, but he had kept all of Kilo back to act as a CP guard and a battalion reaction force. Two platoons of Mike Company, aggressively led by Andy DeBona, had flushed several NVA, but had not been able to engage them with

116

anything more than 60mm mortars. Andy brought his company main body back to the battalion perimeter in the afternoon and set in for the night.

Two platoons of India Company under the company commander, Captain Wayne Coulter, were patrolling west and northwest of Nha Tho An Hoa when, at 1150, they began taking small-arms fire from three sides. The initial burst wounded three India Company Marines. Coulter immediately established a base of fire with M-79 grenade launchers, M-60 machine guns, and his 60mm mortars. The main body attempted to attack one of the enemy positions, but two Marines were shot dead. The enemy fire was so intense that Coulter's troops were unable to recover one of the KIAs from a deep bomb crater. As the company was consolidating, a Bird Dog flew in overhead and the AO radioed that he had spotted an NVA bunker and six NVA soldiers in fighting holes. While the AO called in a fixed-wing air strike, at about 1300, India Company formed a perimeter and managed to recover the KIA from the bomb crater. Next, while the fast movers were still hitting the NVA, several helos managed to grab the WIAs. The AO reported that the enemy troops were moving south and southwest through hedgerows. At 1320, a fresh air strike caught the withdrawing NVA, and the AO claimed four confirmed kills. At 1400, the AO spotted a squad of NVA dug in to the west and called an artillery mission, but he could not determine the results. On another pass over the area, the AO said he had located a fresh foot trail and could see many freshly dug bunkers a little over a klick west of the India Company position.

Kilo Company, with one flame tank and three gun tanks, was sent out from the perimeter to link up with India in order to sweep the area in which the AO had seen the bunkers. India withdrew, carrying its dead, to link up with Kilo. During the link-up, Kilo Company, which was closest to the battalion perimeter, turned around and led India out, but the tanks stayed back with India. It was good that they did.

As the India platoons raced after Kilo Company to get out of the exposed rice paddies, Captain Coulter climbed up on one of the tanks to direct 90mm fire back at the NVA who were dogging his heels. After a few rounds had been fired, the NVA fired 82mm mortars from the north, knocking Coulter from the tank and inflicting many casualties on his company. The main body of India Company had to go to ground in the paddies to evade the 82mm fire and protect the wounded.

The India Company exec, Lieutenant Bob Stimson, returned to the paddies from the head of the India Company column, assumed command, and began organizing a defense.

At 1720, an NVA heavy rocket battalion fired fifty 140mm rockets at India and Kilo companies and the battalion main body, which was five hundred meters east of the India Company position. As the rockets and 82mm mortar rounds fell in on India Company, NVA infantry—several companies, at least—attacked through the fire, nearly overrunning the India position. Fortunately for India Company, many of the NVA who swarmed over its position continued on into the woods to the east, chasing Kilo Company and moving in on the battalion main body.

The India platoons were split unevenly between several rice paddies, in several separate groups. By the time they got organized, they had seven new KIAs and twenty WIAs. At 1735, an isolated India squad was directly assaulted by about fifteen NVA supported by mortar fire. The Marines, supported by heavy fire from the larger India perimeter, repulsed the NVA, killing at least seven and possibly ten of the enemy. Taking advantage of the enemy's temporary setback, the India squad broke from cover and rejoined the main body.

From 1720 to 1749, while India Company was landing in the soup, the battalion main perimeter was struck by three volleys of assorted rocket and mortar fire—about sixty rounds of 140mm and about seventy rounds of 82mm—and intense concentrations of machine-gun and small-arms fire. The battalion returned fire at all known targets with small arms, 60mm and 81mm mortars, and with on-call artillery fire. During the exchange, H&S Company sustained two KIAs and sixteen WIAs, Mike Company suffered six WIAs, and Kilo Company lost one KIA and three WIAs.

There was a lull in the fighting between 1745 and 1800, which the battalion exploited to tighten the main perimeter and move a platoon from Mike Company's sector into India's since it was covered only by Lieutenant Bill Cowan's platoon, which had been held back from the patrol. At 1805, Mike Company's 3rd Platoon repulsed a strong NVA assault. The platoon commander was killed and five Marines were wounded. Minutes later, at 1820, six more Mike Company Marines were wounded by artillery.

Fixed-wing air showed up overhead at 1830 and commenced a vicious strike against an entire NVA company the AO spotted in the open. Also, the AO directed fighter-bombers against mortars and a pair of .51-caliber heavy machine guns he spotted about two hundred meters north of the isolated India position. When the fast movers left, the AO claimed kills on the mortars—there was no more mortar fire from that direction—and the entire NVA company. Pilots involved in a follow-up strike claimed credit for destroying one of the .51-cals.

By 1945, the NVA assaults and gunfire were abating. At 2015, Puff the Magic Dragon—a converted World War II transport plane with a gatling-type 7.62mm minigun aboard—arrived on station. He circled over the battalion perimeter, dropping flares and working over NVA-held areas with his awesome firepower.

The battalion perimeter was probed sporadically from out of the dark for the rest of the night. Out in the isolated India perimeter, Lieutenant Bob Stimson took a head count and came up thirteen Marines short. A search of the main perimeter turned up six India Company Marines who had slipped in with Kilo Company and had joined Cowan's 3rd Platoon on the main line, but that left seven MIAs to be accounted for—a very troubling concern.

At 0100, September 8, Stimson's India Company perimeter was strongly probed by many NVA firing RPGs and small arms. They got close enough to throw in many Chicoms before being beaten back. When things settled back down, nine more Marines were added to the WIA list, against which India claimed three NVA confirmed killed and nine NVA probably killed.

Beginning at 0645, Stimson's able-bodied Marines and most of Kilo Company began a cautious sweep of the areas around their lines to look for the seven India MIAs and to count up enemy casualties. As the sweep progressed, it became obvious that the enemy, who had not been heard from since about 0400, was gone. Kilo helped Lieutenant Stimson's wounded India Company Marines back into the main perimeter. Six of the seven India Company MIAs were found dead and the seventh was found unconscious but alive.

A Mike Company patrol found a live wounded NVA private. The Mike Marines also counted sixteen dead NVA and ran across bloody drag marks indicating another eight dead or wounded NVA. They also found an SKS rifle, a light machine gun with ammo, a .51-caliber machine-gun mount, five hundred .51-caliber linked rounds, and other assorted gear. Cowan's platoon of India Company located an SKS with brain matter on the stock, an RPG in a large pool of blood, Chicom grenades, and assorted other equipment. A search around Stimson's isolated India Company position turned up ten NVA corpses and bloody equipment and drag marks indicating twenty additional NVA dead or wounded.

All of the battalion's emergency medevacs had been flown out by 1000. One overloaded medevac helo crashed on take-off, but without further loss. All the KIAs and most of the WIAs were placed on the rear decks of the four tanks, one of which was under tow, and the tanks, escorted by most of Kilo Company, moved out toward the MSR to meet my convoy of trucks, which was just clearing C-2. While Mike Company was left behind to guard the downed helo until it could be air-lifted out, the battalion main body moved out to occupy a new position about a klick south and a klick west of Nha Tho An Hoa.

In all, from first contact until dawn, 3/26 sustained losses of twenty Marines and corpsmen killed and seventy-one wounded. I have no idea how many NVA we *really* killed; no grunt ever believed the numbers the higher headquarters published.

During the afternoon of September 9, as we were preparing to move to yet a new position—no sense giving the NVA gunners more time to zero us in—several resupply helos arrived, and one of them dropped off a passenger. He turned out to be a newly arrived captain, fresh from the States, who had come out to assume command of India Company. After we completed our move that afternoon, and following the battalion commander's brief, I was introduced to the new captain. He was Matt Caulfield, a selectee for the rank of major who had just graduated from the Amphibious Warfare School. In the course of introductions, Matt told us that a major who had also joined the battalion the day before had superseded Carl Mundy as the battalion exec. Word was that Carl planned to fly out from Dong Ha in the morning to take over as S-3. I did not give much thought to the command change in India Company, but I was happy to hear that Carl Mundy was slated to arrive in the field. I thought the world of Major Mundy and I could not think of anyone I would rather have had running the Three shop while we were in enemy territory.

As soon as we got up before dawn on September 10, we went through our usual morning ritual—making sure our weapons were clean and functioning, eating a C-ration breakfast, and undertaking little housekeeping chores to prepare for the day, which entailed another move to another hill somewhere off to our southwest.

The battalion began the day atop and around the base of a razorback hill—Hill 48—at the apex of a V-shaped valley facing off to the west. Lima Company was to lead off with a sweep along the southwest arm of the "V," a series of densely overgrown ridges only fifteen or twenty meters above the valley floor, which was a series of abandoned rice paddies. A platoon from Mike Company was to patrol up a little stream flowing along the southwest arm of the "V" and India and Kilo companies were to remain on Hill 48 in case Lima or the Mike patrol flushed any NVA. If nothing happened, the battalion main body would move in the afternoon along the base of the southwest arm of the valley to its new position.

Lima Company saddled up and started moving at 0730. We humped right out to the first ridge defining the left arm of the valley and immediately encountered dense, progress-impeding brush growth. It took nearly the entire morning for us to advance seven or eight hundred meters from the battalion position to a broad clear area overlooking the valley. When I halted the company for a break and called back to Battalion, I was told to stay where I was pending further orders.

I expected to be moving out again soon, so I made no arrangements to dig in. There was some thin scrub growing throughout our position, so it was marginally shady, though extremely hot. We stayed there for thirty minutes without orders.

The soil was tough, very rocky. The troops were sure we were going to move again soon, so, when I ordered everyone to dig in, effort was half-hearted. I took out my E-tool to set an example, moved one shovelful of rocks, and said, "Screw it, we're probably going to move out anyway."

Then an hour had passed. No orders.

It was hot. I believe someone measured the temperature at around noon and it came up 107 degrees. The heat was so bad that it sapped our strength and our will. I wanted to do something, but I wound up just sitting there, sort of panting in the shade of a little bush. As hot as it was, we all kept our helmets and flak jackets on, so we were sweating like dogs. We had to watch our water supply, so there was no relief from the heat. We simply were debilitated, baking in the heat, apathetic. I didn't know what the hell was going on, what Battalion had in mind, why they were keeping us up there for no discernible reason. I didn't know what to do, so I just sat there and panted.

Yet another half hour crept by. Nothing. I called back and asked, "What's going on?" Battalion replied, "You're going to hold there."

The word from the troops was that they were running out of water. Small wonder. I got out my map and saw that there was a little blue line running through the area at the base of our hill—a stream of some sort. I looked down at the base of the hill to check. I could not see a stream, but, sure enough, there appeared to be a line of greenery about midway through the overgrown rice paddies stretching across the valley floor. If we were halfway lucky, there would be water down there.

I immediately announced that we were going to send down a water detail. I grabbed Sergeant Peck, the platoon sergeant of Little John's 2nd Platoon, and told him he was going to lead the detail. Peck informed a mixed squad of ten or twelve Marines from all the platoons, added a radioman, and began collecting canteens. Within a minute or two, the dozen Marines were festooned with canteens. Under the watchful eyes of a covering machine-gun team, they moved down off the top of the hill and advanced semicautiously the several hundred meters toward the stream. I sort of half watched them, but I was so apathetic I really didn't pay much attention.

Nothing happened. When the water detail returned about an hour later, Sergeant Peck marched right up to me and announced, "Skipper, I smell gooks in that rice paddy."

I thought "Jesus, gooks in the rice paddy!" and asked, "What do you mean?"

"I can smell them in that rice paddy," Peck insisted.

So there I was. I had been sitting on that damn hill for hours. The company was beat to hell by the heat. I looked down at the rice paddy, but I couldn't see anything out of the ordinary. "Screw it," I said, "your nose is out of joint or something. Whatever you're drinking, get me a case of it." Peck shrugged, nodded, and left to help distribute the water.

Meantime, India Company moved out of the battalion position, hiked to the base of the hill we were on by 1330, and started up the next hill to the southwest, which was about a hundred meters from us. We had nothing to do except watch India moving. Right off, I was struck by how small India Company looked, how roughly it had been treated two nights earlier. The only reason I was watching India was because its movement was the only distraction from the heat and my bored misery. I'm sure I could hear exchanges on the battalion tactical net, but my mind was fried; I really didn't have the foggiest idea what the hell was going on, what the point of our move and India's was.

I was watching India's rearguard top the next hill and half listening to the chatter on the battalion tactical net when, all of a sudden, I was brought bolt upright by the sudden onset of heavy, heavy fire at long range. It was all small-arms fire, and it broke out all at once, in a great, distant roar. I was sniffing the air like a bird dog and immediately realized that there was something going on with India Company. Fully alert, without a shred of my former apathy intact, I picked up Captain Matt Caulfield's New York City accent on the open tactical net: "My lead platoon has been shot down."

Wow! Electrifying! The adrenalin hit my bloodstream like a super-conductor. The heat and thirst meant nothing. "My lead platoon has been shot down" sent everyone in Lima Company scrambling for their weapons, got everyone searching outboard for NVA. Before we had fully reacted, the fire-support request nets were starting to come up strong while, on our flank, the heavy volume of fire rose as M-79s and M-60s added their voices to the roar of M-16s and AK-47s.

I grabbed the battalion-radio handset from Sergeant Vogt and called India-6: "Let me fire—let me seal off your flank. I can see your flank. Let me take my machine guns and fire along your flank." To which Caulfield replied, "They're coming in on me, they're coming in on me!"

I grabbed one of the M-60 gunners and pointed toward India Company. He and his assistant got the message, flopped down on the ground, and prepared to open fire. When I looked up, all the M-60s in Lima Company were being readied to support India by fire. In less time than it takes to tell it, my M-60s were firing along India's right flank. I thought we were doing okay, but India-6 came up on the net: "Lima-6, cease firing. I can't tell whose fire is whose." My M-60s instantly shut off. The worst thing in the world is to shoot fellow Marines.

I called Battalion and said, "Lookit, give me your tanks, give me your tanks, and I'll go up on the flank and try to take some of the pressure off India." Carl Mundy came up on the net and replied, "Yes, we'll send them up."

*I*ndia Company had mounted the adjacent ridgeline with Lieutenant Bill Cowan's platoon in the lead. Though it was understrength, Bill's unit was in far better shape than Captain Caulfield's other two platoons, which had sustained serious losses during the night of September 7-8.

As Cowan's platoon crossed the ridgeline, and before the rest of the company closed up, it was hit from extremely close range by fire from many AK-47s supplemented by showers of Chicom grenades. Despite Matt Caulfield's ominous announcement that the lead platoon was "shot down," only two Marines had been wounded; everyone else had naturally ducked and sought cover. Cowan's Marines returned the intense fire with M-16s, M-60s, and M-79s while the main body of India Company rushed to the crest of the hill and set up a base of fire. Shortly, the company 60mm mortars were in action and an AO arrived to begin directing fixed-wing strikes.

That was at about 1500. By 1520, Cowan's platoon had eased back out of the killing zone and joined the main body of India Company on the crest. Medevacs were on the way to pick up the two wounded Marines, and two gun tanks and a flame tank were on the way out from the battalion main body to support a proposed advance by Lima Company to link up with India.

I got the company up so we would be ready—rarin'—to go by the time the tanks showed. In fact, we jumped the gun a little and began an early move down to the nearest rice paddy to link up with the tanks.

As I moved with the center platoon, the AO was calling in the first air strike. For some reason, the jets came in the wrong way. Instead of running parallel to the front lines so, if they dropped their bombs short or long it wouldn't make any difference, they came in perpendicular to—right over—India's line. The F-4B fighter-bombers were trying to snap into their runs, into their final heading, just off our hill. I looked up in time to see one F-4B just as he snapped out to make his final run-in through a little cloud. I could see him wiggle a little to get through the cloud, a move that set him up on the wrong hill—our objective, which the point of my company column had not quite reached. I could see that he was going to drop short. He pickled three or four 250-pound bombs right between India Company and my company. Long before the bombs hit, I screamed, "Get down, get down! He's bombing wrong." There were assholes and elbows everywhere as everybody ran to get under cover.

The concussion from the bombs rolled over us in huge overlapping waves, but nobody was hurt. I went right up on the tac-air net, yelling, "Goddammit, he's bringing them in the wrong way, he's bringing them in the wrong way."

By the time we were formed up at the bottom of our hill, two of the tanks were up—the third had thrown a track—the bombing had pretty much abated, and the sound of firing from India's hill was merely a dull roar. An H-34 helo passed us like a bat out of hell, coming in low and fast. It disappeared from view for a few minutes, then roared back the way it had come, very low. I presume it had picked up India's casualties.

As the helo passed us—at about 1545—Gunny Almanza's 3rd Platoon was leading Lima Company up India Company's hill. The troops were alert to danger, but their brains were still a little fried and they were missing a few of the finer points I had tried to drive home during the past two months. They were slow getting organized, slow spreading out, and slow deploying flankers. Really, all attention was in the direction of India's hill, from which the sounds of battle emanated.

Almanza's platoon had crossed an overgrown rice paddy, then another, then mounted the far end of India's hill. I radioed India-6 to let him know that we were starting to come up on his flank, and his radioman acknowledged. I looked back then at our former position and saw that my rearguard—Little John's 2nd Platoon—had started down off the top. Just as I was about to redirect my gaze forward, the whole ridgeline that we had been sitting on disappeared under towering detonations—140mm rockets. The whole hill was being dusted off.

We went into overdrive, right up the hill toward India Company. I couldn't have held the troops back if I had wanted to; no one wanted to be caught in the open by a rocket barrage for the second time in forty-eight hours. As I humped up the hill just ahead of Sergeant Mullins's 1st Platoon, Gunny Almanza's 3rd Platoon halted at the top. I had no idea why Almanza stopped, but it was easier to keep going than to try to call him on the company net. All of a sudden, as I neared the top of the hill, I found myself in an old Marine position. That's why Almanza had stopped! There was more than enough cover for the whole company, plenty of holes in which to weather the rocket barrage. As I checked the place out, I found what had obviously served as the company CP.

Almanza's 3rd Platoon was all secure, completely emplaced on the side of the position nearest India Company, which was just on the other side of a bunch of big boulders, maybe fifty meters away, but out of sight. About half of Mullins's 1st Platoon Marines had already reached the crest and they were going into position on Almanza's flank without even having to be told. Prince's 2nd Platoon and the tanks were still on the flat, in the near rice paddy, humping to beat the band.

I turned to my company radioman, Corporal Johnson, and was about to ask for the handset when a terrific volume of fire erupted. It was fairly peaceful one second and then there was this solid *CRACK*—like the Crack of Doom. I had an immediate reaction. I fell straight to the ground—beside Corporal Johnson—and rolled right into the nearest foxhole. *Everybody* who was up was suddenly down. Immediately, the confusion started. People were yelling and screaming, someone was yelling for a corpsman, people were blazing away at targets I couldn't see. It was chaos. And in the middle of the maelstrom, I was trying to figure out what in the hell had happened, what the hell was going on.

I was on my belly in the old fighting hole and wanted to get reports from all the platoon commanders. Corporal Johnson was in another hole about two feet from me. I yelled, "Hey, John, let me talk to the platoons. Give me the handset. Throw it over here!" It was on a rubber cord, so he flipped it to me. As I caught it, there was a tiny lull in the firing, so I sneaked a quick peek over the lip of my hole. All I had time to see was a bush right in front of my foxhole. As I looked, it was shot even with the ground.

The fire was heavy and close. It was really pouring in. As far as I could tell, Lima Company was absolutely pinned. I couldn't hear many of our weapons in action. I tried to call my platoon commanders to find out if anyone was still alive. I got Gunny Almanza, of the 3rd Platoon, and Sergeant Mullins, of the 1st Platoon, and I even located a squad of the 2nd Platoon, but I couldn't raise Little John or the rest of the 2nd Platoon. They had been somewhere downslope when the shooting started. I had a searing hot lump of emotion in my chest as I tried and tried to get Little John on the net. I found myself yelling into the handset, as if that was going to raise the dead. The sense of foreboding was nearly debilitating. As far as I could tell, Little John and two thirds of the 2nd Platoon had been wiped out.

*L*ittle John and the main body of the 2nd Platoon were okay. Moments earlier, after the rocket attack and before the shooting started, they happened to be nearing the top of our hill when Little John turned and saw a line of people jogging across the open area to his left, between Lima and India companies. He thought they were Marines because many of them were wearing American helmets and flak jackets, but he quickly realized that they were NVA soldiers. Little John decided to emulate the World War I hero, Sergeant York. He knelt down and sighted in on a bush the NVA were passing behind. When the first NVA soldier in the line appeared, Little John fired one M-16 round into the enemy's chest. Bingo! One . . . two . . . three . . . four kills for four rounds. But Little John's M-16 jammed and he rolled away out of sight so he could clear the jam.

That's about when the incredibly strong initial burst of gunfire struck the main body of Lima Company on the hill and, I learned later, India Company, too. That's when we landed in what the troops used to call "a world of shit." It was brutal, sudden, and shocking—numbing.

As Little John worked to clear his rifle, he called a two-man M-60 team forward to fire on the passing NVA line. No sooner did the gunners set up than a Chicom landed between them. One Marine was wounded by shrapnel and the second Marine was shot. When the M-60 didn't fire, Little John crawled over to find out why. As soon as he left cover, something deadly thudded into the ground next to him. It might have been a mortar round or it might have been another Chicom. Little John swore he saw a piece of shrapnel heading straight toward his right eye. It's possible; human reactions tend to speed up in battle. He threw himself down to the ground and happened to look at his rifle. There was blood streaming down the barrel, which was hot enough to make the liquid sizzle. Reflexively putting his hand up to the side of his head, Little John discovered that his ear was numb to the touch. Turning to the man next to him, Little John asked, "Do I still have an ear?" The Marine said he did, so Little John let the matter ride and went to work getting his platoon ready to repel boarders. As it turned out, the Chicom or mortar round merely nicked his ear lobe. Ear wounds are invariably very bloody, no matter how big or small they are.

After another moment, Little John was rocked by another close detonation. He instinctively felt his head and his nuts to see if they were okay and then struggled to find out what was going on outside his ringing head. It had not been another mortar round or Chicom; the gun tank that had climbed the hill with the 2nd Platoon and which had not quite breasted the top of the hill, had swiveled its turret around and fired its 90mm main gun—from right over Little John's head—back toward the rice paddies at the foot of the hill.

Sergeant Peck, who had earlier smelled NVA while he was leading the water detail, later told me that he was right behind Little John, also nearing the top of the slope, when he happened to turn around in time to see something really awesome. In Peck's words, "The rice paddy stood up." Just so. As Peck looked on, at least a company of NVA—and most likely one of their little 250-man battalions—stood up in unison from hiding places in one of the rice paddies and launched an immediate running assault down the valley toward the 3/26 main battalion position, at the base of the valley. At that very instant, many NVA on the heights and in other rice paddies opened up on the various parts of Lima Company with a renewed gunfire assault. The gun tank had fired over Little John's head at the passing NVA lines.

The commander of the gun tank opened fire with the .50-caliber machine gun in his turret cupola. He got off about thirty rounds, which I could hear distinctly and which briefly heartened me. Then—*Ba-ROOM*—the tank was blown apart. Little John saw a solid sheet of flame erupt when the NVA, who were very close, opened up with an RPG volley. In fact, the NVA B-40 rockets took out both tanks—the gun tank and the zippo, the flame tank. Armor could not weather so many B-40s fired so close together. Before much more had registered on Little John, the gun tank, which had all our rations aboard, was rolling slowly back down the slope. The driver bailed out of it and Little John's men pulled one dead and two badly injured tankers from the turret. Little John saw that one of the crewmen from the flame tank, who wore no shirt, had a single blister covering his entire back. The zippo, which was burning out of control, was spewing cooked-off .50-caliber rounds from its cupola machine gun.

That was about the time I tried to check in with all the platoon commanders, about the time I started thinking the 2nd Platoon had been wiped out or Little John had been disabled or killed. However, as it turned out, Little John simply was too busy to respond to my call; he was giving orders to his two squad leaders (I had grabbed his lead squad to cover my CP group).

One of the squad leaders was Lance Corporal Anthony Sawicki, a Marine who was always in some sort of trouble with authority. I personally liked Sawicki, but as he was always getting into trouble with authority I had to remain aloof. Little John swore by him, said he was always a good man in the clutch. As Little John began speaking, a bullet hit Sawicki in the head and threw him to the ground. When Little John looked down, he saw that Sawicki's forehead had been shot off. There was a tremendous hole in his head. As Little John knelt there in shock, Sawicki reached up, put his hand into his head, and touched his exposed brain. Then he pulled the hand out and looked at it. Little John kept yelling, "Stop it, Sawicki. Stop it, Sawicki," but the Marine reached into his head again and died. I'm sure he had been killed instantly by the bullet, but apparently his body just didn't realize it for a time.

By sheer dumb luck, the rice paddy below our hill, which the NVA still were charging through, had been targeted the night before by our artillery. An alert FO with one of the other companies saw the NVA begin their charge and placed a call for an immediate mission, firing the entire battery of six 105mm howitzers at C-2 for effect. It was just a matter of ordering fire on a numbered target and waiting for the battery to shift its guns to preregistered coordinates and open fire. However, many and probably most of the NVA evaded the fire.

My own position—the position of the bulk of Lima Company—was tenuous during those first minutes of the NVA attack. We kept trying to establish an orderly defensive position and tie in with India Company, but it was difficult just to get a look around under such intense fire. Long before I had a mental picture of our initial layout, I heard the dreaded cries of "Corpsman, up!" from all around me.

From the NVA standpoint, except for the accurate artillery support, the attack was going beautifully. They were keeping India and Lima companies from linking up—we couldn't even effectively support one another—and they had the two halves of the battalion under intense simultaneous attacks; we couldn't support the battalion main body and the battalion main body couldn't support us. In fact, we couldn't *see* or be seen by the battalion main body. They had their fight and we had our fight. Of the battalion's four infantry companies, only Kilo was in anything resembling a prepared defensive position when the attack commenced.

The NVA attack had caught Mike Company in extended march order, following India Company across exposed ground at the base of the southwest ridgeline, back near Hill 48. Mike Company pulled back into itself as soon as the attack commenced, but it was unable to pull all the way back to Hill 48 to tie in with Kilo Company before the NVA assault reached it. Thus, for all practical purposes, 3/26's four infantry companies were all isolated from one another, though India and Lima could more or less support one another, as could Kilo and Mike. However, the two groupments—India-Lima and Kilo-Mike (with H&S Company)—were isolated from one another, fighting what amounted to two distinct battles.

It was later determined that the various elements of 3/26 came under coordinated simultaneous attack by NVA battalions amounting to a full NVA regiment, the 812th.

Little John moved his 2nd Platoon forward along the edge of the hill and reached across some open ground toward India Company. Fortunately for Little John and his two squads, they came across craters from the earlier bombing by our F-4Bs. That saved them a lot of digging and provided an avenue by which they could tie in with India. The contact was incomplete and tenuous, but it helped our situation by cutting down the frontage each company had to defend.

We did what we had to do. While those who were able returned fire, the rest of us tried to dig our holes deeper. The only way to do that was to scrape the dirt out from beneath our bodies and throw it up on the parapets of our holes. Progress was measured in spoonfuls. As I struggled with my hole, between garbled conversations on the company tactical net, I saw one of those little things that from time to time captured the essence of being a Marine.

Two Marines were crawling past my hole, no doubt under orders from their platoon commander, Gunny Almanza, to fill a gap in our line. Both had fixed bayonets, which probably seems like a small thing to most people, but the fact is that we never fixed bayonets. We used our bayonets only to open C-ration boxes or to play games. But we *never* attached bayonets to the ends of our rifles because we felt they were too short to use properly. So, here come two Marines, crawling past me with fixed bayonets. It electrified me. All of a sudden I realized, "Hey, these Marines know how tough it is!" They were expecting hand-to-hand and they were ready to stand toe-to-toe with the enemy, to duke it out with bayonets and rifle butts.

I instinctively dropped my hand to my web belt and felt my fighting knife, which I carried instead of a bayonet. I couldn't have followed the example of those two Marines—or set one for the rest of my company—if I had wanted to. I did want to, more than anything I had ever wanted. Suddenly, I felt naked and unarmed. I had no bayonet, but I vowed to find one and carry it ever after.

The two Marines passed from sight and I heard people yelling and screaming. I could hear my unit leaders yelling things like, "Get em, get em!" and "Get that fire out there!" and "Pass some ammunition over here"—that sort of thing. The sights and sounds were kaleido-scopic. Everything was happening faster than real life, only it *was* real life, more real than life ever had been. Everything seemed jumbled and out of order, like a poorly spliced video tape running on fast forward. There was a break now and again in the intensity of the fire, but it never really stopped. We used the breaks to move men to cover weak spots or move M-60s to engage specific targets. The thing that really pissed me off was that we never got our 60mm mortars firing. I'm sure the gunners wanted to fire—and would have risked their lives to do so—but we had no ammunition. We had not been able to acquire any before we left Dong Ha, and we had been unable to acquire any since. We had the mortars, but they weren't even much good for braining people.

The NVA—many of whom were dressed in Marine helmets and flak jackets—launched a direct assault on our perimeter. When I heard warning shouts from my troops and looked up to see them coming, a voice in my head said, "Dick, you're not going to make it out of here." But for the actions and examples of a few authentically brave men, that sense of resignation might have proven out.

A little Marine from the 3rd Platoon was manning the foxhole to my right front, seven or eight feet from my hole. He was a character, a kid with a wry sense of humor. He was also extremely good-natured, a Marine who would do anything anyone asked of him. When he had first joined the company, other members of his squad would throw all their extra gear at him and and the poor kid would carry it. It got so that he would be carrying so much extra stuff he would pass out from exhaustion and the heat. I was always on his case, advising, "Goddammit, don't let them do that to you, Marine." But he was that type of kid, so it went on.

Sometime near the start of the fight, I heard the little Marine exclaim, "Jesus Christ, I'm hit! I'm hit!" Next thing I saw, he was waving his foot over the lip of his foxhole while he yelled, "Look, look, look! They shot me in the foot, they shot me in the foot." Pretty soon, a corpsman came crawling by and dropped into the Marine's fighting hole. "Look, Doc," I heard the Marine say in a high-pitched voice, "they shot me in the foot, they shot me in the foot." A few seconds later, a boot came flying out of the foxhole. The corpsman had cut it down so he could get at the wound. As the doc worked, the Marine kept saying things like, "Look, Doc, they shot me. It hurts. The goddamn foot hurts!" Next thing I knew, the Marine, who was crawling past me, stopped to say, "Skipper, they shot me in the foot!"—as if I were his dad and I was going to maybe kiss it to make it better. A short time later, I noticed that he was back in his original fighting hole, just to my right front. Every once in awhile, I heard him say , "Boy, my foot hurts." That's the type of kid he was. He had been shot, he had to say "Goddamn this hurts," but he was back in his position, doing his job.

One of the bravest of the brave was Sergeant David Brown, the platoon sergeant of the 3rd Platoon, a Tennessean who had done his year and, in fact, had missed his plane home that very day because he had been among the first short-timers to volunteer to accompany Lima Company into the field. Sergeant Brown was a short man, about five foot eight, but he was physically and mentally tough. I believe he might have been a draftee, one of the first Marine draftees to get overseas. If he was a draftee and had made sergeant, he probably had a few years of college under his belt. I guarantee, if he was a draftee and a sergeant and had survived a whole year in Vietnam, Brown was one tough, smart cookie. Only the tough guys got to be sergeants and only the smart ones did it in less than a year.

According to some of the troops, Sergeant Brown had crawled out through the brush at the very start of the action and had killed an NVA soldier he found crawling toward our lines. As the fight progressed, I often heard Sergeant Brown shouting and cursing: "Get some people over here!" or "Get some ammunition over there!" or "Get over here!" I saw him at one point, up and about, leading several Marines forward. Suddenly, there was a terrific burst of gunfire and everyone Brown was leading hit the dirt. But not Brown. As soon as he realized he couldn't get forward, he moved in among his men, making sure they were all okay. That was a tremendous display of leadership and guts.

There was a little trail leading right into our position. After awhile, the NVA found the path and started folding in so they could follow it right into our position. I caught a glimpse of several North Vietnamese soldiers as they eased up the trail into a thicket of head-high scrub growth that began about five meters beyond a stretch of clear ground in front of the prepared line of foxholes. At the head of the trail, on our side of the clear area, was a foxhole with two Marines in it. My foxhole—the company CP—was five meters behind that foxhole. Unbeknownst to me, however, both Marines in the foxhole had been killed. There was nothing between me and the perimeter line and nothing between the perimeter line, the clearing, the scrub, and the trail the NVA were about to use to get right into the company position.

The first inkling I had of trouble to my immediate front was when I next spotted Sergeant Brown. Son of a gun, it was like he was standing on the two hundred-yard line at the rifle range. He was just standing there, cool as you please, in the offhand position, with his M-16 tucked into his shoulder, shooting at NVA soldiers who were making their way up the trail. At that moment, the leading NVA were no more than thirty feet away from him. He was shooting them, one right after the other. By the time I looked up, he must have laid out about six or eight of them, all in a nice little pile. Then, just as calmly, he stopped firing, pulled his rifle from his shoulder, stared at the dead North Vietnamese for a moment, and turned around to resume yelling orders and encouragement to other Marines. When he turned away from the front, he saw something he didn't like and stalked beyond my view. A moment later, I looked again when I heard him bellowing a command. He was dragging another Marine—probably a man who was bigger than he was—by the suspender straps. "Get over there," he yelled as he *threw* the Marine toward the foxhole in front of my CP hole. The kid he threw had an M-79. As soon as the kid landed, Brown started chanting, "Shoot! Shoot! Shoot!" The kid was still dazed, so Brown stalked over, grabbed the M-79, and snapped off the 40mm grenade in the chamber. It hit an NVA soldier in the chest and blew him all over the landscape.

I couldn't believe what I was seeing. I couldn't believe it was all happening within fifteen feet of me!

Sergeant Brown disappeared and I didn't see him again for awhile. I heard him yelling from time to time, which made me feel good, because things on our hill were very grim indeed. As I fought to keep control of the company, to keep Lima cohesive and viable, I needed all the encouragement I could get. And Sergeant David Brown provided most of what I needed in that regard. As long as I heard Brown yelling from time to time, I knew we were still in the running.

Somewhere along in there, I heard Sergeant Brown say, "My goddamn rifle's jammed," so I said, "Here, take mine" I wasn't shooting; I was talking on the radio. I had my pistol, which was good enough. I knew we would all be better off if Brown had the rifle.

Next thing I knew, Sergeant Brown yelled "Goddammit!" I naturally looked up. He was lying in a foxhole about ten feet away, but suddenly he was on his feet, uncorking a hand grenade. He reared back and pitched the grenade down the trail leading into our position. There was an explosion, but Brown screamed, "Son of a bitch! I can't get it out!" And before my disbelieving eyes—the fire was as heavy as it had ever been—he stood up and took off his flak jacket and helmet and threw them down because he couldn't throw the grenade far enough with them on.

I was too stunned—too scared for Sergeant Brown—to do anything except watch.

Brown took two grenades out of his grenade pouch, pulled both pins, and let both spoons fly. He had two live grenades and he had to be rid of them in five seconds. He leaped out of the foxhole, ran forward to the trail head, and threw them both at the same time while hurling himself to the ground. By the time he and the grenades hit the ground, both grenades exploded. He had done it that way so the North Vietnamese couldn't throw them back at us. If I had seen John Wayne do in a movie what David Brown did before my eyes, I would have asked for my admission money back.

Sergeant Brown's ongoing performance was not only inspirational, it was the sort of heroism that is known as "above and beyond." He kept doing it—kept uncorking grenades and running them forward. I dropped whatever I had been doing and started yelling, "Brown, get down goddammit! Brown, get down." But he ignored me. Every time he ran up to the trail head, Gunny Bailey also screamed, "Goddammit, Brown, don't do that! Don't do that!"

The gunny was another one. Though he was armed only with a pistol, he accompanied Brown forward every time. Even then it was humorous to see Gunny Bailey with his left hand clasped across his helmet while he fired his .45-caliber automatic pistol right into the faces of NVA soldiers coming through the scrub at the head of the trail. And all the time, *he* was yelling, "Goddammit, Brown, don't do that!"—*bang-bang*—"Get back, Brown!"—*bang-bang-bang*—"Jesus Christ, Brown, cut that out!"—*bang-bang*. I knew the gunny and I knew he was scared shitless, but he ran forward every time Brown ran forward and fired his .45 while Brown hurled his grenades.

Time remained at a standstill—and whirling ahead—as these and a thousand other scenes were seared into my memory. If I had to guess, I would say that Sergeant Brown and Gunny Bailey kept it up for twenty minutes. At that point, Brown ran by my foxhole for the umpteenth time and I looked up, as always, and yelled, "Goddammit, Brown, get down." Then, as I turned to Corporal Johnson to ask for the radio handset, I heard this terrible *thunk*. It was the unmistakable sound of a bullet hitting a man in the head. I knew right away what had happened. I looked up real quick; I snapped my head around. I knew who had been hit.

Sergeant Brown was on the ground, maybe twenty feet from me. He wasn't moving. I thought or maybe said, "Oh shit!" and I crawled out of my hole, straight over to him. I put my hand on his head and ran my fingers through his hair. He had taken a bullet behind the right ear. He was dead.

David Brown was a man, like me. And, like me, he had probably reasoned that this was his day to die. He had nothing to lose, so he staked his claim to the ground on which he stood and challenged the enemy to come take his life if they dared. Well, I don't really know why he did what he did, but I know in the deepest place in my heart that I would not have lived through that bloody afternoon and evening if David Brown had not sealed his pact with God or the Fates, had not laid claim to his manhood, had not done what he felt he had to do or might as well do. I wrote him up for a Medal of Honor, which was little enough compensation for his life. Men who were far from that name-less little hill and who did not see what I saw awarded David Brown's spirit a Navy Cross.

Shortly after Sergeant Brown was killed, several more North Vietnamese crawled into the scrub growth and began throwing Chicoms from ten or fifteen feet outside our position. Suddenly, Marines directly to my front were yelling, "Grenade, grenade!" Everyone got their heads down when they heard that. Then, as soon as the Chicoms detonated, everyone who had them responded with our own M-26 grenades, which were extremely potent. I heard the *crump* of the M-26 detonations followed by the horrible screams of NVA in the brush.

Unknown to me, Sergeant Marshall Jesperson, a 3rd Platoon squad leader, told his troops that the next time the North Vietnamese got close enough to throw Chicoms, he was going to lead them into the thicket to clean the NVA out. I could imagine what those young Marines were thinking about that, but Jesperson was their leader and he knew they were going to obey.

When the North Vietnamese came back up the trail, reoccupied the thicket, and started throwing Chicoms again, Sergeant Jesperson got his squad up and led them into the brush. I heard the fighting. It was horrible. Ghastly. There are no rules in a fight in which you could wind up dead. No rules. Jesperson and his men did it any way they could—bullets, knives, bayonets, rifle butts, whatever. They cleaned out the thicket that time, and again, when the North Vietnamese foolishly challenged Sergeant Jesperson's authority. The squeals of agony were almost too much to bear.

Marshall Jesperson. He realized what had to be done, and he did it. No one told him to lead the way into the thicket, no one told him to kill other human beings up close. He did what he did because it had to be done. More important, those eighteen- and nineteen-year-old Marines followed him. They could have stayed in their fighting holes. No one held a roll call. They followed Sergeant Jesperson into the thicket. That was the key. He led and they followed. How could they not?

I was out checking the lines when Sergeant Jesperson led his second counterattack into the thicket. I stopped off to speak with my 3rd Platoon commander, Gunnery Sergeant Juan Almanza. Gunny was one of the finest Marines I ever served with. A small, whip-thin, dazzlingly neat man from Texas, he was one of the best Marine noncoms I ever commanded. I had put him in command of my 3rd Platoon so the other platoon commanders could see how it was supposed to be done. There was nothing Gunny Almanza couldn't do better than right. He was Old Corps all the way, the perfect role model for everyone in Lima Company, an utterly unflappable leader of men.

When I got to Almanza's position, the firing had pretty much died down for a bit. Jesperson had just cleared out the thicket and Almanza was up with his radioman, Corporal Thomas Krispin, looking around, checking his platoon's position. As the gunny looked around and thumbed rounds into empty M-16 magazines, Sergeant Jesperson trotted up from the thicket with his tongue hanging out from the exertion. When the gunny saw me approaching, he flashed a huge smile and said, "We're getting some, Skipper. We're getting some." I said, "Right on!"

I was going to say more, but right then Doc Bratton, the company's senior corpsman, crawled up to me and blurted out, "Skipper, Skipper, come with me. We got a Marine who's dying and he shouldn't. He's been lightly wounded." I had heard of people with light wounds dying for no good reason. I had heard of lightly injured men getting it into their heads that they were going to die, and dying. Apparently, what the kid Doc Bratton was treating needed was a little motivation. I was it; I was the company motivation machine.

I followed Bratton for about twenty feet, to the side of a Marine who had indeed been wounded. I looked the Marine over and thought that it probably hurt but it didn't look like much of a wound. So I said, "Marine, you're not going to die. Snap out of it. You're going to be okay. You'll be fine. Take it easy." As I spoke, I caught a little red ball tracking across the perimeter. Then there was a blinding orange flash and I found myself flat on my back. Some very heavy concussion had lifted me up and thrown me into the ground with terrific force. Before

I could move a muscle, I heard Sergeant Jesperson bawl, "I'm blind, I'm blind!"

As soon as Doc Bratton and I collected ourselves, we crawled over toward the sound of Sergeant Jesperson's voice, toward Gunny Almanza's foxhole. What I saw was revolting. The RPG had hit Gunny Almanza right in the helmet or on a boulder right behind his head. Either way, everything from the neck up was gone—except for his face. Corporal Krispin had taken a major dose of shrapnel in his chest because his flak jacket wasn't zipped. He was on the ground, coughing up blood and gore, making terrible choking and gagging sounds. Jesperson had his hands over his face and was whimpering, "I'm blind, I'm blind!"

The gunny was dead, no two ways about it. Krispin was in terrible shape. However, a closer look at Sergeant Jesperson revealed that he was not actually blind. He had been blinded by the debris from the gunny's head. In fact, he had been right in front of the gunny, talking to him, when the RPG hit. The gunny's head had taken the brunt of the blast and had saved Jesperson from being sprayed with shrapnel. Everything Jesperson had been sprayed with could be washed off.

Doc Bratton, who treated the company like it was his own private medical practice, waded right into the middle of it. Before the scene had settled on me, he was working on Krispin and talking to him, trying to calm him down: "Krispin, you're not gonna die. Hear? You're not gonna die!" The other doc and I had our hands full trying to get Jesperson calmed down.

For all Doc Bratton's hard work, there was only one way to save Krispin. He and a lot of other Lima Company Marines needed an immediate emergency helo medevac or they were going to die. But there was no way. There was too much fire across the top of the hill to get helos in. I didn't even want to ask a helo crew to risk it. The only good thing that happened to Krispin was that he passed out. It was better for him, not having to be awake with all that pain.

I crawled back to my CP hole and tried to resume my normal duties, but I was really shaken. I had really liked Gunny Almanza. I thought the world of him. As I sat in the bottom of my foxhole—by then, it was nearly deep enough to stand in—I exerted all my willpower on pulling myself together. I was no longer afraid, as I had been through most of the fight. Sooner than some but definitely later than David Brown, Marshall Jesperson, and Juan Almanza, I had passed beyond fear. I was not apathetic or even resigned to death, but I was no longer afraid.

The 3/26 CP in the field, pretty much as I found it the day I first reported in

Major Carl Mundy (*Compliments of Carl Mundy*)

Little John—Lieutenant John Prince (*Compliments of Frank Garcia*)

Members of the Lima Company CP group following our "airborne" assault south of Khe Sanh in July 1967: (*left to right*) Corporal David Johnson, Sergeant Donald Vogt, Lieutenant Tom Biondo

National Route 9 climbing toward Khe Sanh. Everything in view of the camera was "Indian Country."

Lieutenant Jaak Aulik (*top*) and 1st Sergeant Edward W. Miller in the Lima Company
CP tent in August 1967

Staff Sergeant Marvin
Bailey, the Lima Company
gunny for most of the first
half of my tour (*Compliments of Michael Hefflin*)

I took this Hue street scene during a Rough Rider mission. Hue was an exotic, startling contrast to our life in the field.

An unusually spiffy Lima Company stands at ease moments before the 26th Marines' change of command ceremony in mid August 1967. I am front and center.

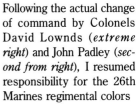

Following the actual change of command by Colonels David Lownds (*extreme right*) and John Padley (*second from right*), I resumed responsibility for the 26th Marines regimental colors

The Lima Company command group takes a break during our sweep through Leatherneck Square in late August 1967: (*left to right*) Lieutenant Tom Biondo, Staff Sergeant Marvin Bailey, me, Sergeant Donald Vogt, Corporal David Johnson, and Lieutenant Jaak Aulik

Corporal Pat Cochran, who was killed in action during the company's late-August sweep through Leatherneck Square (*Compliments of Michael Hefflin*)

Lima Company Marines inspect the gear taken from the two NVA forward observers I killed with a hand grenade in Leatherneck Square in late August 1967

An SKS carbine (*left rear*), an AK-47 assault rifle, AK-47 ammunition magazines, Chicom grenades (*left front*), and a gas mask were among the equipment the NVA forward observers had on them when they died

Artillery Fire Base C-2 in early September 1967. Virtually everything, including six 105mm howitzers, was dug in below the skyline of this vulnerable hilltop position.

Lance Corporal Terry Smith, the Lima Company tactical air control party operator

Lima Company survivors of the September 10 battle south of Con Thien. Sergeant Wendell Mullins is standing at extreme right.

C H A P T E R 16

*T*he main body of the battalion—Kilo, Mike, and H&S companies—had not had a good late afternoon that September 10. That NVA battalion that stood up out of the rice paddy and charged off down the valley did serious damage, particularly to Mike and the battalion head-quarters units, including a penetration that resulted in hand-to-hand combat in the 81mm mortar pits. No wonder we received no support from the main body; they were hanging on by their fingernails and could have used support from Lima and India if we had been able to provide it.

Among the many incredible actions in the fight to our rear was the performance of Captain Andy DeBona, the Mike Company commander. At one point in the fight, Andy dashed forward to lead a squad of his Marines from a shellhole in which it was trapped to the company main line. Unable to get the troops under control, Andy yelled in his commanding voice a chant familiar to every Marine: "Ready on the left. Ready on the right. All ready on the firing line." Most of the young Marines were a year or less away from their drill instructors, and every Marine who heard Andy understood that he was being called to order. From that point, as Andy himself literally fought the NVA at arm's-length distances, the squad withdrew from the edge of panic. Andy was awarded a Navy Cross for the heroic example he set throughout the afternoon.

The battle at the base of the valley remained in doubt well into the evening. Ammunition was in short supply and the battalion main body stood in danger of being overrun simply because the troops on the line did not have enough bullets. The situation was underscored for Major Carl Mundy, now the S-3, when a haggard, bloody Marine crawled up the slope to Carl's vantage point and asked Carl if he had any bullets to spare. Carl was only packing his .45 automatic, but he popped the clip and thumbed off five of the seven rounds he owned and handed them over to the young Marine.

Similar stories abound. The crews of two Ontos Carl Mundy held in reserve until the last minute faced nearly certain death when they drove their thin-skinned vehicles from cover to deliver a blistering rebuttal to the NVA breakthrough with their twelve 106mm recoilless rifles. All the 106s were fired with good effect, but both Ontos were riddled and disabled by a hail of NVA bullets and RPGs. Everywhere, Marine infantrymen stood to meet the NVA with bayonets and clubbed rifles and machine guns. They beat the enemy back, but at grievous cost. •

*T*oward dusk Marine F-4B Phantoms started coming in to hammer the North Vietnamese in our area. The fast movers dropped napalm and general-purpose bombs within seventy-five meters of our position. They came in, one flight of four right after another. Every time one of them streaked in, five North Vietnamese .51-caliber antiaircraft machine guns opened up. I knew there were five .51-cals out there because I could see their distinctive green tracers rising toward the Phantoms. They hit one of the Phantoms. I saw black smoke pour out behind it and followed its progress with my eyes as it turned toward the coast. Some of the troops saw a dark speck leave the airplane and announced, "He's out."

Suddenly, it was dusk. Things were slackening off, but we were still taking some sniper fire. I was about ready to begin breathing easier when Lance Corporal Terry Smith, my TACP operator, crawled up to my CP hole and said, "Skipper! Skipper, I just got the word that there's North Vietnamese in the landing zone." The zone—a little flat place undoubtedly used for that purpose by the previous tenants—was about twenty feet behind my foxhole, in the middle of the company position. Well, that caught me in the solar plexus. I thought, "Oh, shit!" What do you do now, coach?" I couldn't very well merely pass the word to my Marines that there were "maybe" NVA inside the position because it was inevitable that Marines would kill other Marines who were crawling around in the dark trying to pass out ammunition or make sure the lines were okay. If we stopped doing the chores we needed to do, we would weaken our position. What to do?

As I was pondering the alternatives—and perhaps taking too much time figuring the angles—Lance Corporal Smith started crawling off toward the landing zone. "Smitty," I whispered as loudly as I dared, "Smitty, where you going, where you going?" He looked back at me and said, "Skipper, don't worry about it. I'll get 'em with my knife."

I had seen only bad things happen to brave men that day. I couldn't let him do it, especially when I saw he was indeed armed only with his K-bar knife. It took all the balls in the world to even consider such a thing, but I couldn't let him do it. "Goddammit, Smitty, get back in your hole. Get back in that hole now." He did—a little petulantly, but he did. I decided to wait a few minutes more before making a decision, to see if the NVA would act.

Right after I got the word that North Vietnamese might be in the landing zone, I was in my foxhole with Corporal Johnson. All of a sudden, I saw a shadow. I said, "Jesus Christ, John, watch it," pulled up my automatic pistol, and assumed the two-handed crouch. The shadow kept getting larger, so I aimed in on it. It turned into a person. I was squeezing the trigger as the shadow got close enough for me to identify. I was about ready to let the round go when I realized it was Marine. I said, "Goddammit, who the hell's that?"

"It's me, it's me!"

"Who's 'me'?"

"Lieutenant Zappardino." It was Ron Zappardino, the FAC, who had gone out with India Company. He was wandering around trying to find out where his company was. I was very close to shooting him. It was a miracle I held off as long as I did. I asked Zap if he had been over the landing zone and he told me he had just come from there. As far as he knew, no NVA had camped out there.

*I*t had been a terrific fight, and I knew it could erupt in its full glory again at any moment. We were running out of ammunition—we were critically low—so I got Terry Smith up on the tac-air net to request an emergency ammunition resupply. We also had a position filled with wounded men and many of them, such as Corporal Krispin, were in danger of succumbing at any moment. But I also knew that the NVA had set in five .51-caliber heavy machine guns around us and thus could seriously endanger any helos that might respond to our call. But I couldn't worry about them. We needed the ammunition or we would all die. We made it as plain as we could that getting ammo was a matter of life or death. Goddamn if a Marine H-34 pilot didn't come back with "Get somebody in the LZ and mark it for me."

That was Terry Smith's job. Despite my fears that the zone might be crowded with NVA, I ordered him to crawl down there and climb into a foxhole or a shellhole so he could flash his strobe light to mark the zone. Terry sure enough crawled back out of sight and encountered no opposition. He turned on the strobe—which flashed straight up and could not be seen from the ground—and pretty soon we heard the helo. A second later, all five of the NVA .51-cals began hurling green tracers toward the sound. Pretty soon, I couldn't hear the helo.

I was in the bottom of my hole, only twenty feet from the landing zone. I was scared to death for the helo crew. Then I started thinking about what would happen if he was shot down over our position. We would have burning fuel, exploding ammo, and a great big fire to mark us for every rifle and machine gun out there. As I waited and worried, I heard the H-34's engine again above the roar of the NVA small-arms fire. He was right over the zone. As I looked up, I could make out the dim outline of a human form laying prone in the hatchway in the helo's side. I could see a head, chest, and arms. It looked like the man was down, wounded or even dead. It seemed that green tracer rounds were penetrating the body of the H-34 from all angles. Then the helo was gone.

A minute or two later, Terry Smith returned to the CP area and told me the crew chief apparently had stacked the ammo cases right in the hatchway and had kicked them out on the run as soon as the helo edged in over the strobe. The ammo had nearly brained Terry, but it hadn't and he and a handful of volunteers had grabbed it. Unfortunately, most of the ammo the helo dropped was 81mm mortar rounds and chests of linked .50-caliber rounds—useless to us. However, there were a few cases of 5.56mm and 7.62mm bullets, which were being distributed as Terry was reporting to me.

That was the only helo to get over our position that night. We never got one of our WIAs lifted out. The worst case remained Corporal Krispin, the 3rd Platoon radioman. Doc Bratton refused to give up on him; he even set up a shelter half and worked over Krispin's wounds in the light of a hooded penlight. But only the best trauma care in a real hospital could save Krispin, and he died during the night. So did several other WIAs who might have survived if we could have gotten them out in time.

The air strike and resupply were far from the only support we received from around sunset on. When pressure eased on the battalion main body, they were able to devote some time and energy to saving Lima and India. The biggest effort came from friendly artillery bases. We were close to Dong Ha, Camp Carroll, Con Thien, and C-2, so we had a hell of a lot of artillery available to us. I'll bet it was a regiment's worth of artillery by the time they got done laying it on. We were by far the biggest show out there that night. We rated it. Someone told me later that the artillery fired ten thousand rounds to support us. The battalion FO boxed us in and fired constant box barrages to keep the NVA out. We had a curtain of steel around us.

We also requested Puff the Magic Dragon gunships. Puff flew back and forth firing six thousand rounds a minute with his 7.62mm minigun. The show he put on was awesome. He could literally hose an area down with what appeared to be a solid stream of red tracer—a flexible tube of death. It was even more awesome when I realized that the tracer represented only one round in four. Also, the sound Puff made was scary. The whole night was suffused with an eerie, continuous *awwwwww*. I was told that a minute of firing could plow up every square inch of a regulation football field. I heard we used up two Puffs—125,000 rounds apiece.

A big problem we faced was marking targets. We couldn't just bring an aircraft in and say, "Okay, shoot up the terrain." We had no 60mm ammunition, no willy-pete, so we decided to do the marking with our M-79 grenade launchers. Any old flash would do, so the grenadiers fired their 40mm grenades at targets the platoon commanders designated. The pilots and gunners overhead were alert—we maintained very good radio contact—and completed run after run without hitting any of us.

Sometime during the night, an RF-4B photo-reconnaissance airplane came up and gave me one of the truly big frights of my life. I didn't hear him come on station, and no one told me he was there. All of a sudden, the darkness was overwhelmed by a *whoof* and a flash so brilliant I thought we had been nuked. It turned out that the photo plane had launched a brilliant carbon-magnesium flare—followed by four or five more. We found out later that the pictures he took showed hundreds of North Vietnamese bodies scattered around our position. Hundreds of them.

The normal illumination Puff put out for us also had its scary side. The flares went off with a *whoof-whoof-whoof* noise followed by a *thunk* when the expended flare canister hit the ground. The empty ceramic canisters weighed about forty pounds apiece and could kill anyone they hit. No one was hit, but several canisters landed inside the company position.

Unfortunately, the gunfire was too hot to risk a ration run. So we had nothing to eat. It sounds petty, I know, but none of us had eaten since breakfast, and many of us, including me, had not eaten since dinner the evening before. The gun tank that had been hit at the start of the action had been carrying our rations, but it had rolled back down the hill into the paddy field. Naturally, as we later discovered, the North Vietnamese facing us had scavenged the rations. We found empty C-ration cans in NVA fighting holes right around our position. I hope it was all ham and limas.

Between 0300 or 0400, September 11, things really quieted down. When I realized how quiet it had become, I began thinking, "Hey, maybe I'm going to live through this." I did not know if it was the calm before the storm, or what, but I couldn't help thinking—hoping—it was as good as over.

I passed the word that at first light we were going to fire a ten-second mad moment just in case there was anybody out there who needed to be cleared out. I alerted Battalion and we got all set to go. As the very first glimmer of dawn appeared, I ordered, "Okay, shoot it out." We all fired for about ten seconds—that was a lot of bullets— and then we started moving around.

After the mad moment, as I roved through the company area, I immediately began finding dead Marines. I found the two Marines who had been killed in the foxhole dead ahead of my foxhole, at the head of the trail through the thicket. It looked as if two or three grenades had gone off between them. I also ran across Sergeant Brown's body, Gunny Almanza's, and Corporal Krispin's. There were a lot of others. The smell of blood tinged with singed tissue and hair was almost overpowering. I told Gunny Bailey, "I want us to send these dead Marines out of here cleaned up, at least wrapped up." He got them all under poncho liners—as well as he could since they were all frozen in grotesque attitudes. After we got all the wounded lifted out, we staged the dead on the landing zone and waited until there was a free helo to carry them out. After awhile, Terry Smith got word that he had a helo coming in for the dead. As Terry guided the helo in, the terrific downdraft from the main rotor blew the ponchos off. It was a mess. It really got to me—along with my hunger, sleeplessness, and the downer following the night-long adrenalin rush. I felt the sting in my eyes. Though I lowered my head to try to hide the tears, I noticed that many of the Marines in the zone were crying too.

*I*mmediately after we completed the evacuation of our dead and wounded, we started to get ready to move out. Battalion had not told me what was next on our agenda, but I knew there were only two choices: Either we were going to continue on or we were going to get the hell out of there. Finally, word arrived that we were going to pull back to C-2. I cannot describe the feeling of elation I had when that message came in.

We still faced the problem of what to do about the two disabled tanks at the base of our hill. Battalion called me and asked for a status report on them and I told them what the tanks looked like, how charred they appeared. Battalion hemmed and hawed a little and finally told me they were going to send up a tank retriever. Later, as the tank retriever, which was up from Dong Ha, started out from the battalion position, the North Vietnamese started to zero in on it with artillery. It waddled toward us, drawing the artillery with it. At that time, I wanted nothing more to do with artillery, so I grabbed the battalion radio from Sergeant Vogt and yelled, "Get that fucking thing out of here. If it comes any closer, I'm going to knock it out! You know, I don't give a shit about these goddamn tanks. They're destroyed!" Much to my surprise, the tank retriever turned around. That was the last we saw of it.

The battalion command group was back with two companies and we had two companies, India and Lima, where we were. I knew that Matt Caulfield was senior to me—just waiting for his gold major's leaves—but I had more time in-country, so I decided to take charge. I stalked out of our perimeter with my command group and entered India's lines. They were only sixty feet from where we were. I couldn't believe it. We could have joined up during the night if I had known.

Matt Caulfield turned out to be a very cool customer, very confident, but I believe he was a wee bit shaken at the start of his third day in the field. I suggested, "Look, you guys go ahead and we'll follow you." He agreed, and that was that. Without further ado, I formed the company up and moved it out. After awhile, Corporal Johnson pointed out that we were leading and India was following. I snapped at Johnson, told him to shut up, and he gave me a hurt look. When I saw Johnson's face, I knew the pressure was getting to me. I decided to maintain the lead. We were getting off the hill; nothing else mattered.

A lot of the people I talked to later thought the retrograde from our position back to C-2 was the toughest, most physically demanding march they had ever done. No wonder. We had all been without sleep or food for two days and our bodies' reaction to the adrenalin rushes was shocking. But I didn't see it that way. I was so happy to be going to C-2 that I had an energy rush that would have allowed me to do anything. I was walking on air.

As we were walking up the main road into C-2, a Caucasian civilian with a microphone accosted me and said he was with Reuters News Service. He shoved the microphone in my face and said, "How was it?" I just told him that it had been tough out there. I let him off easy.

I later found out that somebody in my little hometown in upstate New York walked up to my dad about a week later and asked, "Hey, isn't your son in the Marine Corps?" When Dad said I was, the other man said, "Well, he's in the newspaper." He gave Dad a copy in which the front-page headline read, "Captain Camp Involved In Fight Against North Vietnamese Regiment—Heavy Casualties." That went over real big in the Camp household until my next letter arrived.

C-2 was on top of a knoll, with no cover whatsoever. They had deep, strong DMZ bunkers, and a trench digger had cut very deep trenches all over the place, each about seven feet deep and very narrow. They were perfect for covering up during an artillery or mortar attack, but we couldn't have fought from them. When we formed up and learned that Lima Company was going to stand fast to guard C-2 while the rest of the battalion moved somewhere else, I ordered everyone to get into the trenches. There were NVA artillery and rockets all over the place out there—as we well knew—and I wasn't about to give their FOs a company-size target.

As the company hit the trenches, I really started winding down. Everything started to hit. The downside of the manic euphoria I experienced getting to C-2 really started to hit me. I went into a bunker my radiomen had turned into a CP and I stayed there all day and all night. I was too numb with exhaustion to think straight. As soon as I got inside the bunker, I sat down on a cot, shed all my gear, and pulled open one of several cases of C rations I found stacked up along one bulkhead. I placed the case of C rations at the foot of my cot and gulped down one complete ration. Then I fell back onto the cot and went to sleep. I half remember waking up periodically during the night, famished. Each time, I sat up, opened up another can of C rations, and gulped it down. It sounds strange, but I swear that by the time morning rolled around, I had eaten the entire case of C rations.

Higher headquarters had promised us relief the next day, September 12. As promised, an advance party from a company of another battalion, 2/4, arrived early and I started briefing them by describing the danger from NVA artillery and rockets. "Lookit," I warned, "this place is under observation and subject to artillery fire. Whatever you do, make sure you bring your people in and don't let them bunch up, particularly on the skyline." The skyline was the big danger because the MSR from Cam Lo ran right up to the top of the knoll and continued on up to Con Thien.

The appointed hour of the relief approached and I ordered Lima Company to stand by in the trenches. Everybody had their gear on and we were all set to go. My command group was down by the base headquarters bunker, in the open but spread well apart. Everyone was waiting for my signal and I was waiting for the relief company to arrive. I strolled to the top of the knoll to see what was going on. I happened to look back toward Cam Lo, which was to the south, and I spotted the dust clouds from the trucks bringing up our relief.

The trucks drove into C-2 through the wire, ran right up to the top of the knoll, and parked, radiator to tailgate. They were right out in the open. I couldn't believe it. As I ran over to tell them to get the hell off the knoll, I happened to glance over to the side in time to see an artilleryman jumping up and down on his bunker. I distinctly heard him yell, "Incoming."

I took three or four more steps and pivoted back around toward my command group. "Incoming," I screamed.

They all recognized my voice and made like prairie dogs going into their holes. My people disappeared so fast even I couldn't believe it. On the other hand, the other company apparently had not been around the DMZ before. The Marines jumping off the trucks just stood there with expressions on their faces that seemed to say, "What the hell are you talking about?"

I grabbed the two nearest Marines and yelled at them, "Get in that culvert." We jumped into the culvert underneath the road—it was a regular drainage culvert—just as the first artillery rounds impacted. The three of us lay there, hunched over, and I thought, "My God, if there's a close round it's going to kill us with concussion." I turned to the two Marines and said, "Lookit, I'll listen and, if I don't hear anything, I'm going to run to the trench and you guys follow me because of concussion." I was sure I was confusing them, but they nodded their heads.

I stuck my head out and listened. I didn't hear anything, so I said, "Let's go," and went roaring out of the culvert toward the nearest deep trench. I was well along into a two-and-a-half gainer when, evidently, a round came in—I didn't hear it—and knocked me ass over tea kettle. A sliver grazed my forearm, just enough to draw blood. As soon as my body tumbled into the ground—I was still in the open—I bounded back up, just like that. There was no hesitation. I executed a pretty nice swan dive into the seven-foot-deep fire trench, right on top of a couple of the kids from my company. I said, "Excuse me," and they chorused, "Yessir."

When the artillery attack slackened off enough, I started yelling for Lima Company to get the hell out of C-2. As the shells continued to fall intermittently, my people raced down the road, a fire team at a time. The other company had arrived; we were no longer responsible for C-2. As I ran down the road beside my radiomen, I glanced down and saw that several trucks were on fire, two 105mm howitzers were burning in the gunpits, and a lot of people were lying all over the ground. It was too bad, but the other company just hadn't understood what the hell was going on up there.

During the afternoon and evening of September 10, 1967, 3/26 lost 34 Marines killed and 192 wounded—more than one man in four. Overall, the four-day operation cost 3/26 55 killed and 262 wounded, over one third its strength.

P A R T **III**

THE WAR

From C-2, Lima Company pulled back to rejoin the battalion of Phu Bai. By the time we got there a day late, the rest of the battalion was pretty well set up. As soon as I reported in, Lieutenant Colonel Alderman told me that Lima Company was going to guard a Seabee— Navy construction engineer—detachment manning a rock crusher and a pontoon bridge across a river. Major Mundy told me that we would be nominally attached to 2/26 for the duration of the mission, but only for operational purposes. For practical purposes, we would be on our own. I didn't think anything of yet another assignment away from the battalion. That's just the way it was. In fact, I was delighted to be getting off on another independent assignment. I liked being on my own.

As we were getting ready to go out on the new assignment, a major, inevitable, and unavoidable problem beset Lima Company— and the rest of 3/26. The battalion had been in-country for just over a year and all the original survivors were getting "short"—to the end of their tours. Thus, the very best men in Lima Company—the survivors— were told to report to H&S Company for temporary duty. Both of my radiomen, Sergeant Donald Vogt and Corporal David Johnson, were among the departees. They and the others had been the stalwarts of the company, but there was nothing to be done. They were going to rotate home. Altogether, Lima Company lost thirty Marines.

The night before we moved out, I told Top Miller that, in the morning, as we moved out, I wanted him to form up the short-timers because I wanted to talk to them. As we formed up the company and got the men on the trucks, I walked over to talk to these thirty Marines. It was a traumatic experience because these guys had really put out. I had a big lump in my throat as I started talking about a few things I wanted to give them in return for their loyal service. "Don't ever forget," I told them, "that while there are an awful lot of people who serve, and serve in Vietnam, there are very, very few who actually go toe-to-toe against the enemy. Always respect yourself for that. Always have pride." There was a lot more I wanted to say, but I was shaken, so I ended with a smile and a rather lame, "God, if any of you are ever close to me or ever run into me, I'll buy you a beer." Then I saluted them and left.

On September 16, the truck convoy drove straight through to the Seabee rock crusher without any hold ups or problems. I had been looking forward to what everyone told me would be three or four weeks of light duty. By that stage of the game, Lima Company was pretty well beat up; we had had some rough fights. We needed time to straighten ourselves out and absorb nearly a quarter of our strength in replacements for all our casualties and short-timers.

Right from the start, the Seabees were great people to be around. They were overjoyed to see us, largely because there wasn't much going on around there. They had had no excitement, and they were pretty lonely.

For the most part, they were happy-go-lucky types, confident about what they could accomplish. They all had had a little combat-infantry training, but they knew they needed us to look out for them. In return, they looked out for us, doing whatever they could to make our stay pleasant and comfortable. The living was decent, well above average. There were enough roomy, airy, screen-sided Southeast Asia (SEA) huts for all of us to live in, and the Seabee cooks fixed tremendous, delicious meals in their, by our standards, lavish mess hall. Of course, we faced the danger of looking like a company of Pillsbury Doughboys, but we were willing to meet the challenge. From the start, it looked like the best possible way to rest up and regain our strength after the trials and tribulations of the war along the DMZ.

There were no Navy officers there; the Seabee detachment was in the hands of several very senior chief petty officers, which probably helped keep things loose. I did nothing to interfere with the Seabees and they did nothing for us that wasn't motivated by friendliness.

The compound was north of Phu Bai and four or five miles south of Hue, on Route 504, which went on into the A Shau Valley. In addition to running the rock crusher, whose product was various grades of gravel, the Seabees maintained a hundred-meter-long floating pontoon bridge across the Hue River. It was our job to defend the bridge against attack by NVA or VC sappers, but we also had to watch over the rock crusher, which was a half mile up the road, on a huge hill. So, we really had two positions to defend. The area was pretty well built up and extensively cultivated. The closest of many villages began beside the pontoon bridge. There was a motley ARVN detachment located in a compound in the village, but we had no direct liaison with them.

The hill the Seabees were quarrying dominated both the rock crusher and the bridge. It was too big to defend all the way around; it would have taken a battalion to do the job right. About the only thing I could do was maintain a squad outpost with a .50-caliber heavy machine gun up there and hope attackers would refrain from shooting down on us if they captured the heights. My hopes were thin armor, but they were all I had.

Making the impossible task laughable was the huge hundred-acre high-walled complex of royal tombs between the bridge and the rock crusher. These were sacred structures, so we were ordered to stay away. That was okay by me, but I wondered if the NVA and VC had similar orders.

I did the best I could. The well-meaning Seabees had built half-assed bunkers, complete with concrete floors and electric lights. The bunkers were big and clean, but I thought they were designed all wrong. Nevertheless, I placed a fire team in the bunker on the far side of the pontoon bridge, which was toward Hue. On the near side of the bridge, I posted one platoon, less the fire team, along with a section of M-60 machine guns and one 60mm mortar. A half mile away, on higher ground, I posted the two remaining platoons and the company CP. If enemy sappers blew the bridge, we would be cut off from the nearest help.

The tactics were obvious: We had to do a lot of patrolling to make sure we could spot the enemy early as he approached us. We also set out a lot of ambushes, and we always had two men out on the bridge, walking back and forth looking for floating mines or swimmers with explosives. As we got into it, the two-man team on the bridge took to chucking hand grenades into the water at weird intervals during the night just in case swimmers were there.

I looked on this duty as an opportunity to retrain the company from scratch. Rather than go static, which was all that was expected of us, I wanted to keep up a schedule of rigorous patrolling and other martial activities. There was a real danger of getting caught by the enemy if we sat still, and I had all those new Marines to toughen and assess. So, in addition to running necessary patrols and ambushes, I began running the individual squads through live-fire training problems up on the big hill.

The training was dangerous, exacting work, fraught with risk of accidental bloodletting, but it was worthwhile. Everyone benefited. The new troops benefited because they got to work with combat veterans. The combat veterans benefited because they had a chance to think about the lessons they had learned in combat. The platoon commanders—Little John and two brand-new second lieutenants—benefited because they were the ones who had to oversee the training and provide safety measures; they got to command troops and work intimately with men they probably would be leading in battle. I benefited because I got to shape the new Lima Company completely in the image I had built in my mind during my six years in the Corps.

The training extended to our normal patrol schedule. Every patrol was led by a squad leader, and every squad leader was required to call in live 60mm mortar fire. That shook down the gunners, many of whom were new, and it got every troop leader used to calling fire.

"The enemy owns the night" was not a meaningless aphorism old salts used to scare the wits out of the green replacements. The enemy indeed owned the night. Given our impossible tactical situation, I spent most of my time with my fingers crossed. I well knew that anything could happen, most probably at night. We were ready for anything. In fact, as events transpired, we might have been a tad too ready.

As soon as we arrived, I put the troops to work digging deep trenches outside each SEA hut. My command group got to sleep in the huts every night, but, of course, the troops manned the perimeter.

We issued each position a handful of hand flares we called pop-ups. They were illumination flares packaged in aluminum tubes, each about a foot long and about three quarters of an inch in diameter. To fire a pop-up, you have to remove the aluminum cap, which was about two inches long and had a sharp, pointed nail in it. The nail had to be jammed very hard into a firing cap in the bottom of the tube. That shot off the flare.

One problem with the pop-up was the loud *swoosh* it made. Everyone within five hundred meters could hear it and, usually, everyone who could hear it—including the approaching enemy—instinctively ducked. Of course, our people couldn't see what was being illuminated if they had their heads down. Another problem was that the sudden bright light ruined everyone's night vision. Once a pop-up was fired, troops manning a line were blind without other pop-ups being fired in succession.

Green troops are particularly jumpy at night, so it wasn't long before the constant random use of pop-ups started pissing me off. They were scared to death, and they were scaring everyone else. They ruined the sleep of everyone who was supposed to be off duty, but, most important, they were giving away our positions and ruining the slim chances of the sentries on the bridge seeing sappers or floating mines. Finally, I passed the word, "No more pop-ups unless the North Vietnamese are physically assaulting the position."

That very night, I went out with my new first sergeant, Top Mabry, to patrol the lines. As we walked along, we nearly stepped into a little foxhole we couldn't see in the dark. The hole was about two feet in front of us when the Marine manning it launched a pop-up that went *swoosh* right past my ear. It just scared me to death. Top Mabry and I didn't know what the hell was happening, so we naturally jumped down into the hole for protection. Nothing happened, so the first sergeant and I accosted the Marine. "What the hell are you doing," we asked in unison. Of course, by then, the young Marine was scared to death because the company commander and first sergeant were in his hole asking tough questions he wasn't sure he could answer. Besides, he had fired the pop-up the very evening of the day I had said he couldn't fire any more pop-ups.

I could feel the kid shaking when he answered, "Sir, I saw something. Honest, sir, I saw something!"

"Hey," I countered in an effusive tone, "that's great, Marine. What I want you to do now is crawl out through the wire and make a determination of how many there are and then come back and tell us." I could see the whites of his eyes get real big. "By the way," I went on, "we'll keep your rifle here and cover you."

He left the hole with the greatest display of reluctant body language I have ever seen, but he gamely crawled from sight and sound, stayed out for a respectable period, and crawled back in to report that he could find no sign of the enemy.

The word got around real quick and the problem got solved. That problem. We had others when the green troops graduated to bigger and better ways to drive me crazy.

One night, I was rousted from a deep, mind-cleansing sleep by a sudden burst of automatic-weapons fire followed by an explosion. As I came out of my rack—real fast—I heard a Marine running down the company street yelling unintelligible words at the top of his lungs, hysterically. The pitch of his voice alone was enough to set everybody on edge. It was particularly scary because we didn't know what the hell was going on. We had heard the automatic-weapons fire, we had heard the *crump,* and now we heard the screaming man. Naturally, we thought that NVA or VC were attacking and the Marine was running for his life.

Everybody in my command group was up and running, and the troops on the lines went to full alert—all without needing to be told. When I got out of my hut, I yelled to Gunny Bailey, "Stop him, stop him!" Immediately, a couple of Marines tackled the guy about twenty feet from me. He kept screaming. As I neared the tussle, I saw that he was waving his right hand and that the tackles couldn't keep it still. Suddenly, I realized that most of the hand was blown away. Big drops of blood were flying everywhere. A corpsman came running over and tried to treat him, but the kid was hysterical. He was beyond reason and thoroughly unmanageable.

Finally, the corpsman got the hand under control and another Marine tried to patch it up. All the fingers were gone and there was a hole through the palm. We tried to calm him down, but there was no talking to this guy. He had flipped all the way out.

I grabbed about half the command group and ran toward the wounded Marine's position on the perimeter line. Though there were no sounds of fighting, I just knew we were going to find NVA swarming through.

We found no NVA or VC, no evidence of anything that might have been an intrusion. However, we did find evidence of an M-26 grenade explosion, but all the damage from it was outside the bunker the injured Marine had been manning. There was no asking the wounded Marine what had occurred; he was completely irrational and never bounced back before a medevac helo arrived. We had to piece it together ourselves, pure speculation.

The Marine's fighting position was above the ground, an open sandbag bunker with a tarp over the top of it, about three feet above the top layer of sandbags. We assumed he had gotten scared by a sight or sound he thought he perceived and, rather than wake up the other Marine in the position, had fired his rifle. Then he had pulled a grenade out and tried to throw it overhand, a common error in a panic situation. Apparently, when his arm came forward, he hit the tarp and the hand grenade fell on the outboard side of the sandbag wall. If we were correct in our assumptions to that point, his follow-through motion extended his wrist and hand out over the grenade as it detonated, and the fragments devastated his hand.

There wasn't enough tension at the rock crusher; there wasn't enough danger to keep the men honest. As the green troops settled into the routine and stopped jumping at every shadow, they became disdainful of the potential danger. In fact, so did the old hands. As a result, I constantly had to inspect all the bunkers because the troops kept hooking up electric lights and running them all night long. The lights destroyed night vision and were visible from a long way off. It was a constant struggle.

Even without the lights, the bunkers were little better than death traps. If the North Vietnamese had hit us, the Marines manning the bunkers would have been bottled up inside. There was nowhere to go. I never resolved the problem. The bunkers were in good locations, but they were built wrong. I expected to be there for only a few weeks and the sort of construction effort we needed would have taken that long. It was stupid, but another reason I didn't order proper bunkers built was for fear of offending the Seabees.

Another major worry was a draw that ran right through the middle of the position. One day, while investigating the draw with several of my Marines, I happened to look up and see where the bark on a tree had been scuffed. I grabbed some branches and hoisted myself up. As I got higher, I could see where the North Vietnamese or VC had built a platform right in the middle of the tree. From there, I could overlook our main position and the position of the platoon down at the pontoon bridge. In fact, kilometers of roadway were well within my line of sight.

There was a kind of peninsula or spit of land that jutted out into the river near the pontoon bridge. The base of the peninsula was set right against the big hill, which made patrolling out to there impossible. In order for us to get there, we had to cross about sixty meters of water. I kept looking at the peninsula and thinking, "Jesus, there's probably something over there and we ought to investigate." The more I thought about it, the more I tried to figure out how we were going to cross over to check it out. But getting there was beyond our means.

Days passed and the peninsula continued to plague my mind. Then it hit me. I had been in a reconnaissance company early in my career and had done a lot of water work, including rubber-boat insertions. I immediately called back to the 3rd Reconnaissance Battalion to see if they had any rubber boats they could spare. They said they did and I asked for three of four of them.

When four rubber boats arrived, I had them dropped off in a covered area which could not be observed from the river or the village on the far side of the river. By then, I had decided to put in a two-platoon assault. I also had decided—what the hell—to make it a night operation.

I quickly learned that there was only one man in the company who had ever used rubber boats before—the company commander. So, I showed the troops how to inflate the boats and ran a few drills to teach them how to paddle them. I selected several steersman and taught them how to control the boats. Unfortunately, since I did not want to tip my hand, I ran all the drills under cover, on dry land. It looked good, but I had no idea what might happen when my armada became seaborne.

At sunset, we began getting ready to go. There wasn't much to do, so we continued to practice. At H-Hour, 0200, in the pitch dark of an utterly moonless night, I whispered orders for my raiders to hoist the inflated boats onto their shoulders and carry them down to the river. As soon as the boats were hoisted by about twenty of the eighty-odd members of the raiding party, the rest of the group spread out and patrolled along the road leading to the bridge. It was exhausting work for the men carrying the heavy boats, but the road was clear and we made our way to the crossing point without incident.

We set in several M-60s to cover us, launched the boats, and climbed aboard. It was pitch dark and very, very quiet.

I was in the lead boat. The plan was for the Marines in my boat to reconnoiter the beach and then call in the other boats. I motioned my paddlers and steersman to ease us out into the stream. To my amazement, though the current was reasonably strong, the paddling was accomplished with a minimum of noise.

I had practiced the landing maneuver countless times as a recon-platoon commander in Hawaii before the war. I knew every move. But practicing ain't the same as the real thing. We had to cross sixty meters of open water. If anyone was on the peninsula, and if they heard or saw us coming, we would be in the open, with no place to hide, when the shooting started. I began thinking that maybe this raid wasn't such a good idea after all. "What the hell are we going to do," I asked myself, "if they open fire?"

Nothing happened. We got to the peninsula, dropped over the sides, and spread out to provide security. I signaled the other boats, which were standing off the beach, and they landed in a pretty fair approximation of silence. We had set up a perimeter by about 0400 and then hunkered down to await the sun. The tension was beyond belief. We had no idea what we were facing and most of the troops were poor swimmers—if they could swim at all. If we lost the boats, they would be trapped. Nevertheless, despite the tension and honest concerns, I knew that the troops were having a ball. I was. Getting there had been so different from the daily grind. We were all scared, but we were exhilarated.

Nothing happened. We started our sweep at dawn and we found nothing, no signs of any habitation, no signs of military activity.

Nothing. After five or six hours, we reboarded the rubber boats and paddled back. We conducted an identical raid a few weeks later, but it wasn't the same.

About a week after we set up, the Marines patrolling the bridge spotted three suspicious characters moving in. The sentries challenged and the three Vietnamese men started running. Both sentries opened fire with their M-16s on full automatic. One of the fleeing men flopped into the river, but the other two escaped. A thorough search did not turn up a body, but the searchers found a quarter-pound block of TNT, all ready to blow. I have no idea what they thought they were going to accomplish with four ounces of TNT.

Another day, one of the Marine sentries guarding the bridge inexplicably fell into the river and drowned before anybody could get to him. We were not able to find him until, days later, his bloated, decomposing corpse surfaced nearly a mile downstream. What a terrible tragedy!

One morning, a Vietnamese civilian man came up to the guard bunker across the river, yelling and screaming in Vietnamese. We didn't know what the hell he was saying, so I had him blindfolded and brought into the position. We took him into the radio bunker and called the 2/26 battalion CP to see if they had a Vietnamese interpreter. They did, and they put him on the net to speak with the hysterical civilian. It came out, between the yelling and screaming, that the man said a North Vietnamese battalion had walked out of the jungle and marched into an area two or three miles away from our position.

When the story finally emerged, I thought, "Well, what the hell, we should find out if this guy is telling the truth or not." I saddled up the whole company except for a few squads, and got set to do battle. I put the Vietnamese man on the point and had him lead the way. My instructions to the pointmen were to follow him, but if guy sneezed or farted they were to blow him away. I didn't know what good that might have done, but I felt better saying it and the pointmen felt better hearing it.

We worked our way down the road a couple of miles, until the civilian stopped at an old construction or work area. There were a lot of old 55-gallon drums strewn around—lots of junk and debris. We searched the area, but we couldn't find any signs of recent occupation or passage by any sort of group, much less an enemy battalion.

Our search carried us to an absolutely gorgeous little stream. It was a beautiful setting, too good to pass up. The troops waded right into the water. We hiked down the stream in water to our chests, as much for the cool peace and quiet as to find the NVA battalion. I finally had to get the troops out of the water because we were getting way off course, and then we had to push through thick, hot brush to get back to the road. We expected to find something any minute, but we never did. After an hour or two, I finally turned the company around.

As we were disengaging from the heavy growth, a Bird Dog that had been shadowing us accidentally fired a marker rocket. No one was hurt when it landed near us, but we spent many anxious, quick-stepping minutes wondering if every fast mover in I Corps was going to drop a load on the telltale plume of smoke.

I have no idea what the civilian had seen or why he led us to that area. There was nothing there and there was no sign that anyone had been there for quite awhile. We went out, we searched, and we came back. Nothing happened.

Per standing orders, we turned the Vietnamese man over to the ARVNs manning the compound in the village across the river. Later that day, some of my troops came by the CP and one of them said, "Hey, sir, we saw what happened to that Vietnamese."

"What happened to him?" I asked.

"Well, he's hanging out on the wire right now."

Evidently, the ARVNs interrogated him and decided he wasn't telling the truth, so they spread-eagled him on the wire that ran around their compound.

A week or so after we arrived at the rock crusher, my sentries called in to tell me that a French priest had arrived at the bridge. I went out to meet him, to see why he had come calling, and was pleasantly surprised to find that he spoke very good English. He told me he was a missionary and lived in one of the nearby villages. He had a very bad limp and, when I stared a little too hard, he told me that he had been in the French Resistance in World War II and had been seriously wounded. He offered to hold a service, so we got all the Catholic Marines down to the CP area and he celebrated mass. The troops were thrilled and he seemed like a good sort, so I asked him to come back whenever he could. He agreed and countered with an invitation for us to visit his church.

The priest held another mass about a week later and, the week after that, we were invited to his church. It was all set, but, the day we were supposed to go, he sent a message: "Don't come." We soon learned that the North Vietnamese had found out about the excursion and had set an ambush for us. Fortunately, the priest's intelligence network was on par with the NVA's.

Near the end of my tour in Vietnam, I learned that during the Tet offensive in early 1968, the North Vietnamese took the French priest, who was just ministering to the needs of the local parishioners, and buried him up to his neck. He died a ghastly death after several days of exposure to the hot sun.

*I*n the early evening of September 27, we received a reconnaissance report indicating that an NVA battalion was moving off a large hill mass about three thousand meters from our compound. There was nothing we could do—they were too far away—but there was plenty our artillery could do. As I listened to the chatter on the 2/26 battalion net, I carried my chair out into the company street and sat back to watch the show. The artillery looked to be right on target. Even if it wasn't, the detonations and flares from a Bird Dog made a dazzling light show. It looked to me like there were many secondary detonations, but the same effect could have resulted from direct hits on rocks. The hill mass was beyond our operating area, so we never got out to check for damage or kills. That was the province of another unit, and we never heard any news. But it didn't seem to matter. What mattered was the effort.

*T*he only live action of the tour directly involving Lima Company came when I happened to be on top of the big hill, inspecting the squad .50-cal position up there. I was speaking with the squad leader when one of the lookouts happened to spot several NVA soldiers as they crossed a rice paddy over a thousand meters from us. I thought, "What the hell, let's try a little sniping with the .50-cal," something I had read about in a book on the Korean War and had always wanted to try my hand at. We cranked in the elevation and fired one round. The range was so great I needed my binoculars to see where the round hit. It was a little off, but it got the attention of those NVA soldiers. I'm sure they hadn't heard the round being fired, but they sure saw the geyser it lifted up in the paddy water. We got closer to the struggling, wading NVA soldiers with the next two rounds, but that really got those people moving. I believe they became airborne as they legged toward the nearest treeline. Finally, I had the gunner open fire on full automatic, but he was way off. No score, but it was good sport. For once, we had them in our sights, which was reward enough.

We stayed at the rock crusher far longer than anyone had antici-pated, until the very end of October, about six weeks in all. After we were completely acclimated to having fun in the sun in that quiet little backwater, the 3/26 CP sent word that we were to pack up and rejoin the battalion at Camp Evans.

CHAPTER *18*

When we returned to Camp Evans—named for Lima Company's first KIA in Vietnam—in the closing days of October 1967—just in time for my twenty-seventh birthday, on Halloween—we found that there was a beautification program going into effect. The newly installed camp commander wanted everything done by the numbers, as if we were Stateside. I have no idea why, except maybe he didn't have anything else to do. It was bullshit. He wanted the rocks around the base headquarters compound painted, he wanted the bunkers just so, he wanted the whole place "beautified." The battalion was going crazy trying to meet his demands because the staff felt we had to show our discipline. I could be wrong, but I think maybe the camp commander lost sight of our primary objective—finding out where the enemy was and then destroying those rascals.

The battalion was having a hard go of it. The staff just wasn't getting along well with the camp commander. The result was that Camp Evans was not a nice place to be hanging around. Morale in the battalion was lower than a snake's belly.

For my own part, I experienced a serious downer at the battalion staff meeting my first evening in. As I looked at the assembled officers, I saw very few familiar faces. Except for Major Mundy, I saw no one who had been with the battalion when I had checked in at the start of my tour, in late June. I barely knew the battalion commander and had had only one conversation with Captain Matt Caulfield, the India Company commander. The Kilo Company commander had been around for a few months, but I had never really worked with him. Andy DeBona had been rotated home out of Mike Company a week after the September battle near Con Thien; his replacement had been the battalion logistics officer for a few months. The exec, Major Joe Loughran, was new; he had arrived the evening before Lima Company went out to save the battalion in September. The S-2 was another new face, and my good friend, Captain Tom Early, the communications officer, was days away from rotating home. I looked at all the new faces and I felt alone. As I thought about it, I realized that, though junior in rank to all the other captains, I had been with the battalion the longest.

November 10 is the Marine Corps birthday. No matter where in the world Marines are, we celebrate. Except for mounting squad- and platoon-size perimeter sweeps and close-in security patrols, Lima Company had remained inside Camp Evans with most of the rest of 3/26, and we were still there for the birthday party. Except for a squad patrol we had to detail, the entire company got to chow down at the mess hall.

The battalion had a tremendous meal lined up. We even had aluminum trays, just like at a Stateside mess hall—and they served the biggest steaks I had ever seen in my life. There were potatoes, vegetables, ice cream, and cake. It all tasted pretty good, too.

During the early part of the meal, the 3rd Marine Division commander arrived to give us a peptalk. Unfortunately, he thought he was talking to the 4th Marines, which was sort of true because 3/26 was temporarily attached to the 4th Marines. However, the general started going on and on about the glories of the 4th Marines, and he never mentioned the 26th Marines. The battalion had only operated directly under the 26th Marines commander once, briefly, at the time I joined the battalion. However, we knew who we were, and we sure weren't the 4th Marines. I found myself getting pissed off at all the good things the general had to say about "you men of the 4th Marines" and blah, blah, blah. It looked to me like everyone else was pretty pissed off, too.

Despite the division commander's gaffe, it was getting to be a wonderful evening. There was a tremendous sense of camaraderie, not to mention the tremendous sense of wellbeing that resulted from eating such a good meal under nearly Stateside conditions.

The general left early and we continued to eat. However, about halfway through the meal, Gunny Bailey sidled up to my side and said, "Skipper, we got a problem."

"What's that, Gunny?"

"Well, sir, one of the men from the squad that's on the patrol tripped a booby trap. He had a traumatic amputation of one of his arms and one of his legs. Blown off. Sir, he died about five minutes ago."

I was floored. There we were, celebrating one of the great things Marines celebrate in life. We were celebrating being alive as much as anything else, having one good time in that miserable goddamn experience. So a few guys got shortchanged. That's the Marine Corps way, too. Nothing's perfect. But getting shortchanged *and* killed—that was too much. The dead Marine had just joined the company; I hardly knew who he was, but I grieved for him.

Battalion notified me one afternoon a day or two after the birthday party that Lima Company was to mount a squad patrol down to a village less than a mile from the main gate. The Marines were to see what they could see and then establish a night ambush along a trail we knew the NVA and VC were using.

As soon as Lima Company had arrived from the rock crusher, I had checked in with the S-2 to learn everything I could about the area of operations around Camp Evans. The news was grim. Because we weren't allowed to go into the mountains around the base, and the NVA knew exactly how far we could go, patrols in the area had been beset constantly by booby traps and hit-and-run ambushes. Patrols out there had been in no major fights, but they had been bled slowly over time with nothing to show for the losses. I knew that we were facing a time as frustrating as our brief sweep out at Co Bi-Thanh Tan in August. The big difference was that we were getting into the monsoon and we would thus have to contend with crappy weather that could keep our combat air and helicopter support grounded.

I randomly selected the squad to run the patrol. It turned out that there were only nine men in the squad because of rotations, extra duty around Camp Evans, and leaves, but most of my squads were short troops for similar reasons, so nine men was about as good as I could do.

The squad went out, spent the night outside the village, and reported in the next morning that it had had no contact with the enemy but that the men had found a cache of brand-new punji stakes near the Vietnamese village. The company had been inactive for days and I was getting bored, so I told the squad leader to stay where he was, that I would be down as soon as possible. I did not expect to do much; I just wanted to get out of that damned oppressive Camp Evans.

I ran over to the battalion S-2 and told him, "Hey, my patrol found some new punji stakes. I'm going out with a few men. Does anybody here want to go out?" The S-2, a newly promoted captain who had been with the battalion for a little over a month, replied, "Yeah, sure, how about if I go out with you?" While he was rounding up a few of his Kit Carson scouts—former enemy soldiers—I ran back to my company CP and rounded up one of my radiomen and a few other Marines who happened to be around and who wanted to get out for a bit.

As we walked down the road from the camp, we were passed by many vehicles. It was a busy road and an easy walk out to the village, which was less than a mile from the camp gate, up a little side road. We found the ambush squad without any difficulty, and the squad leader took us out to where he had found a pile of punji stakes— sharpened bamboo stakes that the VC usually smeared with dung and planted in covered pits to trap the unwary traveler. The punji pit was a crude but extremely potent weapon.

After we gawked at the little cache of stakes, the S-2 and I agreed to have a look through the rest of the village, which was just a little place, maybe twenty-five or thirty huts. The Kit Carson scouts got right into it, quizzing the women and the old men who seemed to be the only residents of every Vietnamese village I had ever seen. Of course, no one knew anything. They didn't know anything about any punji stakes, they hadn't seen the village's young men in an awfully long time, they had no idea if there were any VC or NVA in the area, they were just simple rice farmers who sometimes made a few extra piasters selling things to Marines in the nearby camp. I am sure, if we had asked them, they would have told us that they didn't know where all the infants the women were holding had come from.

I had heard it all before. I knew nothing was going to come of it, so, when the S-2 gave it up, I suggested that we all return to Camp Evans. He couldn't think of anything else he wanted to do, so he nodded his assent. "Okay," I told the squad leader, "saddle them up and let's move out." We started up the trail that ran from the village to the main road.

We were moving in a double column with maybe twenty-five feet back to front between each pair of men. I was about six places from the front of the column when I reached a turn at the corner of the village. Everything looked good, but I had a feeling. I hesitated for a moment or two, but something definitely didn't feel right, so I finally opened my mouth to say, "Let's get off the road," when there was a terrific explosion about twenty feet in front of me.

Where had I heard this before? I didn't know what caused the explosion; I just dropped to the ground and hugged Mother Earth, waiting for the noise to subside so I could begin figuring out what to do next. No noise followed, so I looked up, straight at a Kit Carson scout who was was sitting in the middle of the road, about ten feet in front of me, holding his bleeding head.

Before I could do anything more, our corpsman ran by me and stopped beside a large gray lump off to one side of the road. I scooted to my feet and followed the doc. As I ran, I yelled, "Watch out, doc, there may be mines."

The gray lump was a Marine, Private First Class Smith, the company clown, a short, squatty radioman who always had a joke. He had happened to draw duty the afternoon before as the ambush patrol's radioman. There was a huge smoldering crater in the left track of the road and Smitty was lying on the edge, so I assume he was the victim of a command-detonated mine because he was carrying a radio. The enemy usually tried to get the unit leader, and unit leaders usually had a radioman in tow. If that was their intention, they got the wrong radioman. My radioman was in the column right behind me, but he had not come into sight around the corner when the mine was detonated.

As the thoroughly dazed Kit Carson scout tried to apply a bandage to his head wound, the corpsman dropped in beside Smitty, but he balked. He didn't do anything, he just stared.

Smitty was the most hurt person I have ever seen. The sheer magnitude of the explosion had blown his left leg off, even with the trunk of his body. His right femur was still attached, but there wasn't any flesh on it; it was just sticking out of the end of his body, naked and bare. All the flesh on his right forearm was hanging loose and the wrist was shattered. All his clothing had been blown off him;

everything—the radio, flak jacket, his pack, every stitch of clothing. He was covered with fine gray powder.

I was shocked. I didn't know what to do, so I asked a stupid question: "Smitty, are you okay?" What a stupid thing to say! But, to my utter disbelief, he replied, "Skipper, I'm hurt."

I kept thinking, "My God, what are we going to do?" The corpsman was just kneeling there, unable to act. It was then that I realized there was no blood. We figured out later that heat of the explosion must have cauterized all his arteries and blood vessels. So there was no blood. Big deal. What the hell could we do?

I started yelling at my radioman, who was about twenty feet away, "Get an emergency medevac. Get an emergency medevac out here right away. Get 'em going!" As I stared at poor, helpless Smitty, I heard the radioman calling in the emergency medevac. Then Smitty said, "Skipper, I can't breathe, I can't breathe." I'm sorry to admit that he was so badly hurt I didn't want to touch him—I just didn't want to touch him—but I forced myself to reach over and take his head in my hands. Slowly, the doc and I started moving him around, straightening him out. He was trying to sit up, but he had no leverage, he had no legs.

I kept saying, "Smitty, you're okay, you're okay. You're hurt, but we're going to get you out of here." And he kept repeating, "Skipper, I can't breathe, I can't breathe."

I don't know why we tried to move him around—maybe because he said he couldn't breathe where he was—but that's what we did. I think the doc and I felt we had to do something, anything. It was not a good idea to move him, but we did. We were very gentle. I looked up once and saw that the doc had tears coursing down his cheeks. I didn't look again; I felt embarrassed and I felt like I was about to start crying, too. After we moved him, we took off our belts, but Smitty didn't need tourniquets; he wasn't bleeding and there was no place to secure them. We were just doing things to make ourselves feel better.

I started hyperventilating, so I began yelling at the radioman. "Get that goddamn helicopter out here," I demanded, "Get it out here!"

As it turned out, Battalion had responded to our call by asking that a doctor be sent out aboard the helicopter so Smitty's treatment could begin right away. It was the right thing to do, but nobody told me about the delay the stop by the aid station was causing, and I felt so anxious and guilty and helpless that I reacted by yelling and screaming and carrying on at my radioman, whom I am sure was feeling as badly as anyone—knowing, as he must have, that it could have been him on the ground and Smitty calling in the medevac. He kept telling me that the emergency medevac had been declared, but I kept yelling at him. Suddenly, I found myself stalking up the road toward him. I grabbed the radio handset and yelled into it, "Gimme the goddamn battalion commander!" I didn't even use the call sign. "This is Lima-6, this is Lima-6. Give me the Six," meaning that I wanted to talk to Lieutenant Colonel Alderman.

Finally, I heard, "This is the Three." It was Major Carl Mundy, the battalion S-3.

"Goddamn it," I yelled, "get a goddamn helicopter out here. We've got a man who's dying."

There was a little pause and then I heard Carl say, "Calm down, Dick. We've got a bird coming in."

"We've gotta have that medevac. We gotta have it!" Then I threw the handset at my radioman and stalked back to Smitty's side. When I got there, I noticed that there was no one else around—just Smitty, the doc, and me. Everyone else was steering clear, facing outboard, ready to defend themselves and us. It was a good excuse for not looking at poor Smitty.

Finally, we heard the helicopter. It was an old H-34, with a huge open hatch in the side. As it landed, I was up and running the twenty-five or thirty meters to grab the doctor as soon as he touched the ground. By the time I got there, though, the doctor had passed me in the opposite direction. So, I grabbed the handles at one end of a stretcher and pulled so hard I yanked the two people holding the other handles right out of the helicopter. They untangled themselves and we ran to Smitty and helped lift him onto the stretcher. I don't remember doing it, but we got him to the chopper and slid him onto the deck. He was just lying there. His head was lolling to the right and I saw the shattered right wrist at the end of the bare, fleshless forearm. He looked tiny on that stretcher, half the length of a whole man. That huge white femur was protruding out from his torso. I heard him say "Skipper," so I leaned down to hear the rest. "I'm going to be okay, Skipper," he rasped. "I'm going to be okay." I was too choked up to respond, but, as the chopper lifted off, I gave him the thumb's up and waved.

It was dead quiet. The chopper was gone and there was nothing left to do there, so I formed up the troops and got ready to head back toward the main road and Camp Evans. As we were leaving, I happened to glance at the crater. There was something green hanging on a bush, so I sent the Marine next to me to investigate. I was sure it was Smitty's flak jacket. A minute later, the Marine came back, emptyhanded. "Skipper," he stammered, "I don't want to touch that flak jacket. Part of Smitty's laying in it."

That did it; I was over the top. "Fuck it," I groaned, "let's get outta here."

I don't remember the walk back to Camp Evans. I dumped my gear on my rack and went over to the company CP. Everybody there was very quiet as I sat down behind my field desk. There was no conversation. I just sat there for five or six minutes, trying to collect myself and get my thoughts together. I'm not sure I knew where I was.

After awhile, Top Mabry walked into the CP hut and said in a very kindly voice, "Skipper, I've got Smith's things here."

I don't know what the hell I was thinking, but I said, "You know, First Sergeant, I don't get his personal effects unless he's dead."

Top Mabry did a slow take and looked down at me. "Yessir, I know that, sir."

It finally hit me. I got up without saying a word and left the CP hut. I don't know when the tears began—right there or after I got to my room—but I found myself sitting on my rack, bent over from spasms of sobbing I could not control. I don't know how long I was out of it, but I finally heard someone walking on the wood deck of the hooch. I tried to pull myself together as I looked up to see who it was. Through my veil of tears, I made out the face of the battalion chaplain.

"Dick," he said, "I think we should talk."

I don't remember what was said, but I slowly turned around an got myself pulled together. On the outside. Inside, for all the years since, I have carried the image of Smitty's death deep inside me as a sign of my frailty. I knew it then, clearly, that I never should have let the patrol proceed up that open roadway. I could have said something sooner. I should have. If ever a group of Marines was ambush bait, that patrol on that open road leading out from that village was the best example I ever heard about. I wasn't a snotty, overtrained, inexperienced young captain anymore. No captain then in 3/26 had commanded a company in the field more often or for more days than Dick Camp. I knew better. Smitty died because I didn't speak up in time.

C H A P T E R 19

I began hearing rumors that 3/26 was going to mount a full battalion sweep to try to locate the regional NVA headquarters in the foothills of the nearby mountains. Then I got the official word. At the staff meeting that evening, Major Mundy discussed the plan, which basically called for a couple of companies to hump into the jungle and then leapfrog their way through the growth along the ridgeline. Lima Company was to stay out in the rice paddies, paralleling the main body. The more the S-3 talked, the better I could see that the sweep wasn't going to be a real big deal. I sort of figured the staff was laying it on to get out of town until the camp commander got bored with his beautification program.

I started thinking about the plan and finally said, "Why don't we hold Lima Company back and, if the rest of the battalion runs into anything, we can fly up in helicopters and rappel in wherever we're needed to cut off the enemy or surround him, or whatever." This caused a great deal of gasping because the staffers thought they already had come up with a pretty good plan, but for some reason or other, Lieutenant Colonel Alderman said, "Well, maybe we should consider what Dick has put forward." In the end, he bought the plan as offered. Unfortunately, I became persona non grata with Major Mundy for a little while after that.

At that time, the only people in the Marine Corps who knew anything about rappelling were reconners—and not very many of them. I was the only former reconner in the entire battalion and, thus, the only member of the battalion who knew anything about rappelling out of a helicopter. I had to teach the entire company how to do it, and the memory of my first helo lift into the hills around Khe Sanh in July almost made me recant.

As I got to thinking about it, I realized that we sure as hell didn't want to rappel a whole company into the jungle, one man at a time, especially when there might be some unfriendly people at the other end of the rope. I was really starting to wonder about my sanity when, for reasons I never learned, the entire sweep was canceled by higher headquarters. Not even Major Mundy's original plan would be executed.

Next thing I knew, Lima Company was ordered to go out and sweep down toward the unfriendly mountains. Major Mundy asked me if I wanted to go right out that afternoon or wait until morning. I decided to start out that night, in the dark, so the NVA wouldn't know where we were going until we were already there.

As if there wasn't enough to do that day, the camp commander insisted that every unit in Camp Evans conduct what was known as a troop information briefing. Apparently, an awful lot of explosives were being sent home through the mail, which was obviously dangerous. So, the word was that I had to brief the company about the dangers of sending stuff home through the mails. We lined up the whole company and swore that we were going to shoot them at dawn and the postal service was going to kill their families if they shipped any more explosives home. Then Top Mabry went down the company roster and had every man who heard the briefing sign the roster as proof that he had heard the new rules. (Naturally, four or five weeks later, we got the word from higher headquarters that the postal authorities had intercepted a parcel that had a block of C4 plastique explosive, an illumination grenade, and some ammunition in it. We had to check the company roster to see if the Marine who had mailed the parcel had signed the roster. Sure enough, he had. The parcel had been sent the very day we had conducted the briefing. When we added it all up, we realized that we had given the troops who were only thinking about mailing explosive goodies home—and maybe those who had never considered it—a reason to do so right away. We notified higher headquarters that the malefactor indeed had been briefed, but we added a note that we thought the matter should be dropped because that Marine had been killed the day before we received the inquiry.)

After we got the troop information brief out of our hair, I took the opportunity to reiterate all the little rules and regulations I had imposed on Lima Company during my first weeks aboard as the skipper. This was important because the upcoming sweep was to be the first company-size operation since we had joined so many new troops following the big September fight. For example, I told the troops that I did not allow Marines under my command to carry ammunition across their chests. For the slow learners, I repeated that ammunition had to be carried where it was supposed to be carried. Machine-gun ammunition, for example, was to be carried in ammo cans until we needed to use it—because the dirt that tended to infiltrate the links jammed the machine guns. I wanted grenades to be carried in grenade pouches, and so on. I told them that anyone carrying a pistol had better not have a round in the chamber unless his position was in imminent danger of being assaulted. The .45-caliber automatics scared the hell out of me; they were always prone to accidental discharges for no apparent reason. Over the years, hundreds of Marines have been killed or maimed by their own .45s.

We completed the brief and turned the troops loose to get ready. We ate an early dinner that evening and finished our preparations.

At 2200 that night, we started moving out of Camp Evans. It was one of the darkest nights I can remember. It was so dark that each man literally had to hold on to the belt of the man in front of him in order to keep from going astray.

We got six or seven hundred meters along the trail in the dark and quiet dead of night when, out of nowhere, I heard a *bang*—a gunshot. There was no use being coy, so I loudly whispered toward the source of the noise, "What the hell was that?" There was a brief moment of scurrying, but no response. "I said, 'What the hell was that?' "

Gunny Bailey responded in a loud whisper: "Skipper, one of the men just shot himself."

Oh, Lord! "What?" I whispered back. "How in the hell did he *shoot* himself?"

"Sir," the gunny replied very sheepishly as he reached my side, "I hate to tell you this, but he had a round in the chamber of his pistol and somehow or other when he bent over or squatted down, the pistol went off and bullet went right down through the fleshy part of the top part of his leg. It went in just about at the hip and exited just above the knee, through the fleshy part of his leg."

I followed Gunny Bailey down the column to where a corpsman was working over the wounded Marine. Fortunately, the kid was not injured badly, but the wound obviously hurt.

I was madder than hell. Goddamn, I was mad. The only thing I could say—and kept repeating—"Why the hell did you have a round in the chamber?" I knew it was a stupid question, but the dumb shit had exposed the company's position and endangered us all. I was hopping mad. The Marine was scared to death and he hurt like hell, but I wanted to humiliate him a little.

In the end, the incident cost me a whole squad, which I detailed to evacuate the wounded man. I was not about to call in a medevac only seven hundred meters from the camp gate, and I damn sure wasn't going to turn the whole company around, so I had the Marine's squad fashion a litter and carry and escort him back. Of course, they all got the night off.

I had a handful of Kit Carson scouts working with the company. They were former North Vietnamese soldiers or Viet Cong fighters who, for some reason or other, had rallied to our side. They had all been screened and trained in a special school before being used as scouts and advisors. I figured they knew NVA tactics and could keep us from walking into something, so I put them up with the point. I wasn't sure I trusted them, but I could not think of a better place to put them than the point, where their professed expertise could save their lives and, thus, ours.

It was coming up 2300 and we were about a mile from the camp gate when a burst of gunfire erupted from near the point of the company column. As soon as the first burst sounded, everyone was on the ground and most of us were yelling the usual important question, "What the hell is going on?" After several minutes of "What the hell is going on," I finally got the word from the point that the Kit Carson scouts had heard some Vietnamese voices and had opened fire on them.

We couldn't find anything, which forced me into a quandary. It was pitch dark out and many hours away from sunup. We had had two shooting incidents in an hour and the whole countryside clear to Hanoi must have known where we were, how many of us there were, where we were going, and how fast we were getting there. I had no idea what I should do; should I form a perimeter and stand fast until dawn, or should I keep going? I added it all up and decided to keep going.

Less than a hundred meters after we got going again, the point made a left turn and went through a wide thicket of bamboo that was bisected by the trail. As I moved into the bamboo grove, I found that my hair was standing up on my arms and underneath my helmet. Then I *smelled* North Vietnamese in there. I knew exactly what I was smelling; I had smelled it before. It was a combination of wood smoke and fish.

I knew we were going to get hit. I got real tense—involuntarily sucked in my breath—but I had to keep moving. The troops around me picked up my tension, and they got tense; I could hear them sucking in air. Pretty soon, the whole column was tense. The feeling was palpable. We sort of slowed down and speeded up at the same time—got our senses out to maximum range and leaned forward toward the end of the bamboo grove.

Nothing happened.

Immediately after we eased on out of the bamboo, and unknown to me, the point started moving toward a stream. As they got there, someone detonated a large mine that injured eight or nine of my men plus three or four of the Kit Carson scouts.

The mine triggered a sort of organized pandemonium as the company, which was spread back along the trail, started doing all the things that had to be done in that sort of situation. Simultaneously, we were all trying to figure out what the hell was going on, set up a perimeter to protect the casualties, provide aid for the casualties, and set in to protect ourselves against possible infantry or mortar attacks— all without making a hell of a lot of noise even though we knew they now knew where we were.

The only way to treat the casualties was to turn flashlights on. It was too dark even to see the wounds, much less treat them, without the lights. So, right in the middle of the makeshift perimeter, the corpsmen were using their flashlights, marking the spot for NVA gunners far and wide. They tried to put ponchos over the lights and the wounded men, but the efforts were half-assed because the ponchos were small and barely covered anything. There was an immense amount of noise and confusion going on to help the enemy if they were out there. Pretty quick, the docs were telling me things like, "Skipper, we got to get these casualties out of here." Some of those people were very badly hurt.

Clearly it was time to give it up. "Okay," I told the new senior corpsman, "get the helicopters. Tell them we've got some emergency medevacs. Let's get these guys out of here."

I had Lance Corporal Terry Smith, my TACP operator, get to work calling in the medevac request while I put plenty of other Marines to work clearing and marking a landing zone. We set up the vertical strobe and turned it on at the sound of the first helo. It was noisy, dusty, and confusing, but we got all the wounded out without drawing fire. Enough was enough. As soon as the last of the helos was gone, I moved the rest of the company a few hundred meters off the trail and set up a night-defense perimeter.

We spent the next morning monkeying around, sweeping hither and yon. We didn't run into anything. I believe we must have inadvertently worked our way out of the area the North Vietnamese usually booby-trapped. We found nothing, and nothing found us.

Eventually, we worked our way out to an old French fort that had been there since the 1940s or 1950s. From there, we patrolled out toward the area 3/26 had swept on its very first mission in Vietnam, over a year earlier. The battalion legend had it that Lima Company had been the first unit into the area and the command group and an Ontos had been blown up by a 500-pound bomb the NVA had set out as a command-detonated mine. The mine had killed the company gunny, the exec, and a few others and had blown the Ontos to smithereens. One of the dead was the Marine for whom they had named Camp Evans. When we passed through, the biggest piece of the Ontos we found was about four feet by two feet. Scars from the blast were still evident on the trees, and the crater was still clearly visible. The troops, who had all heard the story, gawked and rubber-necked to the exclusion of all else.

Right around there, one of my Marines crapped out on us.

The Marine Corps has ways of dealing with men who temporarily lose heart—a good kick in the ass usually does wonders—but this kid obviously had absolutely no balls left. Gunny Bailey indeed kicked him in the ass, but he just sat down in the middle of the trail and refused to budge. None of the usual remedies—threats against his life, the usual Drill Instructor's taunts—were working; the kid was not responding.

At length, I decided that a little *real* authority would turn the tide, so I went up to him and asked in my best surly tone, which was pretty well developed by then, "What the hell's the matter with you?"

"Sir," he whined and blubbered through real tears, "I can't make it."

"Get on your feet, goddammit!"

The gunny had been right; he wasn't having any of it. "Bullshit," I told the gunny, "get him the hell out of here." But as I was turning I had a thought, "Hey, wait a minute," I said to him, "what do you have in your pack?"

It turned out that this shitbird's pack was filled with cans of fruit, especially fruit cocktail, which was extremely hard to come by. It figured that a complete pissant like this kid would have been hoarding it. "Gunny," I said, "pass all this out to the real Marines."

I left and Gunny Bailey took all the kid's food, grabbed his canteens for good measure, and sort of drummed him out of the company; he told him to go fend for himself.

It had to be done, and done brutally. The kid was a dead loss and the gunny and I both knew that we had to set an example and a standard for the rest of the men, who certainly had reason enough to feel a little fainthearted after our clusterfuck of the previous night.

I wasn't sure I wanted to know what was going on, but I felt I had to leave it to the gunny; it wasn't a matter for officers. I never heard about that Marine again; I suppose he had the good sense to trail along behind the rearguard as we hiked back to Camp Evans that late afternoon, and that the gunny had the good sense to let him. He wasn't killed or hurt—I would have heard. He just sort of disappeared.

*T*he battalion had a real hard-luck company. It seemed that everything it did somehow came back to hurt it.

One time, the intelligence dope said that an NVA infantry battalion was going to cross into the Street Without Joy area from the mountains. Battalion loaded the hard-luck company aboard trucks and sent it out in a larger convoy that was going down Route 1, toward the Street Without Joy. As the convoy was getting into low hills where it would be shielded from observation, the hard-luck company jumped off the trucks and went into hiding. A truck with a quad-.50 also pulled out of the convoy and the troops from the hard-luck company camouflaged it.

That was in the afternoon. Sometime around midnight or 0100, lookouts using night observation devices or starlight scopes reported that they could see whole units of NVA moving toward them.

It seemed to the company commander that an NVA battalion was on the move, exactly the way Intelligence had reported. But, instead of opening fire with artillery, the company commander started calling in illumination. By the time his FO had adjusted all the illumination, the NVA were long gone. The company went to all that trouble, laid a really good ambush, and the company commander screwed it up by passing up a perfect setup for artillery because he wanted to close with the enemy and score the kills with his infantry weapons.

Stuff like that, losses like Smitty's, the Marine who died during the birthday party, and the bullshit beautification program—a whole raft of shit—was getting the whole battalion down. We were fighting the war, but we weren't getting anything done.

Another time, one night around the time Smitty was killed, the hard-luck company sent out a listening post and a squad-size ambush. For some reason, the ambush went out first, followed by the listening post. The ambush squad got lost and ended up somewhere in the vicinity of the listening post. Inevitably, the listening post reported back to the company CP that it had movement to its front.

The first thing the company commander did was call the ambush squad and ask for its position. That was the right thing to do, but the squad leader reported the wrong position. So, the commander gave the listening post the okay to open fire. The fire from the listening post wounded or killed the first two or three men in the ambush squad. Then the survivors in the ambush squad did exactly as they had been trained to do—they got on line and swept through the listening post and killed or wounded everyone in it. The hard-luck company lost a half-dozen Marines killed and wounded in an intramural firefight.

It was easy to laugh at the hard-luck company, but we came awfully close to a tragedy during one night march. We sent a squad out to set an ambush and then started moving the entire company under cover of darkness to a new position. The idea was to sucker the NVA into our original bivouac so the ambush squad, set in on an overlook, could spring a trap. Well, someone on the point of the main body zigged when he should have zagged and we blundered around in the dark until someone yelled, "Who's that?" The response, in English, was, "Yeah, and who the fuck is that?" There was a lot of tension, but we quickly established that the point of the company column had nearly trampled over the ambush squad, which was waiting until it could see the white's of the enemy's eyes before opening fire. Only the silhouette of the point's helmet saved him from getting drilled at the start of an intramural firefight that, thank God, never quite got off the ground. Close. Very close.

CHAPTER 20

There were big changes at the beginning of the last week of November. Major Carl Mundy rotated home and Matt Caulfield, the battalion's senior captain, was promoted to major and moved up to the S-3 billet. That very day, the main body of the battalion moved to Co Bi-Thanh Tan, but Lima Company was detached again and sent north to the extremely hostile My Chanh area, toward Hue, to conduct ongoing search-and destroy sweeps and ambushes.

Though we would continue to be supported out of Camp Evans, we were to live full time in the field so we could efficiently break the company down to run daytime sweeps and nighttime squad ambushes along trails and around the local villages. On a typical evening, after a day of marching and an afternoon of digging in, we kept back at least one platoon and the company command group and then sent out five or six ambushes and some listening posts from the rest of the company. Hard experience had taught us that the NVA and local VC cadres were constantly running small units through there, and they had the whole area covered with fiendish booby traps. Word was that an entire NVA battalion and who-knows-how-many VC were in there, living off the land. The local civilians were almost entirely in the Communist camp. The very few ARVN enclaves in the area were fortified and static, merely guard posts at bridges and other vital road links.

Lima Company's move to My Chanh exactly coincided with the onset of the monsoon. In that part of Vietnam, "monsoon" is a fancy name for a river of water the falls on people, places, and things. Whole weeks could go by without sight of the sun. So, if life wasn't depressing for a lot of man-created reasons, it was because nature dropped the monsoon on us.

I was surprised by how cold it got. My blood had been thinned out by the long months of heat, and then it got cold and windy and wet. I was usually chilled to the marrow and, right off, the docs were treating Marines who had come down with all kinds of colds and winter diseases. We never got a chance to take off our boots, so, within days, we started getting cases of immersion foot—as effective a casualty as a gunshot wound.

*W*e tried a few cute variations on the standard ambush techniques. Late the first afternoon in the field, one of the ambush squads left the company bivouac, hiked out into the countryside, and made a big display of setting in for the night. Then, after dark, we sent another squad out to a knoll about a hundred meters from the first squad. When the second squad was set up, the first squad left its position and sneaked over to the second squad's position. That way, if the NVA had the first squad zeroed in—as we hoped they had—any hostile action that was meant to hit it would hit nothing. Next, while one squad held the second position, the other squad moved out to set up another ambush that would bag any enemy moving in against the abandoned site in a crossfire.

We didn't get any activity that night, but the whole thing worked so smoothly I decided to keep trying.

The next night, the decoy squad had just moved in with the backup squad when they reported, "Hey, we've got movement coming across the stream. It's coming towards us. Permission to open fire."

The Marines were on a small knoll, covering a trail that came across a stream about a hundred meters away. It was a very good position. I asked, "How far away are they?"

"Oh, a hundred meters," the patrol leader estimated.

I thought it over for a half second and replied, "No! Don't do anything. Hold your position. Keep reporting."

Moment by moment, the quarry got closer to the ambush. At length, they were within thirty meters. The patrol leader said he had very good targets, so I gave my approval to commence firing. They opened fire right away, a really huge volume of fire, that went on for over a minute. When the firing died down, the patrol leader asked if he could lead the patrol back in. The ambush was blown, so I told him to come on in.

Next morning, I went out and inspected the area around the ambush site. There was nothing there. I am certain to this day that the squads had faked it, that they hadn't really gone out to the position and that the whole shooting fracas was an excuse for the patrol leader to get in out of the rain.

*T*he weather was miserable, absolutely indescribable. It rained all day every day. Even on the hills, the water was ankle deep as it ran off in torrents. There was no chance to dry out. The only dry part of me for days on end was the top of my head—because I kept it parked beneath my helmet, the only truly waterproof item of clothing I owned.

We got a huge pile of mail one afternoon and someone left the canvas mailbags out in the rain, on the ground outside the company CP dugout. I was so cold and miserable that I finally grabbed one of these mailbags, slit the bottom open, slipped it over my legs, and tied it off—just so I could get the little extra warmth the wet canvas might provide.

I was luckier than many of the troops because I usually manned the poncho-topped company CP at night. Most of the troops were out in it, humping over muddy, slippery knolls or lying in a foot or two of water for hours on end, exposed to constant wind and driving rain that was so heavy I still can't believe I saw it, much less that I lived in it.

If the rain was depressing, picture us eating nothing more than two C-ration meals a day. Half the time, we couldn't even get the little C-ration stoves going, so we mostly ate cold food out of cans that tended to fill up with rainwater faster than we could spoon the unappetizing food into our mouths. Pretty soon, we were sending Marines to the rear because they had dysentery and a bizarre variety of stomach and intestinal ailments. More shit to think about, more shit to get us down. I started kidding that if the slide on my pistol hadn't been rusted shut, I would have shot myself.

I had about reached the low point when, one morning, I got the word that the company supply sergeant was coming out from Camp Evans to drop off some gear he said we needed. After I sent a detail down to meet his truck on the MSR, I started wondering what he could be bringing us. We hadn't asked for anything, but I had my suspicions.

Sergeant Ricky Bender, the Lima Company supply sergeant, was absolutely unique. He was the classic supply sergeant from right out of the best war novels. He was a thief of the first order, but I never gave him trouble because he was also one of the most good-hearted souls I ever met. His thieving was dedicated to supporting the company. I am convinced Bender never personally profited from his escapades, that his only aim in life was providing aid and comfort to the good guys—Lima Company.

Once, long before the monsoon, when the battalion rear was still at Phu Bai, I had dropped by his hooch during a Rough Rider stopover. When I got there, Bender was deep in conversation with an Army bird colonel and several lesser Army officers. When they noticed me, they all looked like a bunch of kids caught perusing dirty pictures. Right away, they all started talking about—get this—the weather. Bender even started whistling! I walked out. I found out later that Bender was trading enemy weapons the company had captured to the Army officers in return for gear we needed but couldn't get through Marine Corps channels. Over time, he produced piles of warm foul-weather gear and a raft of other good stuff.

Another time, Sergeant Bender had come up to me and said, "Skipper, you know, you don't need to carry that rifle." So I asked, "Yeah, Sergeant, and why is it you think I don't need to carry this rifle?" And he said, "Because, sir, I got a new one for you." In short order, he produced a still-rare CAR-15, a hot little weapon designed for use by Army unit leaders; it was really a very short, very light M-16 rifle with a short flash suppresser and a telescoping stock. I can imagine how he came by that. Another time, he got me a beautiful Browning 9mm pistol, which had to be worth about six hundred dollars. Once again, I never asked where or how he got it.

So, there we were, out in the godawful monsoon. We'd been out there for days, growing mildew in our crotches and between our toes, miserable, cold, and drifting toward suicide. I knew the sort of man

Bender was, but I couldn't imagine what he might have found that would possibly brighten our day. Then, lo and behold, the working party returned from the MSR with cases of—apples! Not only were they apples, they were beautiful, bright red, crispy Washington State apples. Every man in Lima Company got one. And there were cases full of graham crackers wrapped in waxed paper and still crispy and fresh. Every man got five or six packages of graham crackers. Apples and graham crackers. Wow! The only things missing were milk and naptime.

It doesn't sound like much, but Bender's thoughtful little surprise bounced Lima Company's morale gauge up to full. Suddenly, things started going right. The day ahead looked bright and cheerful. Everyone was smiling. I do believe I heard singing in the rain!

At that time, there was a countrywide sunset-to-sunrise curfew in effect. It made our job easier. Anyone who wasn't us who was moving around after dark could be shot on sight. It was no secret; everyone in Vietnam knew about it—the good guys, the bad guys, and all the undecided guys. The dusk-to-dawn curfew was the way of the world.

The evening of the day Sergeant Bender sent the apples and graham crackers, we sent out only one ambush squad, a minimum effort so we could keep morale as high as possible. In due course, the squad leader reported that he and his men were in position. An hour later—well after dark—the squad leader radioed in to say that his troops could hear movement coming toward them. The movement got louder and and louder, and, finally, the squad leader triggered the ambush.

I heard the firing start and then abruptly stop, so I immediately came up on the company net to ask, "What the hell is going on?" There followed a few moments of confusion, but the squad leader soon came back with the word that his squad had shot at three civilian women and several children before they realized what they had in their sights. The squad leader had done a good job of getting his men under control, but not before one of the women had been shot. The squad leader wanted to know what to do, so I asked questions until I determined for sure that the woman was alive. I directed the patrol to bring all the women and children back to the company CP and then I had my battalion radioman request a medevac helicopter to evacuate them.

The Marines in the ambush squad wanted to do the right thing, but they were very unhappy with having to bring back the children and uninjured women, who were all crying and screaming and who could very easily have attracted a bad-guys ambush to the squad and on into the company area. However, nothing bad happened and they all arrived in due course. The company senior corpsman checked the wounded woman over and found that she had been shot through the hip. The 5.56mm M-16 round has a very high velocity, but it tends to tumble when it hits something as solid as bone. So, rather than making a neat little hole, the round that had struck the woman's hip had excavated a ghastly tunnel through her lower body.

We got the helo in and, though the woman was quite shocky by then, we got her out alive along with the children and the other women. As soon as the helo was gone, my officers, senior staff, and I had to get the Marines in the ambush squad calmed down. There was a lot of guilt going on there, but, of course, everyone involved said about the same thing: "Well, I didn't shoot her. I don't know who did, but it was sure somebody else."

Life and death go on. The very next night, we sent out another ambush patrol. The troops went out early to a decoy spot, but they moved well after dark to a small knoll that had a trail across the summit. As the last man in the ambush was squatting down, getting ready to set in on top of the knoll, he happened to glance over his shoulder just in time to see the outlines of several conical straw hats bobbing up the trail. He never gave the previous night's tragedy a second thought. He saw the hats, he knew people had to be underneath them, and he opened fire. The Golden Rule of Combat in action: Do unto them before they do it you.

I heard the gunfire, so I got on the radio and asked, "What the hell's going on?"

After a minute or two of dead silence, the squad leader responded that his getaway man had just killed a woman who was dressed in black pajamas and wearing a straw hat with camouflage on it. She also had an AK-47. He repeated that the woman had on a camouflaged hat and was carrying a Communist weapon. There was no sign of anyone else, but the woman was definitely enemy, and she was definitely dead.

"Bingo," I thought, "we finally scored." I didn't waste two seconds thinking up our next move. "Ambush the body," I ordered.

That sounds cruel, but it was the way of the world. I could be almost dead certain that her friends would be back to recover the body and the weapon—if for no other reason than to keep them out of our hands and off our scorecard.

I was wrong. Her friends left her. In the morning, the ambush squad left her, too. We all felt a little cheated with only the one kill, but by then most of us were thanking God for any small favor.

We were miserable. That morning was the fifth or sixth consecutive day in the field, in a rainstorm that never once abated. We had lost a dozen troops to immersion foot, which required fairly long-term treatment and recuperation. It had gotten to the the point where I didn't think the company could last one more night out there. It was very grim.

I was thinking about calling in to beg Battalion to let us back up to Camp Evans, but they beat me to the punch with news that we were going to be joined by a PRU—Provisional Reconnaissance Unit—team for a special mission.

I knew about the PRUs. Each squad was composed of a half-dozen Vietnamese or Cambodian thugs and a Marine noncom who may or may not have been in command, depending on how tough he was. They were very bad fellows. In fact, the bunch that entered our perimeter were the meanest-looking outcasts I ever want to see. There were six of them, and they looked like they wanted to kill us for the hell of it, to keep their hands in.

Battalion told me that they were sending the PRUs because, next morning, we were to cordon off and hassle a nearby village known to be completely dominated by the VC. Apparently, someone higher up thought our own Kit Carson scouts were too meek to conduct interrogations.

That night was completely miserable. Not only did we have the usual problems, we had to keep an eye on the PRUs and plan the cordon-and-sweep operation into the VC-dominated village. We were all done in, and this had to happen!

At sunrise, I sent off two platoons and held one back. The two platoons swept in and cordoned the place off—formed a half circle around it and connected up with the ARVN compound that was fifty or sixty meters on the far side of the village. Then I led the remaining platoon and the PRUs through the ARVN position and out the gate toward the village. On the way through the ARVN compound, a Marine advisor who lived there helpfully advised us to watch out for booby traps.

We started walking along the dirt road between the ARVN compound and the village through ankle-deep mud. As we walked, I saw one spider hole after another—brazenly displayed fighting holes covered with woven wicker covers and camouflaged with branches and leaves. If it hadn't been raining so hard of late, I have no doubt that the holes would have been occupied by gunmen. Only the flood saved us.

That place was bad. I had never seen anything like it. There was no pretense. The place was hostile, absolutely up-front hostile.

The PRUs were in the lead, which suited me. As we entered the first ring of spider holes, the Marine noncom with the PRUs turned and said to me, "Try to walk where we walk." Nothing to it; only a fool would have been doing otherwise after the booby-trap warning the advisor with the ARVNs had issued. If one of the PRUs got blown up, I'd know where not to step. Until then, I knew just where to put my feet. They all left huge footprints in the deep, sucking mud.

We were all feeling pretty antsy as we approached the first hut. Two of the PRUs went inside and the rest of us stopped where we stood. As we warily held our weapons at the ready and scanned everything in sight, sounds of a terrible verbal imbroglio erupted from the hut. Following much high-pitched screaming, the PRUs burst out with a woman in tow and braced her in the middle of the street. Then they entered the next hut. There was more yelling and carrying on, and they came out with another woman, whom they stood beside the first one. They did the same thing in hut after hut, until there were six flinty-eyed women standing in formation in the street.

By then, I was thinking, "What the hell is going on here? This doesn't smell right."

There were no men in the village, young or old. Typically, I knew, the young men were in the ARVN or out with VC, in which case they were hiding. So, all we had were the six women. There were six PRUs, so I started thinking this whole operation might have been a way for the PRUs to get some women for the night. Beyond that, I had no idea what might be going on.

All this was going through my mind when the battalion radioman said, "Hey, Skipper, it's the Six," Lieutenant Colonel Alderman. I responded to the call sign and the Old Man said, "The trucks will be at the place they met you the other day"—the place at which Bender had met the working party—"We're bringing you in."

"Okay," I thought, "bullshit's over!" I yelled in my best parade-ground voice, "We're going home, we're going home." Everybody in the platoon around me started cheering. We were getting out of the goddamn water. The company radioman called one of the platoons, and they started cheering, and then he called the other platoon. Everyone was cheering.

I didn't want to be out there one second longer than necessary, so I got out my map, hunkered down underneath a poncho my radiomen held over my head, and plotted the shortest crow's-flight line between the village and the pick-up point. When I saw that we needed to pass right near the hill on which the VC woman had been killed two nights before, I decided to look her over with own eyes, even though doing so would take an extra three or four minutes. I still thought we could beat the trucks to the rendezvous.

We started right off toward the knoll and very quickly I found myself in a rice paddy, about sixty meters wide and a hundred meters long, in water to my chest. It looked good on paper, but, ah, what the hell, we were wet to the marrow anyway. The company was all spread out behind me. I was point. I don't know how that happened; maybe it was my turn, maybe I was making like an old plow horse who could smell the barn.

As I reached the middle of the rice paddy, I heard a machine gun open fire. Right away, bullets threw up little geysers in the water off to my left. I didn't have to ask; I knew exactly what the hell was going on. What I didn't know was what the hell to do next.

It was easier to continue forward than to change direction, so I made a beeline for the far edge of the paddy. Behind me, my men were making all sorts of independent decisions. The only thing we had in common was the desire to get the hell out of the line of fire.

I never felt so sluggish in my life. I couldn't duck more than a few inches or I would have drowned, and I found that any ducking at all just slowed my progress through the water. I was terrified, but, hell, I was a Marine—an amphibious warrior—so I reached around to my belt, grabbed my bayonet, and snapped it onto the end of my rifle. I heard four or five little *snick*s; the Marines around me were following my example.

Seconds later, I reached the dike and jumped out of the water, keeping low so I wouldn't present a target. Immediately, other Marines barreled out of the water and started looking around for something to shoot at. I glanced at them and saw that all the riflemen had fixed bayonets. God, I felt good!

Pretty soon, there were thirty or forty Marines spread out along the paddy dike, all with fixed bayonets. There was no more gunfire—there had been only the one burst—so I yelled, "Let's get over the dike and see what's going on."

It was like another World War I movie. Everyone stood up and leaped over the paddy dike, rifles at the ready. Instantly, I found myself on reasonably solid ground, face to face with one of the company's M-60 gunners. The M-60's field of fire was directly across the rice paddy.

I knew the answer before I asked, but I blurted out anyway, "What the hell is going on here?"

The M-60 gunner related, very sheepishly, that he was part of the cordon around the village. He had been detailed alone to set up in a graveyard overlooking the village and had climbed up on top of a big cement tomb, at which point he promptly fell asleep. He swore some VC had gotten close to him and had thrown a grenade which hit him in the side with enough force to knock him over one side of the tomb. The grenade, if there was one, had not detonated. In any case, he had been rudely awakened—he might simply have rolled off the tomb in the middle of a bad dream—and the first thing his startled eyes had seen was a bunch of armed people people wading right at him through the rice paddy. He had fired before he thought, which was pretty common in that time and place, not to be faulted entirely.

Of course, it was us he had fired at, and he had stopped as soon as he realized who we were, after only one brief burst. Miraculously, nobody was hurt. The terror I had experienced was mitigated some-what by my opportunity to lead an actual approximation of a real-life amphibious assault—the only one I ever led—but on balance one I could have done without.

I had had enough adventures for the day, so I bypassed the dead VC woman and made a beeline for the road, stepping smartly all the way, in the middle of the company pack, where I belonged. We did indeed beat the trucks to the rendezvous, but not by enough to count. It took the company about thirty seconds to hop aboard so we could get the hell out of there.

Dry clothes, hot showers, and good, hot chow awaited us at Camp Evans.

C H A P T E R *21*

As soon as the company got back to Camp Evans, I got ready to head out for my five-day R&R leave. It seemed like I had been working out the details almost since my arrival in Vietnam at the end of June.

We had our choice of four or five spots around the Pacific rim, and the expense of getting us there and back was on the government. The choices were Australia, Taiwan, Korea, Hawaii, and, I believe, Singapore. Of course, it was possible to fly anywhere out of those places if one had the time and the cash. I have since heard of Marines who got shipped to Hawaii and flew home to the West Coast for a few days. That was strictly forbidden and carried a heavy punishment for those who got caught, but it was such a good idea I wonder now why more people didn't do it.

The R&R stories were always wild, and some were even true. One of my favorites, which I believe is true, naturally involved that paragon of sophistication, Sergeant Ricky Bender, the Lima Company supply sergeant. Bender went to Australia, but since he was a cut above the average serviceman, he arrived in the Land Down Under with a stake of about two thousand dollars in cash—and only five days to spend it. I guess he had a little extra to unload at the last minute, for he arrived back to the airport to meet two other Lima Company Marines—corroborating witnesses—in a chauffeur-driven limousine with a magnum of ice-cold champagne, a gorgeous woman draped over him, and dressed in a tuxedo. As the limo pulled up to the departure gate, Bender kissed the girl, guzzled the last of the champagne from the bottle, got out, stripped off the tux, and jumped into his uniform for the flight back to Danang. What a guy!

Like everyone else, but particularly since I was a company commander, I had to submit a set of dates to be approved by the battalion adjutant. I have no idea why just about any set of dates wouldn't have been okay since no captain and certainly no company commander had been with the battalion as long as I had, but it was necessary to pay obeisance to bureaucratic procedure. Of course, since I had arrived in Vietnam on the same day as Little John, who still had my 2nd Platoon, I suppose I might have nosed him out as a privilege of rank. In any event, getting the dates set with Battalion was a good deal easier than working out all the other details with Marjorie, my wife. We discovered very early that mailing information back and forth and making decisions at such long range was extremely difficult because it took an unbelievably long time for mail to get between Vietnam and Indianapolis. Often, the news that crossed back and forth ceased to be timely by the time it had cycled through the erratic military postal system.

Fortunately, at many of the larger bases, such as Dong Ha, it was possible to phone home on MARS, a short-wave radio-telephone system that was run by Marine volunteers in their spare time. Sometime in early November, when Lima Company was on light duty around Camp Evans, I had managed to get a day off so I could phone Marjorie from Dong Ha. It was nothing like a normal two-way phone conversation; we had to use standard radio procedures which was a big pain because, of course, Marjorie didn't have a clue about radio procedures; she kept forgetting to say "over" and such arcane phrases and words. The call was timed and that kept getting in the way because she kept talking or waited too long to begin talking and every sentence got chopped off at both ends and had to be repeated. Of course, as a combat Marine I had learned that the only way to deal with problems like that is to yell. I noticed that all the Marines using the MARS system while I was there yelled, but actually the sound quality was superb. Just as my turn came, the big guns in the base opened with a fire mission, so I had big *boom*s going off behind me, and I was further put off—since I really did have to yell—by how public the conversation got; there were a dozen Marines lined up behind me and the MARS operator actually had to listen in. In fact, it got downright embarrassing because, big macho Marine that I was, I couldn't bear to scream "I love you" above the sound of the outgoing artillery. That lack of expression tended to make Marjorie tense.

It was a given that we were going to meet in Hawaii. We had first met in Hawaii, while I was serving with the 1st Marine Brigade and she was flying as a stewardess. The implication of a second honeymoon was so obvious to both of us that there was never any question but that we would meet in Honolulu. Frankly, the thought of taking leave in an Asian city seemed ridiculous, given what I had been doing for a living since June.

We painstakingly got the details worked out and I even got back from My Chanh in the nick of time to get a night's sleep. But there was a flaw in the plan, one I could not have foreseen.

About two weeks earlier, the adjutant had confirmed my departure date and had casually mentioned that I had to have my summer khaki uniform when I left because they wouldn't let me board the plane to Hawaii if I was dressed in utilities. No problem, I thought, I had a set of khakis in my seabag, which was stored in the battalion supply shed, with all the other officers' seabags. I even checked to make sure my seabag was all squared away. So, came the big day—I was just in from My Chanh and due to leave the next morning—and I dropped by the battalion supply officer's hooch to claim my seabag. The supply officer sent a supplyman out to get the seabag and, after a long wait, the Marine came back and whispered something into the supply officer's ear. They buzzed back and forth a few times and then the lieutenant turned to me and said, "Jesus, Captain, I'm awfully sorry, but we can't locate your seabag." He said it in such a way as to imply that the matter was closed.

I knew what the regulations were and I wasn't about to have any bullshit. I told him in no uncertain terms that he and his supplymen had better find my seabag or I'd have them up on charges for stealing. I was so distraught, I was past boiling rage. I was hours away from getting out of that goddamn country, out of that goddamn monsoon, and the only detail keeping me from getting out was my lost khaki uniform. I believe I was still ranting and raving when they brought in my seabag. I'm sure that the lieutenant, who had every reason to fear for his life, called out every supplyman on his roster. I'm sure they tore the battalion supply shed apart in their search. So what; I got my seabag and my precious khaki uniform. Case closed.

*U*nfortunately, the only ride out of Camp Evans I could find—all routine flights were called because of the rain—was in the back of a truck on its way to Dong Ha. On the way to the truck, I handed all my gear over to Top Mabry and turned the company over to my exec. I intentionally avoided the battalion CP because there had been a few snide comments from all the senior officers who wouldn't rate leave for months. I didn't want to be hassled, and I damn sure didn't want to be confronted with any pleas that started or ended with "Sorry, Dick."

I caught the convoy and immediately started to unwind. For the first time since the end of June, I had no responsibilities. I was just back from an absolutely grueling, worrisome week in the rain and cold, and I was taut. But I felt myself loosening up as soon as we passed through the Camp Evans main gate. A quarter mile later, I was feeling exhilarated. The only bleak spot was having to share the ride with an occupied body bag. By the one-mile point, I started having mixed feelings. I was off to five days with my wife in an American city and I was sharing the first leg of my trip out with a Marine who was only going home dead. I was sorry for the dead Marine, sorry for his family, but, God, his presence in the back of that truck made me feel especially good to be alive, thankful to be whole.

I found another convoy between Dong Ha and Danang, and quickly got myself on a waiting list for a flight out of Vietnam. Though Marjorie was also starting out that day, I wasn't overly concerned about a delay in getting a flight because the clock didn't start ticking until my feet touched the ground at my destination. There was nothing going out that evening, so I hiked down to the III Marine Amphibious Force compound and found a rack in the bachelor officers' quarters. I was anxious to get going, but I realized what a world of good an extra night of calming down would do for me.

The sprawling, bustling Danang military compound was a different world, a little military city in which everyone wore green and everything looked military, but which more closely resembled a Stateside military base than anywhere else I had seen in Vietnam. There were places in the base, I heard, where officers could not pack sidearms.

As soon as I dropped off my gear, I went out to see what I could see. Right off, I ran into a couple of old buddies who took me over to an officers' club called the White Elephant. I'm no drinker, so I passed up that part of the offering but there was a huge, busy snack stand that served up just about every goodie I had been dreaming about for five months. I started out a little on the tentative side, with a plate of ice cream. It tasted so good, I ordered some more ice cream. And that was so good, I ordered more. And more. As my buddies drank themselves into a mellow state, I stood beside them at the big-people's bar and stuffed my body with ice cream.

At one point, I noticed that an officer standing next to me was wearing a gorgeous, clean set of utilities and spit-shined boots. I, on the other hand, was not quite up to the Danang standard; my utilities, though recently laundered, had a patina of ground-in dirt and my boots were a little on the muddy side. But this guy was gorgeous, a poster-picture Marine officer if one ever lived. I knew the type; I had been one in my younger days. As I was sizing him up, I saw that he was sizing me up. There was no question where I had been. "Jeez," he finally blurted out, "I'd *love* to be out there in the field, but they won't release me."

I smiled politely and rejoined, "Well, you can have my pistol—and everything else. I'll swap jobs with you. I'm good at things, and what I don't know I can learn."

With an absolutely serious expression, he replied that he sure appreciated the opportunity but he was all tied up with a big special project and just couldn't get loose. I know what he meant: He was too valuable doing what he was doing to give in to his animal instincts. Such loyalty, such devotion to duty.

When I finally boarded my flight out of Danang the next forenoon, I ran smack into Captain Phil Reynolds, with whom I had attended Reconnaissance School early in my career. I was so elated to be leaving Vietnam that I believe I could have flown out without the airplane. I actually started laughing out loud for no apparent reason—a little dementedlike, to judge from the expression on Phil's face. We stopped over for fuel at Clark Air Force Base, in the Philippines, and then flew straight to Hickam Field, Oahu.

I was crazy with anticipation and longing. I tried to act cool and restrained, but I saw Marjorie as soon as I got off the plane, and I made a beeline toward her. I was almost through the gate when an

MP stopped me and said, "You can't see your wife yet, sir. You've got to hear the indoctrination brief."

I couldn't believe my ears. It was absolutely asinine. Did they expect me to pay attention to a boring brief when I knew my wife was sitting in the next room, listening to another version of the same brief? "Bullshit," I said to the MP, "you go listen in my place." I walked past him, deeply embraced Marjorie, and guided her straight over to a bank of chairs.

I was floored by the mixture of emotions that were coursing through me. First of all, I was aware of how peaceful and normal everything seemed. Fresh from the killing fields, I was suddenly immersed in real life, surrounded by the subject matter of every night's dream. I thought I had come down during the long trip out of Camp Evans, but I realized then how wound up in the war I still was. I consciously told myself, "This is the real world. You don't have to be on edge. You don't have to worry about anything. You don't have to be alert for anything." I was there, for real, and I felt great.

After getting my land legs, I allowed Marjorie to lead me outside. It was absolutely gorgeous; the weather was perfect, it was all green, there was no monsoon, I couldn't spot any shellholes, and nobody was trying to kill me. It was a splendid, sparkling afternoon, peaceful and secure.

I immersed myself in my marriage, in the few days of peace and solitude I had been awarded for living so long. I ate normal food and tried to engage in normal conversation. We talked about Katherine, our young daughter, and Marjorie's folks, my folks, and all our brothers and sisters, but I kept getting back to stories of Vietnam. I didn't know and I didn't care if Marjorie wanted to hear some of those stories—because I ran out of funny ones real fast—but I was driven to tell them, to get them off my chest. I had been the boss for five months, the lonely commander, a source of inspiration to 140 other Marines with no source of inspiration of my own, beyond what I had in me. I needed to talk, to heal some of the suppurating wounds I did not know I had until I started talking.

I was grateful for Marjorie's softness, for her humanity. Even if she didn't—couldn't—understand what I was talking about or why I was talking about it, she gamely listened. It plainly shocked her to hear the things I was saying, but she listened. I hadn't known how much I needed to unload until I was actually doing it. I felt so good—for the first time in five months, I felt good, period. I just felt good. Such a little thing, feeling good. I hadn't even noticed it was gone until I started feeling it again. Good. I had had no idea how callous I had become, how deep the bruises ran, until I started feeling good.

We had a fine five days, though always in the back of my mind I knew the minutes were ticking away, that I would be back in the shit very soon. After the second day, I started counting it down. I couldn't help myself. I no sooner started feeling human than I started getting ready to go back, started getting harder, tougher, more distant. I started putting on my mental armor. By the fourth day, I was ready to go back. There I was, in beautiful, peaceful, secure Hawaii, in my wife's soft arms, and I was thinking about the killing, the mutilation, the fear, and the ever-present empty longing to be home, safe and whole—in my wife's soft arms—without the sentence of death hanging over my every move, my every decision, my every breath.

Marjorie and I went out to Trader Vic's one night and we spotted Lee Marvin, the actor and former combat Marine, a few tables away. I wrote my name, rank, and unit in a matchbook and passed it over to him, and he came over to talk and signed an autograph. I wasn't a bit shy because I was a celebrity myself; a year or two earlier I had appeared with Nancy Sinatra and a Marine honor guard on the Ed Sullivan Show!

For our last dinner in Honolulu, we went out with Phil Reynolds and his wife and we all agreed to meet back at the airport when it was time to go. Next morning, Phil and I put our wives on the same plane back to the mainland and then took a taxi over to Hickam to get our flight back to Vietnam. When we checked in, they told us that our flight had been canceled and that there was nothing else leaving that day. We were incensed; we had put our wives on a flight to the mainland only an hour earlier and we were being forced to stay alone in Hawaii for a whole extra day! We must have been crazy; we were angry because we had to be away from the war for a whole extra day?

I called Marjorie that night to make sure she had gotten home okay and she asked, in surprise, "Well, where are you?" When I admitted, "I'm in Hawaii," I caught all sorts of static because of my bad planning, especially when she described the winter weather in Indianapolis, and the fact that she had arrived home to find that Katherine had developed a bad cold and her mother hadn't told her because she didn't want to spoil our vacation. Real stuff, it was all real stuff, and I was on my way back to fantasyland, back to the land of the smoking gun.

Phil and I left for the war again the next day. There were no more hitches or glitches.

The Lima Company 60mm mortar section undergoing instruction at the Seabee Rock Crusher in mid September 1967. In the center, pointing, is the section leader, Corporal Brady.

A Lima Company platoon during a prepatrol brief at the Seabee Rock Crusher

Lima Company lived in these Southeast Asia huts at the Rock Crusher

One of the awful bunkers built by the Seabees at the Rock Crusher

A punji pit uncovered by a Lima Company patrol near a hostile village near Camp Evans in early November 1967

The routine sweep through the hostile village turned into tragedy minutes after I took this photo. Lance Corporal Smith, the radioman who was killed that day, is standing on the extreme left, with his back to my camera.

The mine crater on the roadway between the two kneeling Marines is where Lance Corporal Smith was mortally wounded

Sergeant Ric Bender with the CAR-15 carbine he secured for me (*Compliments of Ric Bender*)

Lima Company Marines inspect the body of one of the NVA officers killed by Lieutenant Nile Buffington's 1st Platoon on January 2, 1968. I am in the center of the group, bending down, in the soft cover and flak jacket. Lieutenant Buffington is right behind me and, at the dead man's head, pointing, is Little John. (*Compliments of Ric Bender*)

All five of the dead NVA officers after they were brought in from in front of the Lima Company's lines (*Compliments of Max Friedlander*)

Khe Sanh Combat Base from the air, looking north. Khe Sanh ville is in the left foreground and the 1015 ridgeline, including Hill 950, is in the background.

The Lima Company lines before the siege, in December 1967

The Lima Company CP tent
before the siege

Marine sharpshooters stalk NVA from the combat base trenchline. Note the stand-up emplacement and, in the center of the photo, a cleared area and rows of barbed wire barriers. (*Official U.S. Marine Corps photo*)

Captain Richard D. Camp, Jr., USMC

C H A P T E R **22**

As soon as I checked into overnight quarters in Danang, I ran into one of the artillery FOs I knew from 3/26. He had a bandage on. Two nights earlier, at around 1830, December 7, Lima and Kilo companies had been running a sweep near Co Bi-Thanh Tan and had been hit by about fifty rounds of Communist 82mm mortar fire. Fortunately, only five Marines had been wounded, all superficially, including the FO, who was on his way out for R&R. I asked where the battalion was and he said, "Well, when I left this morning, they were scheduled to go back up to Khe Sanh."

I was elated. To me, anything was better than going up along the DMZ or working out around My Chanh. I had spent most of my first two months in-country around Khe Sanh and, compared to the lowlands and the coast, I really liked the place. It was relatively quiet and peaceful, and I really had never run into the enemy up there. As far as I was concerned, the Khe Sanh plateau was just about the garden spot of Vietnam.

Next day, December 10, I engaged in a series of short helicopter hops to track the battalion down. I left Danang for Hue, then I flew to Camp Evans, then up to Dong Ha, and finally wound up at Khe Sanh. The battalion main body had pulled in the previous afternoon and was sitting around waiting to go out on a sweep to acclimatize the troops to the rugged highlands terrain.

The word when I checked in at the battalion combat operations center was that the NVA had started building up along the adjacent Laotian border and that they were eventually going to try to overrun the combat base. I inferred but was not told outright that there was some hard intelligence backing that surmise, for I could not think of a place farther removed from possible Communist political or strategic objectives than isolated Khe Sanh.

*I*mmediately after our return to Khe Sanh, I got the word that Battalion wanted Lima Company to conduct a sweep south of the combat base, toward an old French fort near the hamlet of Khe Sanh. We started out early in the morning, right down the road toward the ville. After we passed through the ville, we cut off the road and walked through a village occupied by friendly, anti-Communist Bru montagnard tribesmen. In was a typical Bru village; the houses were built on stilts in the foliage beside the road. Unlike the lowland Vietnamese, the Bru men were at home and the women did not run at our approach. There were friendly children everywhere. The smiles and waves we received from them made it feel good to be back on the plateau.

As we worked our way out of the village, we started to get into heavy scrub growth, which led into the heavy jungle. After several hours, we were navigating through the awful jungle by compass and dead reckoning; there were no reference points to be seen. I actually had to climb trees a few times to help me figure out where the hell we were. After about six or eight hours of this, my battalion radioman chimed up, "Yo, Skipper, it's Battalion. They want us to return to base camp." That sounded weird, so I called Battalion and, sure enough, they confirmed the order. I couldn't figure out what the hell was going on, but anything was better than heaving around through that damn jungle.

It took us most of the rest of the day to get back to the combat base. When we arrived, I went over to the battalion CP to find out what the heck had brought us back there—what kind of emergency. They told me that Regiment had felt the company needed a little experience in navigating through the jungle. Bullshit. I pressed the matter and someone said that the real reason was to keep us from getting bored. Lima Company sure wasn't bored. The only symptoms of boredom I saw were at a higher level.

Over the next week, we checked in new troops, including a new gunny to replace the rotating Gunny Bailey. We also continued to ease the battalion into a routine of humping up and down the steep, jungle-choked hills and ravines. The weather was brisk, but more refreshing than the oppressive lowlands monsoon. It rained a lot, and the usual morning overcast sometimes never lifted. The combat base had taken on a personality something like an Old West boom town. The population had effectively doubled since our last tour and there was an air of expectancy that clearly was being generated out of the 26th Marines' regimental command post, which, along with the airstrip, was at the center of the burgeoning effort.

On December 20, Lima Company and the battalion Alpha command element, choppered to one of the massive ridgelines northwest of the combat base. We set up a little base camp and, first thing the next morning, December 21, Lima Company took off to sweep over the adjacent knoll, which was almost out of sight on the far side of a steep, narrow, jungle-choked ravine. After we jumped off, two of the other companies flew out and, while one guarded the base camp, the other swept over to the knoll on the other side of the valley.

Around midafternoon, when the word passed down the column that the point had broken through the jungle to the open summit of the knoll. I redoubled my efforts in anticipation of seeing daylight after the dank, dark, hours-long march. As I neared the summit, however, the hairs stood up on my arms and underneath my helmet. It had happened before, during that ill-starred night march down near Camp Evans; my brain knew before my nose that I had smelled the enemy.

I immediately crouched down with my rifle at the ready and flicked off the safety. As I looked back to check my radiomen, I saw that they had done the same. All three of us, and Marines farther back who were reacting to our reactions, were looking high and low, sniffing the air, trying to get a fix on whatever my internal onboard radar had whiffed. Wood smoke and fish—it was out there, but there was no movement, no other clues. We eased on up to the summit of the knoll and found the vanguard crapped out, oblivious to what my senses had triggered.

We took extra precautions when we set in our night defense. Unlike when I had overseen setting in my first night-defense position nearby in the last days of June, I had a well-oiled, Camp-trained company to undertake my every whim. There was no questioning me, no dogging the effort; I was king of the hill—of any hill Lima Company occupied—and my every utterance was law.

We dug deep and beefed up the sentry rotation. We were ready for anything, but nothing happened. Still, I had the unshakable conviction that we were being watched, assessed. If nothing else, I wanted to make a good impression. Out there, I had learned, good impressions saved lives; they sent the enemy looking for easier victims.

The whole sweep was uneventful. We spent three days humping the hills and the battalion sustained only one casualty, a Marine in another company who tripped his own booby trap. I heard he detonated an M-26 grenade while he was trying to retrieve it from the trap. Reputedly, it blew off an arm or leg. I used the incident to reiterate to the troops my ironclad rule against setting homemade booby traps around the Lima Company perimeter, that I was unalterably opposed to them.

On the morning of December 23, we got the word from Battalion that we were going back to the combat base. The main body, including the other two companies, was going to head back along the ridgeline, but the Old Man wanted Lima Company to follow a parallel route lower down, right through the jungle.

Needless to say, I wasn't real hot for the idea because humping through the jungle really is doing it the hard way. But I had no choice, so we moved off the ridgeline and slipped—literally—down the wet, steep, brush-choked walls of the defile. It took a long time to come in for a landing, and the effort of defying gravity really did us in. When we got there, we discovered that there was nothing like the cool air up above; it was close, humid, and hot. Some of my people nearly panicked when their overworked bodies started panting and gasping for air.

I was different than most; I had always liked working down in the jungle because it was quieter and, most of the time, cooler than the hilltops. The part I hated, though, was the way the trails and steep inclines tended to channelize a company column and prevent deployment of flankers. The threat of ambush, a constant source of worry, was particularly oppressive because we had continued to sense the enemy's presence despite a singular lack of hard evidence. He was out there, okay; there was no doubt about it.

Another major difficulty we encountered during every jungle jaunt was reckoning our position at any given moment. It was very difficult to see anything outside the jungle, and it was usually so close inside that we couldn't pinpoint landmarks that showed up on our maps. Unless we found a break in the canopy that presented a useful vista or were following a stream, we relied solely on our compasses and a purely estimated rate of march. It is very difficult to navigate in the jungle.

As we got formed up on the floor of the high-walled gulch, we discovered a well-beaten, five-foot-wide trail with ample signs of recent activity on it. That got my attention. I radioed Battalion and told them what we had. They said, "Follow it."

That sounds like a reasonable request; go see where the enemy is by following the enemy's trail. But the men who gave the order were way up there and the men who had to obey the order were way down here. Somewhere up that trail, I knew, was the enemy. He had been dogging us for days and he had to have a vague idea that we might find the trail. If I were him, I would have the trail outposted and ambush sites scoped out or even manned.

We got moving very slowly, very cautiously. The air was still and quiet, and about the only sound I heard was my own breathing. There wasn't even a whisper along the company column; necessary orders and inquiries were passed by means of standard arm-and-hand signals and little improvised pantomimes. The only human voices were those of my two radiomen, who were whispering reports to Battalion or responding to Battalion's inquiries with whispers into cupped handset mouthpieces. I never even heard a twig snap.

All of a sudden—oh, man!—we stumbled into a bunker complex. There was no shooting here, as there had been in another Khe Sanh valley in early July. The squads and platoons fanned out silently and searched through more bunkers than I had ever seen before—forty or fifty, of every size and description; there were living bunkers, cooking bunkers, medical bunkers, and fighting bunkers. There was no sign of the enemy and, though the bunkers were reasonably new and well maintained, no signs of habitation or recent use. We whispered the estimated coordinates to the regimental combat operations center and eased on up the trail to see if we could find more of the same or climb out of the box, whichever.

We kept moving up the five-foot-wide superhighway, finding one bunker complex after another, each about the same as the first one—

new, well-maintained, large, and blessedly deserted. I figured that each could house and support a 250-man NVA infantry battalion. Pretty soon, we had discovered housing for more than an NVA regiment.

At length, we came upon a swift stream that was twenty or thirty feet across with water two or three feet deep. To me, it was a pretty major waterway and I was not about to storm across. I shook out the lead platoon, sending security squads to either side of the trail and out along the stream in both directions. Then I sent over a few Marines to check things out. They found nothing and signaled that the crossing was clear. Next, I sent over the middle platoon. It spread out up the trail and up and down the stream, mirroring the efforts of the vanguard platoon on the near side. When the middle platoon was in position, I sent the remaining platoon over and then started drawing in the first platoon and pushing it across the stream. After it passed through the security cordon on the far side, the security cordon folded back onto the trail and the company proceeded ahead.

While all the moving and waiting was going on, I stopped to look around. Except for all the Marines defiling the place, the scene along the stream was beautiful, a paradise. I could even hear the cries of jungle birds. It took my breath away.

A little way up from the stream, I began thinking that it was starting to get late and that I absolutely did not want to spend the night in the jungle-choked, enemy-possessed defile. It took me all of about two seconds to decide to call Battalion and ask for a way out. I think they were chastened by what we found, because I had not quite finished making my request before Lieutenant Colonel Alderman's radioman told my radioman, "Come on up."

Easier said than done. If going down had been an unguided ballistic drop, there is no way to describe climbing out of that defile, up slippery, muddy, steep, jungled walls. It was agonizingly humid and oppressively hot. We had to maintain a single company file, which meant the troops at the end of the line had less to hang on to and a slicker path than the vanguard. We also had to maintain a reasonable vigil, with weapons unslung and a decent interval between the men. Since I had not dared to stop for water at the stream, we were about out of the vital nectar and it was only a matter of time, I feared, before we started having heat cases tumbling out of the column.

When I bulled through to the top of the knoll, one of the Marines who had preceded me nudged me and said, "Hey, Skipper, look at all this shit." It took me a moment to focus through the sweat in my eyes but, sure enough, the ground at that spot looked like a garbage dump. My bet was that a succession of Marine reconnaissance units had spent a few days each working out of there. War casualties had certainly cut into the quality of training and discipline the reconners were receiving. It sure wasn't the same as when I had been a reconner. There were C-ration cans and an assortment of junk all over the place, in various stages of decay. It was easy to see why lazy reconners would keep coming back; the place was easily defended. But it was plain stupid, suicidal. There were no secrets out there, not in NVA-land. I couldn't conceive of using the same camp twice in the same lifetime. As soon as the company was formed up and the men had taken a little breather, I got us the hell out of there.

We worked our way down the back slope of the knoll and then up an even higher slope, toward the dominant open ridgeline. It was extremely hard going, a very tough hump. I knew the company had about had it by the time we got to the top of the big knoll, especially the machine gunners and mortarmen, with their heavy loads of ammunition, so I gave the order to set in as soon as we found a spot wide enough to support the company. We even found a source of fresh water.

If we had been super-compulsive about setting in on previous afternoons, then we were postively anal that night, after seeing four NVA battalion bivouacs along a road nearly as wide and worn as the section of Highway 9 that climbed and traversed the plateau.

Nothing happened. Next morning, December 24, we rejoined the battalion main body and started the relatively easy hump back along the ridgeline to the combat base. With rest breaks, a few stream crossings, and a steep descent off the ridgeline, we made it back home in about six hours, by 1500, in plenty of time for Christmas Eve.

We went into position along the outer combat-base perimeter and chowed down on—yuck—C rations. I'm sure the regimental staff ate well that evening, and so might have the combat units that had been there long enough to have set up mess halls. But we had nothing of the sort. As usual, our camp stoves were in the rear because we lacked trucks to haul them to Khe Sanh. No one offered us an ounce of Christmas spirit.

I was looking forward to a miserable evening when, lo and behold, Top Mabry and the new company gunny stalked into the company position yelling, "Mail call! Mail call!"

Well, maybe there was hope. Next thing I knew, the company postal clerk was at my side asking, "Hey, Skipper, where do you want I should put all these boxes?"

"Jesus," I gasped, "what boxes?"

"Hell, sir, I got a big bunch of boxes here for you."

"Well, hell, put them right here in the company CP," indicating a hole in the ground.

I couldn't believe my eyes. There must have been thirty or forty boxes, each bearing the postmark of my tiny hometown, Wolcott, New York. Each box had my name on it in a different girlish scrawl. Thoroughly buffaloed, I began opening the boxes at random. Every one of them was filled with homemade cookies, and every one of them had a Christmas card enclosed with a note from a different member of the local Brownie and Girl Scout troops. The whole town didn't have but fifteen hundred residents, and I figured there must have been nearly three hundred pounds of cookies.

Merry Christmas! Old Santa Claus Camp grabbed a dozen volunteers and started passing cookies out to every man in Lima Company. Then, to round out the magnificent Christmas Eve, a few of the men started passing out—can you believe it!—eggnog from the dozen cans of frozen mix Regiment had had flown in for each company in the combat base. Then other Marines who had received goodies from home in the mail started throwing their stuff into the pot. Together with the two- or three-week accumulation of letters we received, it might just have squeaked by as the best Christmas Eve ever experienced by a company of Marines in the field.

And it wasn't over. It was a beautiful evening—warm, but not too warm, and startlingly clear, with a dazzling view of the shimmering heavens. As my command group sat in the open, munching cookies, slurping eggnog, and reading our mail, we started talking. Rank and position came off as we exchanged news from home, as if we had always been family, as if we were brothers and cousins camping out in the woods near home.

As I felt my heart suffused with the Christmas spirit, I got to thinking that I should at least invite the platoon commanders over to share the warmth, so I made the rounds and soon wound up at the 2nd Platoon CP. "Where's Lieutenant Prince," I asked his platoon sergeant and radioman. They didn't answer, so I repeated in an expressly good-natured tone, "Say, where's the lieutenant." They looked like a pair of cats who had swallowed a pair of canaries. "Now, dammit," I rasped in mounting exasperation, "tell me where the hell Prince is?"

"Well, uh, sir," the platoon sergeant stammered, "he's, uh, well, you know, sir, he's unavailable at this time, sir."

"What do you mean by 'unavailable'?"

"Just unavailable, sir."

I pressed the matter and they finally fessed up. Little John's goodie box had contained several plastic baby bottles—to prevent breakage— filled with his favorite spirits. By the time I came visiting, he was about fifteen sheets to the wind, dead drunk. I was pissed off, but there wasn't a hell of a lot I could or wanted to do about it right then.

Probably, my command group and I were about the only people in the company on watch that night. I hated to admit it, but I really had no idea what was going on. Fortunately, we had a quiet evening.

Around midnight that gorgeous moonlit Christmas Eve, the NVA probed the Marine platoon from 1/26 that was outposting the radio-relay station on the northern 950 ridgeline. While the whole rest of the plateau was clear, Hill 950 was socked in beneath a layer of, it seemed, perpetual fog. When the NVA hit the outpost, my command group and I saw muted tones of tracer—red for us and green for the NVA—and bursting hand grenades flashing in the fog. Now and then, the tracer broke through the fog and streaked across the clear sky, resembling shooting stars as much as the fallout of war. All the while, the tactical net burped little static-riddled exchanges between the embattled Marines and their concerned battalion commander. After ten or fifteen minutes, the color and noise died away and the valley returned to peace.

We had spent the day tracking the enemy. Then we had returned to safety. Over there, five thousand meters from me, Marines and NVA soldiers, were fighting for their lives. And over here, my little war family was eating cookies, drinking eggnog, reading letters from our loved ones, sharing in the fellowship of man. I hardly knew what to make of the contrast.

P A R T **IV**

THE SIEGE

C H A P T E R 23

*E*arly on the morning of January 1, 1968—New Year's Day!— I woke up and felt great to be alive. As soon as I opened my eyes, I said to myself, "By God, I gotta do something!" When I bounded out of my foxhole, everyone in the company command group looked at me as if to say, "What the hell's going through this guy's mind?"

I just had this *thing!* I knew there was a shower unit set up all the way down at the end of the runway, clear at the other end of the combat base, an easy mile and a half from the company position. As I figured out what I wanted to do, the command group of Marines just stared at me, waiting to hear the good news.

"Shower call," I ordered. "We're gonna take the company down for shower call." I immediately saw their reaction in their eyes. "Aw, Jesus," they were thinking, "this madman's got a wild idea now."

Very reluctantly, Top Mabry and the platoon commanders called out the whole company and told the men what we were going to do that morning. Half my men . . . three quarters of them . . . *all* of them! . . . had to be thinking, "Who the hell wants to take a shower?" I knew they would think it was a pain in the ass, but they had no choice. When the company commander said, "We're all going to take a shower," we were all going to take a shower.

Actually, it was a pretty good idea. All of Lima Company, myself included, lived in dirt foxholes. What with the pre-Christmas operation and all the routine digging and patrolling since then, everyone smelled to high heaven. The only way anyone had to get himself clean was to fill his helmet with cold water and sponge himself off. Shaving went the same way, using cold water from a helmet. At Khe Sanh in late 1967 and early 1968, Marines just did not think a lot about taking showers.

I ordered everyone to form ranks. We would all be taking our weapons, but not our gear; we were going to leave all that back in the company position with a few sentries to make sure it stayed there.

It took a lot of yelling, a huge amount of griping, and no end of kidding, but we finally got the whole company lined up—staff, officers, the whole shooting match. I put them through the whole routine: the noncoms formed the squads, the platoon sergeants formed the platoons, and the first sergeant formed the company. Then I took over the company from Top Mabry and the platoon commanders took over from the platoon sergeants. When the entire formation was set—there was 130 or 140 of us formed up—I right-faced all of them, just like that, and started marching them south through downtown Khe Sanh.

When we hit the main perimeter, I could literally hear everyone in the formation thinking, "Oh shit, what the hell are we gonna do here?" As soon as we got on the packed-earth, all-weather Seabee road through the combat base, I gave them "Double time!" Immediately, I heard the moans and groans going back and forth through the entire company.

I was sure the troops were going to mutiny, but they surprised me. The moaning and groaning stopped as soon as one of my noncoms started chanting cadence. Before I knew it, we were all chanting. And as we chanted, I saw Marines from other units start to look at the company. And the more people who looked at the company, the straighter, the more powerful, the more in-step the company got. You could hear my Marines thinking: "This is an *infantry* company! This is *Lima* Company, Three-Twenty-Six, coming down the pike."

By the time we got to the artillery battery that was about a half mile from the company position, my Marines were shouting at the top of their voices. This was really it! The morale went sky high.

We were still in pretty good formation after running all the way down to shower unit. By then, in addition to the chanting, most of my Marines were cheering themselves hoarse and laughing. I ordered "Halt!" and the platoon commanders, first sergeant, and platoon sergeants repeated the order. The formation got a little ragged then, but I thought the troops brought it off pretty well. Then it was down to the work at hand. I ordered everyone to strip down to their boondockers, and pretty soon we had 140 Marines with only their boots on standing on the roadway next to the shower unit.

The shower unit knew we were coming; they had the water heated and ready to go. We all lined up and hit the water, lathering up as we went. I had not had my body in touch with so much water since Honolulu, not to mention *clean*. It felt absolutely great, an absolute luxury! It was sheer heaven to be able to scrape all that crud and dirt off. The water was scalding; just fantastic. As the layers of mud and crud came off, we got very relaxed, very mellow.

As we came out the far end of the showers, we were motioned over to a big mound of clean clothing the shower unit had set out. They would keep our dirty stuff, wash it, and provide it for the next unit while we got the clothes the last unit had left behind. Of course, there was a big rush to find utilities that would fit. No one had sized the clothing; there was just one big pile of it. So we all rushed over and started trying on stuff until it all fit, basically. That was an opportunity for more grab-assing, more griping, and a little payback by the troops on the officers and noncoms.

When everyone was dressed in utilities that more or less fit, we formed the company again and marched it back to our position. I still felt great and everyone's morale was sky high. The company was really tight.

As soon as we got home, I called over the first sergeant and the exec and said, "Goddammit, let's have a football game!" There was no bitching and moaning now; everyone was ready to get physical. We all went at it again. As we were choosing up sides, the battalion chaplain, who had once been a semipro football player, showed up and asked if he could play. Of course, I kept score. I knew better than to get out there and roughhouse with the troops.

It was a hell of a football game, what with sixty or seventy men on a side. The chaplain knocked some of those lads looser than their shoestrings; he went through the line like crap through a goose. They all loved it.

It was just one of those rare days that is absolutely perfect. We even had a good meal that night. After dinner, I was trying to figure out how I would ever top a day like that. I was not able to come close to a solution, but the NVA came to my rescue; they provided the means for making this memorable group high absolutely perfect.

During the week between Christmas and New Year's, 3/26 had been fully integrated into the defenses of the Khe Sanh combat base. The resident battalion, 1/26, had been maintaining a number of static company-size positions in the hills and running patrols since its arrival the previous summer, but there were strong indications of an NVA build up no doubt leading to an attempt to overrun the base, so 3/26 had been called back to take over manning the hill positions and lend a hand building up a formal defense line around the combat base itself, leaving 1/26 free to conduct more, more-distant, and stronger patrols.

Kilo Company was sent out to Hill 861, approximately northwest of the combat base, overlooking the Khe Sanh plateau, and India Company was sent out to Hill 881 South (881S), approximately to the west, overlooking both the combat base and "neutral" Laos. Lima Company was assigned a fixed section of the base perimeter line—a bubble, really, at the western end of the runway—and Mike Company was held in reserve within the base. Also on line around the base were Bravo and Charlie companies, 1/26. Delta Company, 1/26, was the regimental reserve. Alpha Company, 1/26, maintained a platoon security post on Hill 950, north of the combat base, where the radio-relay and electronics-eavesdropping center was located. The remainder of Alpha Company guarded the regimental command post and its important structures and stood ready to provide a perimeter reaction force. In addition to the two Marine infantry battalions and two Marine 105mm artillery batteries (Alpha and Charlie batteries, 1/13), the Army maintained a small, tough cadre of Special Forces people. Known as Forward Operating Base 3 (FOB-3), the Green Berets were charged with running a tough little Civilian Irregular Defense Group company composed of local Bru montagnard tribesmen employed as scouts. There was also a detachment of Army dual-40mm antiaircraft vehicles (dusters) and quad-.50-caliber antiaircraft vehicles, a Marine tank platoon, an Ontos platoon, a Seabee detachment, and assorted Marine and Air Force personnel manning the airfield facilities. Altogether, Khe Sanh was a bustling concern with, I would guess, three thousand full-time residents.

As we did every night, Lima Company got ready for its night defense. In the fifteen or twenty minutes before dusk, we had our usual stand-to. Everyone got all his gear laid out in case we got hit during the night. I had dug my own foxhole, which was where I slept alone. It was four feet wide and six feet long, a little cramped for me. As was my custom, I spoke briefly with the radiomen and everyone else in the command group before I hit the sack at about 2200.

Somewhere around 0100, January 2, I woke up on sheer intuition just as the company radioman crawled over to me and whispered, "Skipper! Skipper! Get up. The First Platoon listening post hears something." It was SOP in Lima Company that when a listening post made contact or heard something, the situation immediately belonged to the company commander.

A listening post was a fire team—four riflemen—which was sent out by each platoon to monitor a likely avenue of approach on our lines. We usually had three or four listening posts out on any given night, depending how many avenues of approach we had to cover.

The alert had come in from the 1st Platoon listening post, which was screening the company right flank. One member of the fire team had heard something and had immediately alerted the company radioman, who immediately alerted me.

The company and battalion radiomen shared a big hole near my hole; it had tarpaulin stretched over the top in such a way as to make it absolutely lightproof. As I crawled to the radio bunker, I whispered a call for Corporal Brady, my mortar-section leader. As soon as Brady crawled up beside me, I whispered, "Brady, get your ammo humpers up and have them stand by." The 60mm ammo party was my reaction force, the group of Marines to which the company commander had immediate access in case something happened. I could use them to stop a breakthrough or reinforce a listening post—whatever—without having to steal men from the rifle platoons.

Next, I rolled beneath the radio-bunker tarp and dropped into the hole. As soon as I got there, one of the radiomen gave me a handset and I called up the 1st Platoon listening post, which was "Lima One-One"—the first listening post of the 1st Platoon of Lima Company.

"Lima One-One. Lima Six." I waited, but there was no response. "Lima One-One. Lima Six." No response again. I tried it two or three more times, but the listening post was not answering—or could not.

I was sorting out options when we heard two clicks from the handset. Someone in the listening post had keyed his own handset twice to tell us he was alive but did not want to talk. I came right back up on the radio and said, "Lima One-One. Lima Six. If you hear this transmission, key your handset twice."

Click. Click.

I knew the fire team could not talk but that they were listening to me.

"Lima One-One. Lima Six. When you can talk, let me know what's going on."

And then we waited. The adrenalin went straight through me. I had four Marines out there who thought they saw or heard something. It was darker than pitch. I had no idea what was coming in on them, and maybe they didn't either. I worked up a lot of empathy for those four Marines, but there was not a thing I could do until I heard from them or until something happened.

I was listening so hard I almost missed the faint whisper coming in over my handset: "We see something. Out."

That was enough for me. I was galvanized to action. "Brady," I loudly whispered, "Brady, get your people up and get them ready to go." At the same time, I called the 1st Platoon commander, Lieutenant Nile Buffington: "Lima One. Lima Six. Are you monitoring this transmission?"

"Lima Six. Lima One. Roger that."

"Lima One. Lima Six. Did you personally put them out?"

Buffington replied that he had put them out and that he knew precisely where they were.

There was a small draw that came out of a valley seventy or eighty meters from our main line. There was a tree there we called the Hanging Tree because it had an odd-shaped, bent-up limb. When Buffington told me that the listening post was out near the Hanging Tree, I knew right where it was.

"Lima One. Lima Six. Stand by. I'm going to send a reaction force down to you. You take it over. We might go out and reinforce the listening post, depending on what they've got out there."

Typically, a listening post was like a grape. If we did not get them in on time, they stood a good chance of being swallowed up as the enemy moved right up to our main line to launch an assault. On the other hand, if we pulled a listening post in too early, we would not know what the hell was going on right in front of our line. Timing was everything.

My solution to this age-old quandary was to try to reinforce a listening post that had detected movement on its front. Doing so would offset the possibility of its being overrun if it stayed out too long. It also might be given more time to report everything it could hear and see. In the best of all worlds, a reinforced listening post just might provide us with a sizable force in the enemy's path or even in his rear.

This was an extremely delicate operation. We had practiced it several times in the past, but this was the first chance to do it live.

As soon as I made my decision, Corporal Brady sent his ammo humpers—eight Marines in all—down to the 1st Platoon command post.

There was one little flaw in the plan. The eight men in the reaction force were all apprentice mortarmen—not riflemen. Moreover, they were all very junior in rank, all privates first class and lance corporals, if that. All of a sudden, they were faced with the very real prospect of having to advance beyond our prepared defenses in the dead of night. Once they were in the open, they would have to locate a well-camouflaged friendly position they had never seen. If they got that far, there was a good chance that they would have to duke it out with who-knew-how-many NVA Regulars. I knew that the ammo humpers were pretty excited about what they faced, but they were all I had. Short of defending a key sector during an all-out attack, there was no way I was going to thin out my platoons manning the main line.

The adrenalin was coursing through everybody at this stage.

After Brady sent out the reaction force, I finally got back in touch with the listening post. During the course of five or ten minutes—time was going fast _and_ slow—I spoke with the fire team twice more. During the first transmission, the team leader out there was whispering so low that I could not make out what he was saying. But the last transmission was, "We see something. Six of them just walked by us." Then there was a pause and the team leader asked, "You want me to tell you what they're armed with?" I knew that he wanted to make sure that I knew that he wasn't bullshitting out there.

"No. Hold your position. We're gonna reinforce you."

Next, Lieutenant Buffington came up on the net to tell me that he was with the reaction force. I said, "Lima One. Lima Six. Take them out. Be careful."

I now had a four-man Marine listening post standing by near the Hanging Tree. One officer and the eight ammo humpers were going to work their way out to the listening post. I had an unknown number of NVA out there, too—at least six. The situation was extremely dangerous.

While I was waiting to hear back from Buffington, I had the battalion radioman contact Battalion and let them know what we had. When he got through, I told them at Battalion, "We have some friendlies out in front of the wire. Alert the line at Khe Sanh so they don't start shooting at our people out there." Battalion verified that they had heard and understood my transmission, which is not the same as assuring me that my Marines would not be endangered by other units if they were heard or seen.

I was tense from waiting, so I told Corporal Brady to break out his 60mm mortar illumination rounds and prepare to fire them immediately on my command. I had no sooner said that than, all of a sudden, Lieutenant Buffington came up on the net: "Lima Six. Lima One. We made contact with the listening post." So, that part was over with. Lima Company now had a dozen Marines and a very good, experienced lieutenant out in front of our lines.

Brady reported back that he had the illume broken out. I told him, "Have them standing by to fire."

We had three 60mm mortars in the company position, all under my direct control. Brady actually had a round "hanging" in each tube—that is, a gunner was holding a round at the mouth of each tube, ready to drop on command. There is no faster way to get the first rounds up.

As soon as I knew Brady's mortars were set, I told Buffington to get all his people on line, that as soon as we started the illume he was to sweep through the area where the listening post fire team thought they saw the North Vietnamese. We were all set to go. Buffington was then about seventy or eighty meters in front of the 1st Platoon line, about a hundred meters in front of the company CP.

There was another wait. Then Buffington came up on the net: "Lima Six. Lima One. I'm ready to go."

I turned to my mortar-squad leader, "Brady, start the illumination." No sooner said than one of the 60mm mortars popped the first illumination round.

I was staring as hard as I could, dead ahead, into the harsh white magnesium light of the illume, but I could not see anything. I hopped out of the radio bunker for a better look, and my radiomen stood up next to me. I was waiting for something to happen, but it was dead quiet out there. The only thing I heard was the *thung* of the second illumination round being fired as the first one started to wane.

All of a sudden, there was a burst of fire, ten or fifteen rounds. This was followed a half beat later by a terrific volume of automatic-weapons fire. It all sounded like one continuous roar, and I do not think it lasted for more than a few seconds. Then there was nothing, absolutely nothing; dead silence. The next thing anyone heard was me yelling into the handset, "What the hell's going on? What the hell's going on out there? Tell me what's happening out there! What's happening, Lima One? What the hell is going on?"

Suddenly, I heard Buffington's voice break into my stream of questions. He was yelling at the top of his voice. I heard him on the handset and through the air. We did not need the radio.

"We have contact. We can't figure out what's going on."

I tried to sound calm. "Tell me what the hell's happening!"

Before Buffington could answer, an Army duster—a pair of 40mm automatic cannon mounted on a tracked armored chassis—opened fire from our right flank. I could not hear anything except the 40mm guns. I was afraid that the Army people were blowing away our people. The only thing I could do was call Battalion and scream at them to get the Army to knock off the fire, that we were trying to find out what was going on with Buffington and his crew.

The duster kept putting out rounds, but somehow I managed to hear Buffington's next radio call: "We're down; we can't see anything."

The Army duster was still throwing rounds out there, so I yelled into the handset, "What've you got?" But Buffington said he had no idea. "Well," I asked, "is anybody hurt?"

"No, not that I can tell."

"Okay, then, bring them on in, bring them on in." I was not sure he could hear me over the continuous roar of the Army duster. "I said bring them all in, bring them all in before somebody gets hurt."

I did not get an acknowledgment that I could understand, but I passed the word up and down our line to watch for friendlies trying to reenter the company position. About ten minutes later, someone told me that Lieutenant Buffington was back inside our wire. He had come back in through his own platoon's lines because they knew him and knew where he was. I sent word for him to come straight to the company CP, and he and the ammo humpers and the original fire team got to me all at once within a minute.

I was going to ask what happened, but the whole bunch of them started talking a mile a minute before I opened my mouth. They were all incredibly hyper, and they all wanted to talk. I could see the adrenalin pouring through them. They were all bunched up in front of me, jabbering away, talking with their hands. They looked like a bunch of escapees from an asylum.

There was no way they were going to wind down on their own any time soon, so I yelled, "Shut up, goddammit! Sit down!" That snapped all of them out of their high. They all sat down—fell down, really—and I said as calmly as I was able, "Okay, Lieutenant Buffington, tell me what happened."

Buffington told me that he had gotten all twelve Marines formed up in a single line and started moving them forward to sweep out in front of the listening post. All of a sudden, almost as soon as the first illume round popped overhead, the Marine in the middle of the line, right in front of Buffington, stopped in his tracks. Instantly, the entire line stopped with him. Then the Marine said, "Who's there?"

Nothing happened, but the Marine kept staring at something straight ahead, so Buffington closed up on the Marine, stared ahead over the Marine's shoulder, and said, "You fuckers better say something."

And that is what they did: one of the NVA soldiers fired about fifteen rounds right over Buffington's head. Fortunately, there is a tendency to fire high at night. Buffington said he felt the rounds whizzing past his head.

Every one of the Marines had set his weapon on full automatic, and each man had eighteen rounds in the magazine. That is thirteen Marines with eighteen rounds apiece. Every one of them instantly opened fire on full automatic. Naturally, every one of them ran out of ammunition at the exactly the same moment. That was when I heard it get quiet all of a sudden.

As soon as everyone had emptied his first magazine, all hands dropped onto the ground to present less of a silhouette. Then every-one started fumbling around on the ground trying to find a fresh magazine, and trying to put the fresh magazines into their M-16s. Of course, when they all fell down, some of them were pointing their weapons one way and others were pointing their weapons the other way. The result was that they were as likely to blow away one another as any North Vietnamese. Buffington was yelling at them, trying to get them squared away: "Where the hell is everybody," and calm questions like that. Everyone was crawling around out there, thoroughly confused, thoroughly scared.

Buffington finished telling the story and I patted everybody on the back while exclaiming, "Way to go, Marines!" and "Well done!" and "Good job! Whatever's out there, I know you just scared the shit of them. You know you alerted the lines. Well done." I made a special effort to pat the listening post Marines on their backs; they had done good.

As soon as I was done passing out attaboys, the fire team returned to the 1st Platoon position, the ammo humpers went off to tell Corporal Brady's mortarmen what great warriors they were, and Nile Buffington and I trekked down to Battalion to give them a brief. I was stunned to see that no one at the battalion combat operations center appeared particularly interested in our story. Noting all the bored expressions, we gave a quick brief and headed home. I could not imagine why they acted that way; it seemed like a damned interesting story to Buffington and me!

By the time we got back to my CP it was probably 0400. I told Buffington to send out another listening post, but not in that same vicinity. Then I jumped into my hole and crashed.

After a few hours' sleep, I called Buffington and told him that we had to search around the Hanging Tree to try to find out what had happened in the night.

As I was getting set to go down to the 1st Platoon area, two of the mortar ammo humpers came over and asked if they could help search for bodies. I told them they sure could, and they accompanied me to the 1st Platoon CP. I guess they had become bored with the easy life of the rear echelon.

I was just rubbernecking while Buffington's people and the ammo humpers were kicking around out in front of the lines. I had even less of a sense of what to look for than they did. I doubted we would find anything; it was always extremely difficult to find any results from a fight because the North Vietnamese were always very good about dragging their bodies off. I happened to be watching the two ammo humpers, who were about seventy meters from where I was standing. No sooner did I take my eyes off them that I heard them both yell, "Skipper! Hey, Skipper!" When I lifted my eyes, they were jumping up and down and yelling, "Come out here quick. Come on out here. See what we got!"

I grabbed a bunch of other rubberneckers and we ran out there at high port. The ammo humpers had found five dead NVA officers, all stretched right out on the ground. All of them had been hit literally from the top of their brain housing groups to their toenails, and it looked like somebody had raked the ground around them. That was the result of all that automatic fire that the listening post fire team and the reaction force had put out. They put out over 230 rounds, and all of them were right on target.

The dead men were all wearing black pajamas and rubber-soled Ho Chi Minh sandals. All of them were really big men, a lot bigger than most Vietnamese. One of them had pulled a hand grenade halfway out of his pouch, and another one was gripping a pistol with his arm outstretched. Rigor mortis had set in, so they were all frozen in the positions in which they had died, like wax statues.

After staring at the bodies for a few moments, I noticed that all their shoulder straps had been cut. The listening post had told us early on that there were six of them. That explained the cut shoulder straps. One of them had survived and he had apparently had the presence of mind to cut away their dispatch cases before he took off out of the area. That is fantastic discipline, particularly if he had been wounded, which was a good bet.

For once, we had the proof of our success. I turned to Lieutenant Buffington and the others. "Let's bring the whole company out here by squads to see the results."

First, I brought out all the ammo humpers who had been on the reaction force; it was important for them to see what they had accomplished. Afterward, everyone else was rubbernecking at the fire team and the ammo humpers, which made them all stand tall. I do not think there was a corporal in the bunch; they were all junior troops.

While the squads were rubbernecking, I told my exec to contact the Marine interrogator-translator detachment and get them out to view the remains and take whatever they needed for intelligence purposes. The dead North Vietnamese were definitely big fish; every one of them was wearing a gold or silver belt buckle, not the standard aluminum type. Dispatch cases, pistols, expensive belt buckles—it was obvious to me that those people were special.

When the intelligence team came out, they even made plaster masks of the dead men's faces. I heard later that all of the dead North Vietnamese were eventually identified by name. Radiomen from the FOB-3 Special Forces detachment on our left flank later told me that the North Vietnamese tactical radio nets they were monitoring went bonkers an hour or so after the kill.

What it all added up to was that we had killed the commander of an NVA regiment and his staff. This was incredibly lucky for Lima Company. The only thing officers as senior as that could have been doing out there was reconnoitering our lines in preparation for a major ground assault.

The only casualty we suffered came to my attention when one of the kids in the listening-post fire team showed me an ugly bruise over the orbit of his right eye, which, he told me, had been inflicted when a bullet glanced off his face. I had Top Mabry write him up for a Purple Heart, and I made sure everyone in the fire team and all the ammo humpers got souvenirs, the gold and silver belt buckles, the officers' pistols, whatever.

January 1–2, 1968, is my idea of a perfect day: Showers for everyone and a major, major kill.

Lima Company had been damned lucky.

CHAPTER 24

During 3/26's summer 1967 tour at Khe Sanh, we had been in a holding rather than a defensive mode. We had had a segment of the base perimeter to man, but that had been pro forma; it was then considered unlikely that the combat base itself would be the object of an NVA ground assault. Our return in December 1967, however, was a different matter entirely. The battalion and an extra artillery battery had been brought in precisely because there were signs of an NVA build up around the combat base, on both sides of the Laotian frontier.

Lima Company's January 2 bag of five high-ranking NVA officers as they presumably scouted our lines preparatory to an attack, set off a fury of activity the likes of which I had not seen until then and have not seen since. It is extremely likely, in hindsight, that the deaths of an NVA regimental commander and his staff on the eve of a planned attack delayed the beginning of the NVA offensive against Khe Sanh. Since the great Communist Tet Offensive of 1968 has been demonstrated to have begun several weeks later than originally conceived, it is arguable that the chance encounter in front of Lima Company's lines on January 2 actually threw off the entire Communist offensive timetable. It is more or less certain that the NVA planned to hit Khe Sanh just before the start of the major countrywide offensive as a way of drawing off the I Corps strategic reserve. Thus, if the attack on Khe Sanh was in fact delayed by our January 2 encounter, it is reasonable to assume that the local delay we caused led to a delay in the countrywide plan.

Whatever may or may not have been going on at levels beyond my ken, it is certain that the destruction of the NVA regimental scouting party in front of Lima Company's line, together with several other hard contacts, set off a furious program of entrenchment around and within the combat base. The order of the day every day for weeks was: "Dig in!"

Within a day or two of January 2, Major Matt Caulfield, who was still our S-3, came over to the company CP with some plans for bunkers he personally had designed. Since Lima was the only company in the battalion with frontage on the base perimeter, we were going to get to build to Matt's specifications.

Matt is bright, but very hardheaded. He made it clear at the outset that he wanted all the bunkers to be built exactly as specified in his plan. I wasn't all that excited with Matt's design. As I pointed out to him. "What the hell are we doing building all these bunkers above the ground?" But he said, "Do it!"

We did it. We began assembling the building materials, which were just beginning to arrive in a stream of helicopters and C-123 and C-130 transport planes that resembled a taxi rank at a busy airport. I figured, what the hell, we would do what we were told, the best job we could. However, as the building materials were piling up and we were about to begin building Matt's bunkers, someone told me that Matt's plan—the only copy—had vanished. I was not disturbed at all by the disappearance, but I swear I had nothing to do with it. Unfortunately, Matt didn't see it that way. He came out to the line and said right out that he thought I was goofing off. That sure got my back up. "No," I flared, "I'm not goofing off."

"Well," he argued, "then where the hell are the goddamn plans?"

"Why ask me? I don't know where they are." Obviously, he thought that I had shitcanned them, that I was deliberately obstructing his grand defensive design.

We got into a big argument, right there, out in the open. There was a whole lot of yelling and posturing. I don't know how it happened; I think the world of Matt. Besides, he outranked me. But the accusation and his attitude hit me wrong. Finally I yelled, "Okay, if that's the way you feel, the hell with it. Get yourself another company commander."

Matt sure wasn't about to stand for that. He yanked me right off the line and we both went off to see Lieutenant Colonel Alderman. I told the Old Man the same thing, but he wound up saying, "Oh, goddammit, you two, quiet down, simmer down." He said it softly, with some amusement, but Matt and I reined in our egos and indeed simmered down. I maintained that I had had nothing to do with the disappearance of Matt's plans and that I didn't know anyone who had. Matt said he accepted that and that he would take the time to draw up a new set. I agreed to continue to stage materials and to build the bunkers as ordered.

There were a few hard feelings about the altercation for some time. It was unfortunate, just one of those things that kind of got out of hand.

As soon as the new plans arrived, the troops started building the bunkers, which were about seven feet tall, two sandbags thick on the sides, and one sandbag thick on the top. In light of subsequent events, they turned out to be foolishly thin-skinned. Their being above the ground only made it worse. But that was in the future. Nevertheless, the real heart of Lima Company's future survival lay in excavation work.

While we were installing Major Caulfield's above-ground bunkers on the perimeter line, the battalion CP itself went underground—underground!—in a little copse well back from the main line. They were so fearful of exposing themselves as a command post that they didn't even allow vehicles into the copse, and they camouflaged everything. They got the Seabees to come up and dig a huge pit which was about the size of a GP tent, about thirty feet long, twenty feet wide, and fifteen feet deep. Then they took inch-thick pierced steel runway matting and covered the hole with it. The runway matting was then covered with dirt and, on top of the dirt, they placed upended expended artillery shell casings filled with dirt, followed by a layer of crushed rock. Then they put one-inch plywood sheets on top of the rock, another layer of filled shell casings, more plywood, and more dirt. The roof of their bunker measured out at over six feet.

I was so incensed over what they were doing up at Battalion that I did nothing to improve my too-short six-foot unroofed CP hole in the ground. When Matt Caulfield's above-ground line bunkers were all built, I made a big show of moving into one of them because I was ordered to. I also made a big show of installing a deep, narrow fire trench right outside the entrance. There was no reason at that stage of the game to send mixed messages. As soon as the S-3's bunkers were done, I got the troops to work digging reinforced foxholes and trenches. This part of Camp's grand design was not for show. I had no confidence in the bunkers and I wanted the best available cover close at hand for my men. For the moment, I could see, the bulk of the new engineering supplies were being expended on the various command posts deep within the perimeter.

In all, the Lima Company sector measured out at close to a thousand linear feet on a curve around the western side of the combat base, in what they called Red Sector. Charlie Company, 1/26, was on our right, covering the entire northern side of the runway, and FOB-3 was on our left, covering the southwest corner of the combat base. H&S Company, 3/26, was to our immediate rear, nominally manning what at that time was a poorly built secondary line. Mostly, that line was manned by 81mm mortarmen, 106mm recoilless riflemen, and headquarters clerks who were off duty from their regular chores.

The digging was done by Marines with their own entrenching tools or whatever long-handled shovels we could scrounge or steal. The only outside help we received was from the Seabees, who came by one day and sprayed herbicide on the brush out to about a hundred meters in front of our lines and told us they would be back in a few days with a bulldozer to scrape off the dead bushes. They were as good as their word, but that was all the help we received.

The digging was brutal, but it was in earnest. Reports of NVA contacts mounted almost daily, though Lima Company had no direct contact with the enemy after January 2. Most of the contacts were made by the Green Berets and their Bru scouts—who worked across the frontier in Laos—or by patrols from the resident reconnaissance company. A patrol from Kilo Company, 3/26, working off Hill 861 found a bunker complex during one sweep in early January, and a 1/26 ambush turned up a dead NVA officer scout whose map clearly showed our defensive line. Almost daily, NVA or signs of NVA were spotted by patrols or even fixed positions working along the arc of hills surrounding the combat base to the north, northwest, and west. And I had not forgotten the four battalion-size bunker complexes Lima Company had located a little farther out on December 24.

I made a point of keeping the troops up to date. All the news translated into some very serious excavation efforts, which is what I had in mind.

Eventually, a small part of the huge cache of building materials reached us so we could adequately defend the hundred-meter field of fire the Seabees had scraped off for us. We got a load of mines, which Marine engineers emplaced in front of our wire and we initially strung a few strands of a particularly brutal new type of concertina barbed wire called German Tape, which had what amounted to razor blades attached.

While we had the usual concerns about rocket or mortar attacks, we concentrated mainly on improvising positions that would withstand infantry assaults. Everything we had seen pointed to the danger of a massive infantry assault once the NVA battalions had completed their move into the area. Given all we knew and could learn during the first three weeks of January 1968, betting on an infantry assault was getting about even money.

One good outcome of the sudden focus on building up the combat base was the arrival of the battalion rear echelon.

Throughout my tour with Lima Company, Marine units were transferred so often and so quickly around I Corps that rear parties almost never caught up. When the battalion main body had been sent up to Khe Sanh in early December, the rear party remained stranded down at Dong Ha. For weeks, the battalion exec, Major Joe Loughran, kept asking Regiment to provide trucks to bring up our rear party and its gear, which included field ranges and other heavy equipment that tended to make life bearable between trips to the field. But, try as he would, Major Loughran never made any progress. One morning, he decided to accompany some of the supplymen up to Khe Sanh so he could beg Regiment to give him trucks to accompany him back to Dong Ha. As the major and the supplymen waited beside the taxiway at the Dong Ha airstrip in hopes of finding a ride in an airplane, an Air America—CIA—C-130 transport plane landed and rolled up to the taxi apron. As it came to rest, the co-pilot opened his side hatch and leaned out to ask, "Anybody here know where Sergeant Bender is?" As Major Loughran stood there wondering, "Who the hell are these guys," Bender ran up and said to the co-pilot, "Yeah, I'm Bender," to which the co-pilot responded, "We've come to pick up your gear." Major Loughran immediately collared Sergeant Bender and asked the usual question officers ask when they're confused: "What the hell is going on?" This was answered by a vague shrug from Bender, so Loughran tried to get specific. "How come this plane—this *CIA* plane—is here to pick up Lima Company's gear?" Caught out, Bender painted a big smile on his face and said, "Oh, hell, Major, load the battalion's gear on, too, if you want to." It eventually came out that Bender had become disenchanted with Regiment's ho-hum devotion to the battalion's needs, so he had spread the word that he had two mint-condition NVA weapons waiting for the first flight crew that would pick up Lima Company's gear and fly it up to Khe Sanh. Good old Bender; he cut straight through the bullshit and everybody wound up happy—except Major Loughran, who went along even though he didn't approve of graft and corruption.

By the middle of the month, the NVA were growing bolder. On January 14, a team from Bravo Company, 3rd Reconnaissance Battalion, made contact with an enemy unit of unknown size on Hill 881N, and the enemy stood and fought. Two of the reconners, including a lieutenant, were killed and four were wounded. On January 15, a Special Forces patrol called artillery fire on about three dozen NVA it found bathing in a stream. This was the biggest artillery fire mission of our stay so far, and it truly impressed us.

Even more impressive was the arrival of the entire 2nd Battalion, 26th Marines, on January 17. The battalion flew in aboard several C-130 transports, which was itself unique in the annals of Marine airlifts at that stage of the war. But it was the mere presence of another Marine battalion that really got my attention. The arrival of 2/26 marked the first time since the end of World War II that the entire 26th Marine Regiment had been assembled in one place at one time. In fact, this was the very first time since its activation just over a year earlier that 2/26 even had served directly under 26th Marines. Word was that the battery of 105mm howitzers that had been supporting 2/26 down south of Hue was also due in within the next few days. If that was true, then the 26th Marines' direct-support artillery battalion, 1/13, would also be whole for the first time in over two decades.

After spending a day inside the wire, the bulk of the fresh battalion moved a few klicks to the northwest to occupy Hill 558—a 558-meter-high hill sitting in the middle of a broad valley that was the best attack route into the combat base. One company of 2/26 was sent on a long patrol to the north and northwest to try to find the NVA.

*T*he NVA the 2/26 company was looking for came calling on their own. On January 19, an India Company patrol sweeping from Hill 881S to neighboring Hill 881N was ambushed by an NVA squad firing automatic weapons. The Marines returned fire and called in artillery. As the big guns were firing, the India patrol withdrew with one Marine dead and two wounded.

Immediately following the fight on Hill 881N on January 19, Battalion decided to send all of India Company to the ambush site to clear the enemy off the hill. The Mike Company command group and two platoons were alerted to fly out to Hill 881S the next day, to guard the India Company position and to be close at hand in case India needed support. I was made privy to the plan, but Lima Company was given no role because of our total commitment to the perimeter defense of the combat base.

When India Company jumped off from Hill 881S toward Hill 881N at dawn, in a pea-soup fog, I tuned in to the battalion tactical net to follow the action, if any erupted. I figured there was a better-than-even chance that the NVA would cut and run in the face of a full-company sweep. Nothing I had ever seen at Khe Sanh could make me believe otherwise, though I was well aware that the stakes had been changing at least since the battalion's Christmas sweep and the discovery of the NVA battalion-size bunker complexes. There was obviously a lot of NVA out there, but there was still some question about their willingness or readiness to get into a big fight.

The instigator of the January 20 sweep to Hill 881N was the India Company commander, Captain Bill Dabney. Bill, who had joined the battalion on the same day as Matt Caulfield and the exec, Major Joe Loughran, had served briefly as the H&S Company commander and the Mike Company commander. He is the scion of an old and respected Tidewater Virginia family whose men had fought in every American war going back to the earliest days of the colony. He is a big, naturally taciturn man, a Naval Academy dropout and Virginia Military Institute graduate who had served an enlisted tour in which he made sergeant. A superb leader of enormous personal stature,

Bill's standing in the Marine Corps was considerably enhanced by his marriage to the elder daughter of the Marine Corps' legendary beau ideal, Chesty Puller.

Out of ingrained habit, I kept up to date on the India Company sweep by means of the ongoing chatter on the open battalion tactical net. Along about 0930, as I was taking a breather in my newly arrived CP tent with the rest of my command group, I heard Bill Dabney's radioman report that his lead platoon was being hosed with automatic-weapons fire, that the platoon commander had reported that he thought he could see bunkers at the source of the fire.

The suddenness of the news—the tone of voice Dabney's radiomen used—made me sit straight up on my rack. This was it; I just knew this was it!

I started yelling for the exec and company gunny: "Get the company ready to go. Alert the men. We may have to go out. Prepare to draw ammunition." In a flash, I was running down to the battalion CP.

When I arrived, I came up short. It was business as usual there; nobody seemed to be the least bit concerned about what India Company had reported. "Jesus," I blurted out, "they've run into bunkers and automatic weapons. It's gonna be a tough go out there." I told them I was getting Lima ready to mount out.

"No, no, no," the battalion commander said, "Stand down. You're not going to go up."

I couldn't believe what I was hearing—we could now hear the chatter of machine guns in the background on the open battalion tactical net—so I stalked back to my CP and told the exec and gunny to stand the company down, that there was no interest in our offer up at Battalion. When we gathered around the battalion radio and listened to blow-by-blow reports of some very serious, very bloody fighting that involved, among other things, a major jet strike within meters of one of India's surrounded rifle platoons. I thought someone would send out the two thirds of Mike Company that was already up there, but that didn't happen either. Except for the jet strike and 81mm mortar support from Hill 881S, India was left to extricate itself. It did, but with grievous casualties. Four Marines, including two of Dabney's platoon commanders, paid with their lives and another thirty-nine thoroughly chastened Marines and corpsmen had to be evacuated. Someone reported that 103 NVA were killed, but I couldn't imagine how a retreating infantry company could take time out to count the dead on a field it was conceding. Maybe the jet pilots counted up the dead, but picture that.

*T*here were three other significant contacts—as they were called—that afternoon.

Unknown to anyone outside the highest command echelons, the local Vietnamese district headquarters—call it a county seat—at Khe Sanh ville was surrounded and cut off. Though a Marine combined action company was there—as was an Army advisory team and various and sundry ARVN units—the action only a few klicks from our base was deemed to be not our problem because it was actually outside the combat base's area of operations and because the combined action company and the U.S. Army advisory team were working for MACV (Military Assistance Command, Vietnam) Headquarters, in Saigon. It turned out that our inattention was to reward the Communists shortly with the very first South Vietnamese political center ever to fall into their hands.

On the north side of the combat base, a recon team was surrounded late in the afternoon by an enemy force of unknown size. The reconners had to pull in really tight and get their heads down to keep from getting hit by the extremely close-in artillery support fired in their behalf. That kept up all night, until the NVA finally let them loose.

More significant than even India Company's fight was the voluntary surrender at the base wire of an NVA lieutenant. Among other things, the NVA officer, who was the executive officer of a 37mm antiaircraft battery no one knew was in the area, said that he had witnessed and nearly fired on Lima Company Marines on January 2, as we were patting ourselves on the back out by the five NVA corpses in front of our line. More important, the lieutenant told his interrogator where many NVA antiaircraft units were set in to interdict the flow of supplies and reinforcements by air into Khe Sanh. Then he gave up the entire NVA infantry order of battle on the Khe Sanh plateau— there were two fresh, veteran infantry *divisions* up there, ready to go into action. Capping the startling catalogue was news that Hill 881S and Hill 861—one staffed by India and most of Mike companies and the other staffed by Kilo Company—were due to be overrun by *regimental* assaults that very evening, only a few hours hence.

When the 3rd Marine Division commander heard all the good news late in the afternoon, he decided that nothing would be lost by believing it. We were put on Red Alert—ready to repel boarders.

Though we, the besieged didn't realize it yet, the Siege of Khe Sanh had begun.

CHAPTER 25

I had a first lieutenant assigned to Lima Company in December who was a fallen angel, a pilot trainee who had washed out of flight school. He joined the company very shortly after leaving flight school, with an official but hardly credible military occupational specialty in the infantry. There were several vacant executive-officer billets in the battalion, but this first lieutenant could not be put into one of them until he acquired a little seasoning, to bring him up to a competence level equal to that of a fresh crop of second lieutenants that had arrived recently from the States. I suppose he was assigned to Lima Company because we were closest to the battalion CP.

Since all my rifle platoons were already in the hands of talented second lieutenants, I moved the new first lieutenant in as my Weapons Platoon commander, a billet we rarely covered. He was eager to learn, but I'm not sure his heart was into being a grunt, an infantryman. Nevertheless, after he had been with Lima Company for several weeks, Battalion decided to move him up to vacant exec's billet in Kilo Company, which was on Hill 861. He left for his new assignment on the morning of January 20, several hours before the NVA defector told his interrogator that Hill 861 was due to be overrun that very night.

It turned out that India Company's bloody sweep toward Hill 881N during the morning and afternoon of January 20 was really an engagement with one of the NVA battalions slated to attack Hill 881S that night. The NVA battle plan was upset and the attack on Hill 881S never got off the ground. Not so the NVA regimental assault against Kilo Company, on Hill 861. That quickly developed into a huge fracas as two NVA battalions attacked from out of a thick fog in the dead of night. The initial assault was so devastating that I believe Kilo Company would have broken if the dazed survivors had had anywhere to run.

The NVA had done a masterful job of scouting the Kilo Company position. The first volley of mortar and RPG fire—the latter from virtually within Kilo Company's wire—struck the company's supporting arms, including a 106mm recoilless rifle, a 4.2-inch heavy mortar, and one or two .50-caliber machine guns. The NVA also blasted the Kilo Company CP at the outset, killing the company gunny and seriously wounding the company commander and first sergeant. About the only key player the NVA missed was the company's enlisted artillery FO, who remained in contact with the 1/13 fire direction center and, through them, the Army 175mm guns at Camp Carroll and the Rockpile. Also, the fact that Hill 881S was not hit allowed Captain Bill Dabney, of India Company, to support Kilo from there with his two 81mm mortars, his one 4.2-inch mortar, and the three 105mm howitzers emplaced on his hill.

The fighting along one end of Kilo's infantry line immediately degenerated into a hand-to-hand struggle to the death. The NVA all but won that fight when the rifle platoon that was first contacted gave way under overwhelming pressure.

Though the Kilo CP was hit by RPGs and mortars at the outset, the new company exec, my former weapons officer, was not hurt, and he clung grimly to his post. Unfortunately, he barely knew a soul up there and had only had a brief tour of the lines. I know that a number of the noncoms under his command didn't even know he had arrived, and by then the noncoms were pretty much running the defense of Hill 861.

The new Kilo exec did the best he could, but he was in over his head. He knew it and everyone listening in on the battalion net knew it. He obviously wanted to take charge, but he was effectively in charge of only himself and his radioman. To calm him down, Matt Caulfield started talking to him in an unbelievably gentle voice. However, when Matt was winding down, he decided to finish with a little rah-rah phrase: "Okay, Kilo Five, take the ball and run with it."

Either the lieutenant was still too nervous or there was static on the line, because he didn't hear Matt's close quite right. I almost fell over when I heard him ask, "Did I hear you say 'run,' sir?"

Major Caulfield couldn't grab the microphone fast enough to tell him, "Shit, no! It's just an expression!" As tense as things were, we all had to chuckle.

One of the most inspiring stories I ever heard about Marines in trouble emerged from the carnage of Hill 861. It involved the Kilo Company first sergeant, Bernard Goddard, a tough old bird on his fourth tour with a combat unit in Vietnam.

Top Goddard was in the company CP when it was blasted at the onset of the action, and a piece of shrapnel severed one the major veins carrying blood from his brain. For all practical purposes, Goddard was bleeding to death, but he was too tough to just up and die, so he grabbed a passing corpsman and asked for treatment. The doc thought the first sergeant was a goner and he knew that there were many who could be saved if he could get to them, so he pulled a hemostat from his aid pouch and clamped off the bleeding end of the vein. "Hold it there, First Sergeant. If it slips off, you die," the doc said as he was leaving.

Top Goddard tried to sit where he was, beside the company CP, but the dead gunny was only a few feet away and Goddard couldn't bear to look at him. He finally decided to risk a move over to the 60mm mortars, where at least someone might see him if he lost his grip on the hemostat.

When Goddard got to the mortar pits, he realized that all the young mortarmen were yelling the Marine Corps Hymn at the top of their lungs. They were so charged up that it looked like the mortars were firing on full automatic. As the first sergeant said later, "What the hell could I do after seeing something like that? How could I die?" So, he leaned up against the mortar pit's sandbag wall, took out his pistol, cocked it, and sat there all night, holding the hemostat on the vein to keep from bleeding to death.

Kilo Company held, but it and the NVA who remained in the wire around the hilltop were hors de combat, not much good for anything. There was some talk during the wee hours of scraping together a relief or reinforcement, but the idea was forgotten in the press of events at the combat base. It turned out that there were a few things the NVA defector did not know or did not tell us.

On the morning of January 21, about a half hour before sunup, I was in the company CP, just shooting the bull with Top Mabry and the gunny, when, out of the blue, I heard *boom, boom, boom, boom*—an endless series of detonations coming from someplace very close. Before I could react, I felt the ground shake and heard the distinctive *shweee* of a supersonic 122mm rocket coming in for a landing a split second after it had already landed.

"Jesus," I warned long after it might have done some good, "incoming!"

The gunny and I were in motion through the door before we thought about it, but Top Mabry, who had never been rocketed in his life, just stood there asking, "What the hell's going on?" As I became airborne through the door on my way to our trench, I yelled back over my shoulder, "Jesus Christ, it's incoming." By then, I was hugging good old Mother Earth. "Get down here quick, First Sergeant."

He jumped into the hole just as five or six more rockets arrived nearby. Then five or six more rockets struck the company area. All three of us—me, the gunny, and Top Mabry—were just sitting there, bouncing around in the hole, yelling at one another, "What in the hell is going on? Where the hell did all these rockets come from?"

From the noise in the air and on the tactical radios, which we had left on and which we could hear between detonations, it was obvious that all or most of the combat base was getting hit. At one point, there was an immense explosion that literally moved the ground out from under us, and then a chain of smaller explosions that sounded like rounds cooking off. Indeed, the combat base's main ammunition supply point had been set off by a direct hit and, as we later learned, the whole other end of the combat base was subjected to the fall of hundreds of our own rounds, which had been set on fire and which were detonating on top of and within Marine positions.

Right in the middle of the whole thing, I heard a call from Little John's 2nd Platoon saying, "Shit, we got a casualty, we got a casualty!" The next thing I knew, four Marines started dragging the wounded man past my bunker. As they did, a rocket impacted right on the edge of one of the trenches. The rescuer who was nearest to the detonation was decapitated and a Marine who was in the trench caught a little piece of shrapnel in one of his eyes, which he probably lost.

I don't know how long the rocket barrage went on, but it stopped as suddenly as it had begun. When I was sure it was over, I toured the company position and counted over forty craters. As I looked around farther out, I could see many fires, especially a huge one where the ammunition supply point used to be.

The first thought that popped into my head as I stood there, hands on my hips and jaw on my chest, was that Matt Caulfield's bunkers were completely inadequate. If the NVA were going to be dumping ordnance on us like they had that morning, we needed to get under-ground in a big hurry. Fortunately, as the shock of that immense first bombardment wore off, my superiors at Regiment, Battalion, and even Division were reaching precisely the same conclusion. Where until then we had been at the end of the system that was doling out building materials, we suddenly jumped to the front along with all the other line units.

Now everyone in I Corps knew it—Khe Sanh was under siege.

*B*eginning on the afternoon of January 21, we really started fencing ourselves in. Over the next few days, we erected a cattle fence, which is composed of steel engineer stakes driven into the ground and wire strung three or four strands high—just like a cattle fence. It marked the boundary of our defensive position. Next was a five-meter open area and then a tanglefoot barrier. The tanglefoot was about twenty feet wide and composed of low stakes driven into the ground in an irregular pattern and strung with calf-high barbed wire twisted be-tween stakes at odd, irregular angles. As the name implies, it was meant to trip attackers, or at least slow them by making them watch their feet. Behind the tanglefoot was another five-meter open area backed by a double-apron cattle fence. Then there was another open area and then a pyramid of German Tape concertina wire—a base of two rolls topped by a third roll. Behind that were our front-line positions. Later, when there was more German Tape available than the battalion knew what to do with, we kept extending the base and raising the height of this barrier, until, in some places, it was five or six rolls high. After we strung our own wire, Marine engineers arrived to seed antipersonnel mines throughout the open areas we had left. Similar barriers were built up in other sectors all around the combat base until we had an impressive continuous belt of mines and wire barriers fronting our trenches, bunkers, and fighting holes.

At the outset, we backed the barriers with a line of foxholes, but the plan was to run trenches between the holes and build fighting bunkers at regular intervals along the trench. Eventually, after weeks of continuous excavation, the trench went down to well over man height, so deep that a firing step had to be installed. Later, also, reinforced living bunkers were dug right into the backside of the trenchline.

Within hours of the onset of the immense engineering effort, it became SOP to try and steal extra wire, sandbags, and sundry materials, particularly those which could be turned into effective overhead cover—runway matting, aluminum cargo pallets, lumber, 55-gallon drums, whatever. In no time at all, front-line units were stealing from headquarters units. There was no remorse, no second thoughts; Marines stole anything they could find to strengthen their own positions.

As we wired and dug and mined and strengthened, we started planting Claymore mines, a vicious antipersonnel package consisting of a curved, oblong case with a heavy steel back, a soft plastic front, and a load of hundreds of steel pellets. When fired by means of trip-wire or on command with a battery-charged detonator, the Claymore sprayed the pellets across an expanding arc to the front, like a big shotgun shell.

After we had installed several hundred Claymore mines, we began building fougasse traps. Each of these consisted of a steel 55-gallon drum filled with a mixture of napalm and gasoline that could be set off with an battery-activated Claymore detonator. A fougasse trap is meant to incinerate men moving across a low area or up a slope. In our sector, we ambushed the little draw leading up to the Hanging Tree with several fougasse drums.

Over the first two or three days, as the troops were stealing building materials and digging in between incessant light-to-heavy bombardments, I began thinking about how much ammunition we might need on hand when those two NVA divisions out there finally got around to attacking frontally. Starting then, we began accumulating all the bullets and hand grenades we could lay our hands on by any means. Eventually, every squad leader had a case of ammunition for every weapon within his squad, and the platoon commander had a case of ammunition for every man in his platoon. I have no doubt that most Marines added considerably to this store by means of individual initiative.

At one point, I thought about what would happen if the NVA penetrated the company position in force. So we started to run wire inside the company position in order to channelize attackers along specific routes we could cover from internal positions. Thus, we had the rifle squads in the first line of defense, then wired-in corridors leading to secondary positions manned by the platoon commanders and their little command teams, and then more wire corridors leading to several positions that could be manned by the company command group and the 60mm mortarmen and such other Marines as Battalion doled out to man .50-caliber machine guns and 106mm recoilless rifles. Behind our defensive sector was a secondary line manned part time by H&S Company Marines.

Until the big January 21 rocket attack kicked off the siege, the battalion compound and most of the other parts of the combat base consisted of a lot of tents, mainly GP tents, set up in the open. Though we lived in bunkers just before the rocket attack and moved underground afterward, the company's tents remained where they had been, in the rear of our position. Behind them were the tents belonging to H&S Company, including the huge mess tent, with its rolled-up sides.

We tried to continue eating under canvas for a day or two after the January 21 barrage, but it became obvious that we would have to give it up. We went over to a predominantly C-ration diet, which we eked out primarily by means of stealing. As the company commander, I did not feel I could be involved directly in the rampant illegal activities, but I firmly decided that "foraging" was not immoral, so I foraged. On one successful journey through the old kitchen area, I located a number 10 can of mustard, which I kept hidden in my bunker. The mustard made everything palatable. Mostly I ate sliced pork or sliced beef with mustard on white bread, but I was willing to put a dab or dollop of mustard on just about any C-ration meal or combination—except dessert, of course. Anything to make the C-rats palatable.

*T*he Vietnamese district headquarters located in Khe Sanh ville fell to the NVA during the night of January 21–22, following a brutal two-day siege. Within hours, the Khe Sanh Combat Base was beset by refugees. On the morning of January 22, after the U.S. Army advisers and the survivors of the headquarters element of Marine Combined Action Company Oscar were allowed into the combat base, we found a small number of Vietnamese Regional Forces and Popular Forces soldiers who had not deserted and hundreds of armed Bru irregulars—and their displaced women and children—camped outside the combat-base wire.

Within hours of sunrise, as more refugees arrived, the area to Lima Company's left front, just outside the FOB-3 wire, was crawling with unsavory-looking armed Asians, any number of whom could have been NVA infiltrators bent upon entering the combat base to launch hit-and-run raids or at least to reconnoiter us. Word came down very quickly from Regiment that all the Asians were to be disarmed and evacuated, but the order was soon rescinded because the South Vietnam government could not agree on where to send them.

Long before Regiment spoke and recanted, several of my colleagues and I went down to the FOB to rubberneck. We saw a lot of Bru, whose features and dress were distinctive, and a lot of other types whose roots we could not begin to guess. Many of the Bru men were armed with AK-47s, brand-new folding-stock models in perfect, mint condition. One of the Bru interpreters working for the FOB told us that his fellow tribesmen claimed that they had ambushed an NVA arms convoy on the Ho Chi Minh Trail and had liberated the AK-47s and tons of ammunition. By then, I assumed that anything was possible, for I had heard that the Bru were rabidly anti-Communist.

Many of the Asians sitting in front of the FOB wire had on bloody bandages, and many appeared to be ill. They just sat there, and I wondered what in the world we were going to do with them. After I heard that Regiment had canceled the order to disarm them and evacuate them to the lowlands, I could not see how so many people could be treated and evacuated under siege conditions. I got into a row with an Army officer because, technically, running the Bru and their families—not to mention the lowland Vietnamese—was the whole reason the FOB was up there. I asked, in sheer frustration, "Hey, why don't you take care of those people," but I did not see the Green Berets do anything for them.

All of the ethnic Annamese—lowland Vietnamese—and several hundred of the wounded and sick Bru were evacuated by air that day, but we did not sleep easy that night with so many armed Asians camped out just the other side of our wire. Next morning, I went back with other Marine officers and demanded of the Green Berets, "Why don't you do something for these people?" Many wounded and sick Bru were still there, but I didn't see anyone even handing out food or water. It looked like most of the AK-47–armed Bru were gone, but those who remained were armed with an assortment of old M2 .30-caliber carbines, a few M-60 machine guns, M-79 grenade launchers, and pistols of a dizzying variety.

I gave up trying to talk to the Green Berets, but after awhile I was called back to the camp gate in the Lima Company sector to see what was on the mind of an Army major who had come calling. Apparently, the major had just shown up and ordered several Marines to accompany him as a working party. Since the man was a major, the Marines had obeyed.

By the time I got wind of the major's impressment of Marines, the Marines each had carried several armloads of weapons from the Asian encampment into the Lima Company position. The Marines had put all the weapons into a truck the major had rustled up but, by the time the major checked the truck, there were no weapons in it. When the major saw the empty truck, he went ballistic.

When I got there, the major was yelling, "Where did those Marines go?" Of course, all the Lima Company Marines in the vicinity were saying, "Hell, sir, we don't know. They weren't from our company." These answers only drove the major over the edge; he was absolutely deranged.

"Major," I cut in, "what's the problem here?" He told me what had happened and I said, "Well, Major, I don't know who the hell they were. You should've asked an officer to get you a working party. Then we'd have known who those men were."

The major went away muttering all sorts of dire threats as I stuck my head into the Lima Company CP to speak to Top Mabry. "Lookit, First Sergeant, I want all those goddamn weapons turned in right away." The last thing in the world any of us wanted was a company of Marines armed with weapons they weren't qualified to operate, particularly those old World War II carbines. Even the M-60s and M-79s were suspect; there was no telling what sort of shape they were in or what weird modifications their former owners had performed. As far as I was concerned, the whole cache was just plain dangerous.

It took several hours, but Top Mabry, the gunny, and the other Lima Company noncoms rousted every man in the company and collected scores of M2 carbines, five or six M-60 machine guns, several M-79s, and a whole bunch of weird weapons I couldn't begin to identify. As I was looking at the stash, Top Mabry caught my eye. I knew exactly what was on his mind. I had all the carbines and other junk carted over to the FOB by a work party escorted by the gunny, but I let the top keep the M-60s and the M-79s, as long as he promised to rebuild them to Marine Corps specifications.

The last of the Bru were flown out by the next afternoon. I heard that the big delay in evacuating the Bru was indecision on the part of the civil authorities about what to do with them once they left their home villages on the plateau. The lowland Vietnamese thought all of the mountain tribesmen were subhuman and they didn't want them living outside their own areas.

On January 22, as the Bru flap was just developing, I saw a huge formation of CH-46 helicopters setting down on the helicopter pad, which was just to the rear of the Lima Company right flank. As each serial landed, Marines in full combat gear ran out, formed up, and quickly moved into the main camp, to our rear. Each Marine had a towel around his neck, the distinctive badge of the 1st Battalion, 9th Marines, which had been in so many bloody battles it was calling itself the Walking Dead.

The new arrivals were so effective at getting under cover that I didn't see any signs of them until the next morning, when the entire battalion marched up the road leading out to the Seabee-run Rock Quarry, which was on a hill about a klick to the west of the combat base, right out in front of the Lima Company position.

I had friends in 1/9, so I went out and stood beside the road, asking officers if my friends were around. At length, I saw Captain Fran Schafer, with whom I had served the year before at Marine Barracks, Washington. Fran saw me at the same time I saw him and he stepped out of the column with his hand outstretched. "Hey, Dick, how you doing?" We caught up for ten or fifteen minutes, until the 1/9 rearguard was passing. Fran told me that the whole battalion was moving into the Rock Quarry to establish an outguard position and patrol base for the vulnerable western side of the combat base. That made Lima Company's line a rearguard position, which was okay with me. There's nothing like having a tough, tried infantry battalion between you and the enemy.

I never spoke with Fran Schafer again. In late March, on his last day before rotating to a safe job in the rear, several of his Marines were struck down in a rocket attack. Fran went out to help bring them in, but a follow-on bombardment killed him and one or two other rescuers. I was told by a friend who went to see Fran off from the Regimental Aid Station that, except for a little piece of shrapnel embedded in his head, Fran didn't have a mark on him, that he looked like he was sleeping.

*I*n addition to the rockets, 120mm mortars, and a growing assortment of artillery—including 152mm howitzers fired from within nearby
Laos—the NVA quickly moved 60mm and 82mm mortars and 57mm
recoilless rifles into trenches very close to the combat base and fired
them at odd but frequent intervals. Everyone quickly developed his
own variation on what we started calling the Khe Sanh Shuffle or the
Khe Sanh Quickstep, from which we could launch ourselves toward
cover at the mere *pop* of a mortar round.

Nearly everybody walked around with his helmet underneath an
arm, to improve hearing. Typically, everyone had an ear cocked
toward the west, toward Laos, where most of the NVA artillery was
set in. Our senses developed overnight: You'd be standing around
talking to someone who also had his helmet beneath his arm, until you
or the other man said, "Shhh" or "Stop talking." It got to be automatic; everyone stopped talking and cocked an ear to the west. If
nothing more was heard after a few seconds, the conversation picked
up right where it had left off. If there was "something" in the air,
everyone in the neighborhood ducked for cover. If I heard nothing but
saw anyone suddenly change direction and head for cover, I headed for
cover, too. It wasn't just me; everyone did it.

Our only effective early-warning system came compliments of the
India and Mike Marines up on Hill 881S, which was the nearest of all

the Marine outposts to the main NVA artillery positions around Co Roc Mountain, inside Laos. The men on 881S usually heard the *boom* of 152mm, 130mm, and 120mm guns, and 120mm mortars as they were being fired. They kept an open line to the regimental combat operations center so the familiar call of "Arty! Arty! Arty! Co Roc!"—which we also heard on the battalion radio—could be passed to a Marine who then activated the base siren. The warning afforded everyone about three extra seconds to find cover, which was the margin between life and death in hundreds of cases. Since we had direct access to the battalion net, we heard the warning as it was being broadcast. Our response got to be Pavlovian; the first syllable sent all hands rocketing for cover.

All kinds of stuff was reaching us from out of the sky, and only some of it was aimed at us by the enemy, as I learned when I took a call from my 3rd Platoon commander, Lieutenant Dan Madison. The conversation began with Dan's call of, "Hey, Skipper, one of my squads is going to surrender." To which I replied, "Okay, Dan, tell me what the joke is." He started laughing and said, "You gotta come over and see this." It turned out that a truck being slung in by a CH-53 heavy transport helicopter had gotten loose right over the company area and had plummeted several hundred feet to the ground. It landed about ten feet from one of the new underground squad bunkers and caused a great deal of confusion for a few moments. When the Marines looked up, they found that the truck had been crushed into a little package, only about three feet high. When Dan Madison ran out to see what was going on, one of his Marines told him, "My God, Lieutenant, if the NVA are throwing *trucks* at us, we're gonna surrender."

Just going to the head presented major obstacles. I believe the NVA recoilless riflemen and mortarmen who worked close in toward the combat-base wire had the shitters all scoped out, but they pretty much withheld their fire during periods of low visibility. You had to time it just right to take advantage of the thick fog that settled in over Khe Sanh nearly every night. The idea was to take a crap in the dark of night or in the morning before the ground fog burned off. After a very short time, our bodily functions kind of organized themselves around the safest schedule. Even under cover of darkness or fog, speed was of the essence. Before I got the hang of things, I was caught in the shitter by random artillery and rocket salvos a few times with my pants around my ankles.

At night, the fog usually was so thick that you couldn't see two inches in front of your face. However, it was long-standing tradition for the company commander to walk the company lines once or twice each night to make sure everybody who was supposed to be awake was indeed awake.

Early on the morning of January 22, a little before sunrise, I was stalking the 2nd Platoon sector alone. There was a heavy dew and it was quite chilly. Most of the Marines I had seen and visited with on that tour were wrapped up to their ears in their poncho liners, but I eventually came across a foxhole in which both Marines had their poncho liners pulled up over their heads. One of the Marines, whom I assumed was off duty, was curled up on the deck, and the other, whom I assumed was on watch, was sort of leaning against the side of the hole. It didn't matter if he was awake because, if he was, he sure couldn't see anything through that poncho liner.

I unslung my rifle and banged the muzzle across the top of the sentry's helmet, just to see how he would react. The contact of metal on metal produced a loud *clang,* sort of like a broken bell. The Marine stiffened to an upright position and started shaking. Then, in a real calm voice, he said, "Who's there?" I almost broke up, but I chewed him out for being asleep on post and instructed him to report to the first sergeant for office hours.

The next night, while everyone was perhaps overly alert to potential danger from the scores of villainous-looking Asians outside our wire, I got to show the whole company everything it needed to know about night vigilance. That night, I selected Corporal Brady, the mortar-section leader, to accompany me on my rounds. It was absolutely white out and we had to feel our way along the trail that ran along the Lima Company lines with the toes of our boots. From the start, we had no idea where we were. Only a little way along, I suddenly felt a tripwire rubbing against my ankle through the canvas material of my combat boot. I tried to stop, but my brain was a little behind the momentum of my body; I couldn't quite make it. Fortunately, the tripwire activated only an illumination grenade.

The illume went off and silhouetted Brady and me in the open—in front of the developing trenchline, which was still mainly foxholes. Brady instantly jumped to the ground and starting making like a gopher, but I remained on my feet, loudly whispering, "Don't shoot, don't shoot, don't shoot! It's me, it's me." I didn't want to look any more suspicious than I already did.

Through the piercing glare of the illume, I managed to make out that we were ten yards directly in front of a machine-gun bunker. I held up my hands, squinted at the bunker, and kept whispering. Finally, a voice from within the bunker replied: "Come on in, come on in. I know who you are."

Brady got up and sort of smoothed out the front of his utilities, as if he was smoothing out his dignity, and we walked in through the diminishing glow of the illume grenade.

I asked the machine gunner when it had dawned on him that the man in the limelight was me. When he replied, "I recognized your voice right away, sir," I asked why it had taken so long for him to say so. There was a long, embarrassed pause and a few furtive glances between him and his assistant gunner. Then the story came out. The gunner, who was on watch, had indeed recognized me right away, but his assistant, who was pulled from sleep by the sudden flare of light and my loud whispering, took a few moments to clear the cobwebs from his head. Meantime, he tried to do what he had been trained to do; he tried to push the balky gunner aside and start firing the machine gun at the human form he saw ten yards in front of the bunker. The delay had been the time it took the gunner to punch his assistant fully awake.

I grabbed Brady and we felt our way back to the company CP. That was the last time I tried to make my rounds in the fog.

The NVA lieutenant who had defected on January 20 was absolutely correct in every detail he offered his interrogators. Hill 861 had indeed been attacked that very night, and 881S would have been had not India Company spoiled the attack earlier in the day. And the lieutenant, who had been an antiaircraft battery executive officer, was dead right about the NVA's plan to bag our airplanes as they came in to land on the airstrip or support the combat base with air strikes.

In the middle of the afternoon of January 21, we heard distant, echoing *booms* and looked to the south in time to see several jets streaking down over the old French fort near Khe Sanh ville—which no one had yet told us was surrounded and in imminent danger of falling to the NVA (and which fell later that day.) As usual, we all stopped what we were doing to stand up and rubberneck.

All of a sudden, my new artillery FO said, "Skipper, what the hell are those black puffs?" Before I could register on them—they were 37mm antiaircraft rounds blossoming in the sky—the lieutenant exclaimed, "Jeez, is that aircraft going in?" One of our airplanes was indeed trailing a thick plume of greasy black smoke as he dropped in around the west side of the combat base. At the last minute, we saw the pilot eject and the parachute open.

Within a matter of moments, several Huey helicopters scrambled from the Khe Sanh helo pad and streaked down toward the French fort. When the Hueys returned, one of them had the downed jet's pilot dangling on the end of a jungle penetrator.

Two days later, January 23, the ridgeline a few thousand meters to our right front was being bombed. All of a sudden, as the aircraft dived in, I could hear the throaty roar of heavy machine guns. Immediately, distinctive green NVA .51-caliber tracer was reaching out toward the fighter-bombers as they completed their runs. One of the bombers was a propeller-driven South Vietnamese Air Force AD Skyraider, nicknamed Flying Dumptruck because it could carry so much ordnance. I believe the AD pilot got target fixation, because he stayed in his dive far too long. Then, sure enough, the green tracer connected with the silver AD and the AD wobbled and tumbled in. The Hueys scrambled and braved the NVA machine-gun fire as the other bombers returned to suppress the ground fire, but the helos came back empty-handed.

Later on January 23, I was watching another bombing mission by A-4 Skyhawks out along a valley just in front the 1015 ridgeline when I heard .51-caliber machine guns as they followed the A-4s through their runs. All of a sudden, one of the A-4s that was trying to pull up out of its bombing kind of curved up and away toward the combat base. As the jet turned parallel to the edge of the plateau off our northern perimeter line, I saw the silvery glint as the pilot popped the canopy, followed by the black form of the pilot as he ejected. He bailed out so low that his chute barely had time to open. The plane kept angling down and eventually exploded against the ground in a huge, fiery ball. Meantime, the pilot fell into some brush right at the edge of the drop-off and the whole combat base thundered with cheers and applause. I later heard that the 1/26 battalion surgeon and a staff officer drove an ambulance out from the perimeter and rescued the pilot, a Marine major who was unhurt but mightily embarrassed about being shot down, as he put it, "in front of five thousand Marines."

Among many strange and thrilling incidents that first week of the siege, the Payroll Caper stands out.

It was SOP in those days that everybody got paid twice a month regardless of the proverbial hell or high water. We had not yet mentally adjusted to the siege when we got word that our payroll was ready and could be picked up from the regimental paymaster. As usual, the junior lieutenant, the 3rd Platoon's Dan Madison, was designated company pay officer.

In those days, we got paid in cold cash. The ritual was to call each man by name, pay him, and have him sign the company roster acknowledging he had received his money. It was a lengthy process, but unshakable in the face of the U.S. military's oldest tradition.

So there we were, right in the middle of the first week of the siege, and Dan Madison shows up with a bag full of U.S. currency—five-, ten-, and twenty-dollar bills. By law, we had to pay the troops right away, so Dan and the company clerk set up in front of a half-finished underground bunker, broke the bills down into neat piles on a two-by-four timber, and sent out the word for the troops to collect their pay.

There was one small problem. Between the time Dan and the clerk starting setting up and the time they ordered "Pay Call," the combat base came under intermittent shelling from NVA artillery and mortars. It wasn't a major shelling, but it was ongoing and it had our attention.

Right off, it was obvious that we couldn't assemble the entire company, so we confabulated for a bit and decided that we could safely call up one fire team at a time. We decided to start at one end of the company bubble and work our way around during lulls in the shelling, which were frequent and lengthy.

The first fire team spread out under cover and Dan and the clerk went through the laborious process of calling out a man's name, identifying him, counting out the cash, confirming the count, and getting a signature on the roster. As each man completed the ritual, he was sent back to his squad's position.

We had a pretty good run to start with, finishing up a platoon and a squad from another platoon. Then there was a little flurry of incoming and everything stopped. On and off, it took us three or four times the usual time to complete the payroll ritual. Now and again, the incoming erupted with such sudden intensity that everyone involved ducked and covered, with no thought about all the cash that was lying around on that two-by-four. A few times, piles of bills got brushed to the ground and scattered.

When it was over, Lieutenant Madison came up several hundred dollars short. Who knew where the shortfall was? Dan admitted that a few close calls had rattled him, so his counting might have been less than exact. Maybe a few bills got blown away in the confusion. Maybe a dishonest Marine had taken the opportunity to grab a little extra hazardous-duty pay while everyone else was scrambling for cover.

Another ironclad tradition is that the pay officer who comes up short pays the shortfall out of his own pocket. Dan was a family man who really needed every cent of his pay, a fact that was well known in the close confines of the company. There was no way he could come up with over two hundred dollars in cash. Well, as soon as the troops heard about it, within literally a matter of minutes, passers-by had dropped bills amounting to nearly five hundred dollars.

When I heard what the troops had done, I hit the roof. There clearly were extenuating circumstances for the shortfall, so I thundered, "Bullshit, we're not going to do it this way. I'm going to write this up and we're going to write off the debit on the books." True to my word, I wrote up a detailed narrative report about the heavy incoming and recommended that the books simply be cleared. We gave all the donations back to the troops and closed our books on the matter.

About two years later, I ran into Dan Madison at Quantico. As we talked, he asked, "Do you remember the payroll incident?" I sure did. I was not surprised to learn that, two years later, the Marine Corps was still after Dan for two hundred dollars to reimburse the government. I wrote another long explanation and finally used every highly placed connection I had to get the shortfall successfully wiped off the books. The fact is that, even in those days, two hundred dollars wouldn't buy a belt of .50-caliber ammunition.

A new captain joined the battalion during the first week of the siege, which happened to coincide with the end of my sixth full month as the commander of Lima Company. I would have stayed forever, but it was decided over my head that I should turn Lima Company over to the new captain and assume duties as the battalion assistant operations officer—callsign Three-Alpha.

Following a last tour of the lines, in a little ceremony in the Lima Company CP bunker, I turned my command over to Captain Bill Hurley, cleared out my gear—including my number 10 can of mustard— and walked down to the battalion CP bunker to go to work as Matt Caulfield's assistant.

CHAPTER 27

My first weeks' work at the battalion combat operations center—COC—was routine. The entire combat base and the hill positions were hit at all hours of the day and night by various combinations of mortar, artillery, rocket, and recoilless-rifle fire. As we sustained an unending chain of casualties—on January 31, for example, Mike-6 was severely wounded in the leg by a sniper as he was checking the troops along the Hill 881S trenchline—we burrowed in deeper and made the best of life.

The COC's duties had been expanded a week before my reassignment because of the addition of Echo Company, 2/26, to our operational control. Echo Company was sent up to Hill 861A—directly across from Kilo Company's position on Hill 861—and ordered to dig in to observe and interdict a possible route into the base that had not been covered earlier. It is possible that I was drawn into the COC to man a billet a little beneath my rank and experience because of the battalion's expanded size and the widespread nature of our deployment—for we oversaw four companies manning three isolated hills and one reinforced company manning three hundred meters of the Khe Sanh perimeter line. Another good reason might have been the decision to split the COC into two parts. The Alpha command element—Lieutenant Colonel Alderman and Major Matt Caulfield—remained in the big main CP bunker, but I was detailed with the exec, Major Joe Loughran, to establish and man a Bravo COC in another bunker. The thought was that we could keep the battalion running in the event the Alpha COC was disabled by a direct hit. The arrangement also provided us with a convenient means to split shifts. Each COC and shift had its own artillery and air advisers, radiomen, and clerks.

Joe Loughran was a hell of a guy, a bluff, smiling Irishman with an Irish temper that was bound to flare up at the oddest times. He had a bottle of Irish whiskey he must have brought from home. Every day, when we called it quits and turned the watch over to the Alpha COC, he hauled out the bottle and poured out a small thimbleful of whiskey for each of us. I have never been a drinker, but I enjoyed the little ritual jolt at the close of each tour.

I had often heard it said that soldiers who stay in trenches too long develop a trench mentality, that they no longer want to go out in open areas. We had to watch out for that, but there was no effective means for doing so. The four Marine infantry battalions at Khe Sanh could not go out and attack two NVA divisions, and the onset of the great Communist Tet Offensive in the lowlands during the last four days of January 1968 prevented the commitment of larger Marine or Army units. The plan that was being developed for Khe Sanh was a full-blown demonstration of the set-piece strategy. It became our job to sit on the hill outposts and in the combat base and draw the NVA within range of our guns or into areas where our air support could get at them. We were the bait.

We lived in trenches so much that we hesitated to get out and around. I could feel the hesitation myself. I traveled everywhere I could in the trenches, even to the head. Pretty soon, we had trenches that went to all our positions. Everyone eventually developed a fear of getting up out of the ground. We did when we had to, but we always listed toward the nearest underground cover—the Khe Sanh Shuffle.

We were always measuring our cover against the effects of direct hits on other positions. One day, Major Loughran came into our little three-sandbag-thick Bravo COC and said, "Hey, Dick, a 152mm shell landed on the hard surface of the all-weather Seabee road. Go down and take a look at it; see what we've got to do to dig in." I walked down the road and found the hole quickly enough. When I did, I came up short and just stood there, staring. It was a godawful huge hole, big enough to park our whole bunker in. It was easily eight feet deep and ten feet in diameter. I couldn't imagine digging effective cover against a 152mm round with entrenching tools and stolen building materials. After a few minutes of utter depression, I shuffled back to the little bunker I shared with the exec and said, in all seriousness, "Major, I think the best thing to do is surrender."

We got right to work expanding our bunker, using the spoil to fill sandbags. We built an outer blast wall, three sandbags thick, with an open space between it and our bunker wall. We added a trench along the inner wall of the bunker, deep enough to hide out in. Then we started adding overhead cover, a process that never abated. I hated being in the ground, was afraid of winding up beneath a collapsed overhead, but I was determined to gut it out. It obviously was better to have more overhead cover than less, though we started hearing stories of otherwise unscathed Marines who were being pulled lifeless from beneath blast-collapsed overheads. We also heard stories of miraculous escapes because of sufficient overhead cover.

Early on the evening of February 4, we heard machine guns firing on Hill 861A, which was occupied by Echo Company, 2/26. This had been going on night after night for a week, and Majors Loughran and Caulfield were about fed up with it. Echo-6 had a splendid reputation for hunting down VC in the lowlands—mainly around and inside the royal tombs near my old Seabee rock-crusher position—but he was breaking rules 3/26 had learned and imposed. The big fear was that the NVA were goading Echo Company into firing at night so they, the NVA, could plot in the positions of Echo Company's weapons bunkers. Matt Caulfield especially was bent out of shape at Echo-6. That evening, I heard him say in exasperation, "Look, I don't want you firing the guns anymore. But now that you've fired them, move the goddamn things so they don't get pinned down or picked off." But Echo Company was building the 861A position from scratch, so they didn't have anywhere to move the guns; there were not yet enough bunkers built.

At around 0400, February 5, I was standing my watch in the Bravo COC, shooting the breeze with Matt Caulfield. All of a sudden, we heard a long burst of firing off in the distance. Then the Echo Company battalion radioman reported, "We're being overrun."

That got my heart going. Everybody dropped what they were doing as Matt yelled into the microphone, "What the hell's going on? What can we get for you?"

As they had at the onset of the attack against Kilo Company on January 20, the NVA had already penetrated almost all the way into Echo's wire and had blasted every known—make that every—weapons position on 861A's narrow nose. They got the M-60, 60mm mortar, and 106mm recoilless rifle on that side of the perimeter in the first volley and followed through with a stupendous battalion infantry assault that swept up to the crest of the hill, right past two other 60mm mortar pits, almost to the company CP. Echo Company Marines with whom I spoke later said that the first inkling they had that the North Vietnamese were inside their positions was when enemy soldiers swarming along the back side of the trenches began shooting their buddies in the back.

Echo-6 was stubborn about stopping the unnecessary nocturnal shooting, but he was a great man in a clutch situation. As Matt Caulfield turned the fire-support problem over to the regimental fire support coordination center, which called in 105s and 175s and even a B-52 strike, Echo-6 sealed off the penetration and started retaking lost sections of this trenchline. The massive pinpoint artillery and air response sealed the NVA breakthrough from the rear—prevented a follow-on battalion from scaling the hill—while Echo Company fought back against the badly hurt NVA battalion that had penetrated its position. This is not to say the bitter fighting was not touch-and-go, for we almost lost Echo Company, but the survivors held until dawn, threw the NVA off the hill, and even weathered a follow-on attack the NVA launched through the thick morning fog.

The February 5 attack against Echo Company was the last time the NVA tried to take one of the hill outposts. It was estimated that they lost nearly two battalions in strength on Hill 861A, about the same number of men we believed they had lost on January 20 on adjacent Hill 861. However, having its ass handed to it was never reason enough for the North Vietnamese Army to back off. Two nights later, they achieved a major victory.

The earliest American presence on the Khe Sanh plateau had been a Special Forces camp established in 1962 on the site of the combat base. In 1966, the Special Forces detachment had been displaced by a battalion of Marines and had set up a new camp at Lang Vei, about eight klicks to the west, toward Laos, right on Highway 9.

The Lang Vei Special Forces camp routinely supported forays by Bru volunteers—and, undoubtedly, Green Berets—into Laos and, possibly, into nearby North Vietnam. There was a vague long-standing promise that the Marines at Khe Sanh would send a relief force to Lang Vei if it was endangered, but the promise was not possible to fulfill once we were besieged. If anything, we figured that Lang Vei would be threatened by NVA whose real intention was drawing the Marine relief force into a massive ambush.

On the night of February 7, Lang Vei was overrun by an NVA assault regiment, supported by a company of light PT-76 armored amphibious reconnaissance vehicles—easily mistaken for tanks. The 26th Marines regimental commander refused to dispatch the relief force, though he did provide some artillery support. The NVA who overran Lang Vei slipped away by dawn and Green Berets from FOB-3 arriving in Marine-piloted Hueys reclaimed the camp and rescued the American survivors.

After Lang Vei, the various Marine battalion and regimental CPs were going bonkers trying to respond to the armor threat that had been unveiled at Lang Vei—the first time the NVA had *ever* committed armor inside South Vietnam. Though we knew we were facing light, thinly armored PT-76 tanks, reports from Lang Vei and aerial observers—or maybe only rumors—indicated that there were swarms of them.

In all of Khe Sanh, including 1/9's Rock Quarry position, we had just five M-48 tanks with one 90mm gun apiece and five Ontos tank-destroyers, each with six 106mm recoilless rifles. Beyond that, a few old 3.5-inch bazookas some battalions still retained, and LAAW light antitank assault weapons, we had no real means to defeat armor. However, faced with a demonstrable threat, we had to start inventing ways to defeat a tank attack. It was left to each battalion to find its own solution.

At length Matt Caulfield suggested, "Why don't we form antiarmor assault teams." So we put out the call for volunteers to stock extra LAAWs in their fighting holes. Then someone purloined a flame-thrower, and several Lima Company 60mm mortarmen volunteered to attack tanks with it. I understand that 1/9 got some magnetic antitank mines and talked volunteers into agreeing to stand in head-high holes in front of the wire so the mines could be affixed to tanks passing overhead—good, useful ideas like that. Damn if volunteers didn't turn up to man every hare-brained scheme!

On February 15, Charlie Company, 1/26's massively reinforced but nonetheless above-ground CP bunker took a direct large-caliber hit. The company gunny was killed, the company CO was severely wounded, and the 1/26 battalion sergeant major was mortally injured. Any complacency we had acquired about our own bunkers was erased and a spate of digging and piling dirt ensued.

On February 23, just as the new round of building was winding down, the NVA gunners opened what was to become the heaviest one-day bombardment of the siege. Between 1100 and 1700, the NVA hit us with 1,307 artillery rounds and rockets.

It was a devastating day—not in terms of casualties, which were blessedly few, but in terms of having to take an hours-long shelling we couldn't do anything about. We just sat in our bunkers and took it. Even our artillerymen, who normally braved incoming fire to respond—at least for the sake of morale—wisely stayed safely in their bunkers that afternoon.

By sunset, I was physically and emotionally drained. All I wanted to do was go to sleep. The adrenalin had been going through me for hours and I was about to fall over.

At last, the bombardment died way and I walked outside, through the remains of the trees that had once shielded the battalion CP from view. I meandered through the trees, looking at the stars and feeling life return to a landscape that resembled the surface of the moon. Then I went back inside and drew two cups of coffee from the perpetual urn. As I was handing one cup to Matt Caulfield, I heard an observer up on Hill 881S announce on the battalion net, "Arty! Arty! Arty! Co Roc." I instinctively hunched my head into my shoulders and wondered half aloud, "So where's this one going to hit?"

The next thing I knew, there was a tremendous explosion and all the lights went out. The bunker instantly was filled with dust and there was an immediate dead silence.

I think I was the first to speak—one of those dumb questions: "Is everybody okay?" It was dead dark in there, so I was immensely relieved to hear people say "Yeah, I'm okay," and "I'm fine" and "No sweat." Everyone had had his brains rattled, but no one had been hurt.

There was just the one round. Until someone got our generator going again, there was nothing doing inside, so we all went out to see what had hit us.

The round had come in at an angle, right between the trees, right through the tent we had erected to camouflage the bunker. It had hit the one-inch plywood outer shell and detonated—just the way we had hoped. There were six feet of earth, wood, rocks, and metal between us and the explosion, but the blast had blown off two feet of all those materials and had taken down the three-ply blast walls we had erected around the bunker.

Two Marines who had been exiting a tent just across the way were saved by the blast walls, which directed the full force of the blast outward in another direction. We found them flopping around on the ground, stunned but unscathed except for a few tiny shrapnel wounds, hardly more than scratches.

We had taken a direct hit from a 152mm or 130mm round, but no one was permanently injured. It was a miracle of foresight and faith in our two main gods, Dirt and More Dirt.

The next day, Joe Loughran and I were rubbernecking outside the Alpha COC, behind the inboard side of the blast wall, joking about this and that, when a small round—maybe a .51-caliber round—impacted within a few feet of us. I heard it go *thunk* and saw the dirt fly up. I looked at Joe and he looked at me, and we both burst out laughing. We were out of control for many minutes.

During the early part of the siege we got a hold of a book called *Hell in a Very Small Place,* by Bernard Fall, the military scholar who had named the Street Without Joy—and who had been killed there while he was out with a Marine patrol. *Hell in a Very Small Place* is the classic study of the French Army during the siege of Dienbienphu. For us, the story was especially poignant because the press was comparing Khe Sanh to Dienbienphu every day we were there. As we read Dr. Fall's book, we could look outside and see the very same tactics developing on the North Vietnamese side of no-man's-land. For example, the book mentioned how the North Vietnamese dug their trenchlines and tunnels right up to the wire of the French outposts. That was what happened at Khe Sanh.

I was monitoring the tactical air net one day and I could hear the pilots describe the trenches they were finding. It was like listening to a lecture on eighteenth-century siege warfare. After that, we could see flight after flight of fixed wing trying to bomb the NVA out of the trenches with napalm and high-explosive bombs and rockets. Yet, day after day, the news from every quadrant was that the trenches were getting closer to the combat-base wire, particularly along the open stretch of ground southeast of the combat base. We continued to read of such things in *Hell in a Very Small Place,* and, as we lived them at Khe Sanh, it became very eerie.

Fortunately, our humor never quite flagged. After weeks of reading about the trenches at Dienbienphu and hearing descriptions of the trenches at Khe Sanh, we started kidding, "Jesus Christ, skip all the middle part; what happens at the end of this book?"

Unfortunately, the end of *Hell in a Very Small Place* describes the surrender of the French at Dienbienphu, so we started kidding that one day we were going to wake up and find that the North Vietnamese had erected their own barbed-wire fence and watchtowers and that we would be ensconced in the Khe Sanh prison camp.

We had a little sign over the Alpha COC that was blank on one side and said on the other, "Tonight's the Night." On those nights we expected to get an infantry assault against our position, we turned the sign over so it could be read. After awhile, it remained undisturbed, with the message side out.

When we heard scuttlebutt that the NVA were digging tunnels beneath the combat base itself, we started warning one another, "Hey, listen very carefully because you're going to be sitting there someday and all of a sudden Nguyen is going to tunnel right up underneath your chair."

It was no joke. Our artillery couldn't even reach their artillery, which was longer-ranged and so well camouflaged that our aerial observers couldn't even find it. And they held several of the dominant ridgelines, from which their FOs could see everything we did inside the combat base and atop several of the hill outposts. They had also cut Highway 9, so everything we needed had to be flown in—all our food, ammunition, equipment, reinforcements, replacements, and medical supplies. All our casualties had to be flown out at enormous extra risk to life and limb, and even the Marines who were rotating home had to risk their lives to be gone. So many planes and helos were hit that they eventually stopped landing C-130s altogether, and I understand that some short-timers refused to fly out, which about says it all.

*T*he decisive support the Marines had at Khe Sanh that the French had not had at Dienbienphu was air support. We had an artillery battalion inside the combat base and the 175mm guns firing at long range from Camp Carroll and the Rockpile, but the real factor in our being able to hold was unprecedentedly massive air support of every type.

Airplanes—including daily parachute drops—and helicopters kept us supplied at livable levels, and they brought in reinforcements and carried out our wounded and dead. Helicopters kept the hill outposts supplied and reinforced, though at exceptionally grave risk. Fighters and fighter-bombers from all the services, but mainly from Marine squadrons, were virtually always on call during daylight hours, ready and willing to handle any target, any sighting, any situation down to within a mere few hundred meters of any of our positions. At night, Marine air ran radar-guided bombing missions against targets identified and pinpointed by radio intelligence, infra-red aerial snooping, photo reconnaissance, or any of a number of exotic supersecret electronic listening devices that had been seeded along NVA trails from within Laos to the base wire.

At any hour of the day or night, two or more B-52 heavy bombers from as far away as Guam, each carrying scores of 500-pound bombs, arrived at such altitudes as to be invisible and carried out "Arclight" missions, saturation bombings of radar-designated kilometer-square areas. So many bombs fell in so small an area that they created brief electrical storms, hence the name, Arclight. NVA survivors of Arclights who were captured or surrendered consistently claimed that whole NVA battalions literally vanished in the maelstrom. As the NVA trenches closed on the combat base from the southeast, Arclight missions were run to within a thousand meters—and, later, to within five hundred meters—of the wire. They scared the hell out of us, and bounced us around a lot, but not one of the bombs ever went astray.

Every airplane in I Corps that came back from any mission anywhere with any bombs aboard showed up over Khe Sanh so our air controllers could use up the ordnance. I know of cases where, in the absence of enough bombs, the controllers asked Marine fighter-bombers to drop their reserve fuel pods on NVA positions and then follow up with strafing runs aimed at setting the fuel afire with tracer rounds. During the day at least, the screeching of jets diving on NVA positions was never-ending.

The 105mm artillery batteries comprising reinforced 1/13 were composed of the bravest Marine artillerymen I have ever heard or read about. Though they knew their 105s and a few extra 155s could not reach the NVA 130mm and 152mm guns based in Laos, those gunners stood tall in the face of incoming and fired on targets they could reach—NVA machine-gun positions, NVA 57mm recoilless rifle positions, NVA 60mm and 82mm mortar positions, NVA .51-caliber and 37mm antiaircraft positions, the expanding NVA trench systems—anything we asked them to hit. It was very important for us to hear the sounds of the outgoing; it kept us sane, kept us in the game. They were all heroes.

The Marine helicopter pilots and crewmen were all heroes, too. Dubbed "mortar magnets" from the first day of the siege, the helicopters that arrived at the Khe Sanh helo pad or any of the hill outposts invariably drew heavy fire. Many of them were shot down or badly damaged and many pilots and crewmen were killed or injured. But they never faltered, hardly ever aborted, particularly if they were coming in to pick up wounded Marines. It says something about courage when they were often guided into one of the Hill 881S landing zones by radiomen on the ground who used the wreckage of a downed helicopter as a turning reference.

Something also needs to be said about the young enlisted Marines who guided the helos in to the hill outposts. They suffered enormous casualties because they often had to stand their ground in the face of intense .51-caliber or mortar and rocket detonations to guide helicopters in and out of tight landing zones. One of the bravest of the brave was Lance Corporal Terry Smith, who had served so nobly with Lima Company during the big September battle and who volunteered to go up to Hill 881S to help there. Terry was always in the thick of it, until one day he stood his ground in the landing zone a little too long and was mortally wounded. He earned a posthumous Silver Star and, many years later, in 1988, the new gymnasium building at Headquarters, Marine Corps, was named in his honor.

The NVA became so good at hitting the helicopters sustaining the hill positions that we had to up the ante with what we called Super Gaggles. A dozen or more fully loaded helos would hover at the edge of the plateau while every available form of fire support—fixed-wing, armed Hueys, artillery, mortars, machine guns, whatever—pounded and pummeled known NVA gun, mortar, rocket, and observation positions in the hills around every one of the outposts. When the NVA gunners and FOs had their brains scrambled and were hugging Mother Earth, the fire lifted briefly and the helos darted in to the one or two outposts for which they were bound. Then, as the helos were unloaded, the intense fire support resumed until it had to be cut off again to let the helos get away. Each Super Gaggle required major planning and flawless timing, so they were not run as often as we would have liked, but they took up the immense shortfall in the supplies the hill outposts required to stay viable. Naturally, medevacs and other on-call helo missions had to be handled the old, dangerous way, without all that fire support.

Aside from the incessant incoming and slow accumulation of casualties, the factor that did the most to keep morale low was eating C rations for every meal, day in and day out. The battalion was blessed with a smart, resourceful mess sergeant—Gunnery Sergeant Billy Ray, known to all as Ptomaine-6—but Gunny Ray's best efforts were done in by the sheer volume and unpredictability of the NVA fire plan. Early on, Gunny Ray oversaw the excavation of a bunker that matched the battalion CP bunker in depth and strength. After the kitchen force went underground, Gunny Ray was capable of producing banquets, but he lacked supplies—it was easier to fly in cases of C rations than anything else—and he could not be sure his hot meals could be delivered to H&S and Lima companies. They certainly could not be lifted to the hill outposts. So, after several heart-wrenching letdowns, Ptomaine-6 got going on the next best thing. Whenever he could get flour and sugar—which was suspiciously often—he produced mounds of cookies and cakes, which were distributed far and wide. The C rations we lived on were pure puke, but the fresh cookies and cakes were pure heaven.

One day we got the word that the combat base had received an air drop of Coca-Cola. It worked out that every man in the combat base rated one can of Coke. They passed out the warm soda all right, but we had to pay dime apiece. What bullshit!

They also flew in what we called SP packs, which were filled with health and comfort items such as candy, cigarettes, shaving cream, toothbrushes, and toothpaste. According to long-standing directives, each SP pack was supposed to last one platoon for twenty days. We needed anything for a lift, but the good old Marine Corps stuck right to the schedule.

Even getting replacement socks was an ordeal. I understand that no new socks ever reached the hill outposts, and I know that every sock in one load that was passed out inside the combat base had stamped across the heels, "U.S. Army rejects."

We got C rations and bullets in ample quantity, but not much else. Some of the extra goodies we did get bordered on the ridiculous. A special lift of ice cream, a touching gift from one of the Marine air groups, melted on the runway either because no one wanted to get killed retrieving it or because no one could figure out a fair way to get some to everyone—as in, If everyone doesn't get his fair share, no one gets any.

All this was simply great for the morale.

We had scout dogs at Khe Sanh. Before the siege began in earnest, they were used to patrol the wire or accompany reconnaissance patrols into the jungle. A dog has a very sensitive nose, so we really felt safe with them out on the lines. Eventually, we had five or six dogs, and they all happened to live in the 3/26 CP area.

Unfortunately, the dogs were kept at Khe Sanh a little too long. I'm sure no one thought to evacuate them. As the siege deepened, we found out that either the tension that was communicated from Marines or the incoming itself started sending the dogs over the edge. They spent all their time howling and crapping all over themselves. Finally, someone thought of evacuating them, and it was done.

When I heard that the dogs were gone, I figured, what the hell, I'd do the same thing. When I told the battalion surgeon that I had begun howling at the moon and crapping all over myself, he told me to knock it off and clean up my act. They sure as hell didn't evacuate me.

We suffered casualties. One day, one of the battalion radiomen said, "I gotta go to the head." His relief, who happened to be standing around doing nothing, took over for him and he walked out. After a long interval, someone said, "Hey, where the hell is the duty radioman?" We couldn't figure out where. It turned out that the Marine had stepped out of the bunker just as incoming rounds hit around the CP. He was wounded and evacuated, and we didn't even know it until we had turned the place upside down.

Our battalion supply officer, who was stationed safely in the rear, at Dong Ha, called one day and said he was being transferred and he wanted to fly up to say good-bye to one and all. Well, no one in his right mind just flew up to Khe Sanh unless he had to; half the replacements stampeding out of helicopters each day never made it off the helo pad in one piece. As soon as Major Loughran heard the lieutenant say he wanted to come, he radioed Dong Ha and told him, "Don't come up here. There's no reason to. We appreciate your sincerity, but we know you only want to say good-bye, so don't come up here. That's an order." The lieutenant ignored the warning and flew up anyway. The plane he was aboard was shot down on the approach and everyone aboard it was killed.

It was madness, but the R&R schedule was maintained despite the danger inherent in getting out and back. We had to send people out regularly to conduct important business in the rear, but I thought it was madness to risk life and limb for a little "liaison" in Singapore or Hong Kong. Or was it? I don't know that anyone turned down his leave.

Sergeant Ric Bender, the Lima supply sergeant, was on his way back from a foraging expedition in the rear when he met up with a Lima Company corpsman who was on his way back from R&R. The two decided to travel together, but they got nowhere for a few days because the flights they hopped up to Khe Sanh were canceled or had to abort because of heavy incoming. It was a typical homecoming story; troops always tried to get to Khe Sanh, but the system was imprecise. After awhile, the corpsman admitted to Bender that he had "a bad feeling" and that "I just don't want to go back up there." Bender counseled him—"Hey, you gotta go up there; you'll be a deserter if you don't."—but the corpsman persisted: "I really feel bad about this. I just don't want to go up." Bender couldn't talk the doc into continuing the journey with him, so he left him in Danang and advised him to return when he felt up to it. Bender arrived safely, but the doc never reported in. We investigated and eventually learned that he had pulled himself together and had followed a day or two behind Bender. The doc was aboard the same plane as the supply officer, and he perished.

C H A P T E R *28*

*O*ne day toward the end of March, near the close of my ninth full month in-country, Major Loughran tracked me down and asked, "Hey, Dick, how'd you like to be an aide?"

"To who, sir?"

"I don't know, but a message just came out asking for volunteers from the Third Division who want to be a general's aide. You should apply."

"Aye, aye, sir! What the hell does an aide do?"

"Well, I don't know, but how'd you like to do it?"

"Major, I'll do anything to get out of here."

*F*ive or six days after my talk with Major Loughran, by which time I had forgotten about the offer, one of the radiomen got a hold of me and said, "Hey, Skipper, you got a message and orders to report to Dong Ha for an interview to be an aide."

The only problem was that I had to leave that day and it was about 1000 before the radioman tracked me down. It was the worst possible time of day to try to get a flight out of Khe Sanh because it was precisely the time the fog lifted and the NVA mortars routinely dusted us off. I was undecided for a few minutes, but I finally came down on the side of risk; it was now or never. I told the exec I was leaving right away.

"Hell, Dick, you can't go down to the big city looking like that. You at least need to put on clean clothes."

Who would have thought? After three months in the mud and filth of Khe Sanh, I no longer noticed my down-at-the-heels appearance, or anyone else's, for we all looked the same. I had no spare utilities, no clothing that wasn't permeated by Khe Sanh's distinctive red dust. I put out a five-alarm plea and someone finally came up with a clean set of utilities that looked like they might fit. The trick, however, was finding a place clean enough to change clothes.

After searching the battalion area, I finally wound up standing right on top of the CP bunker, where I removed my filthy trousers and very gingerly pulled on the fresh pair. So far so good; I still knew how to dress myself. But I no sooner got the trousers zipped and buttoned than *swish . . . boom*—a large-caliber artillery round fell to earth just outside the nearby base wire. For some reason, I thought it might be a friendly round. Shit, I couldn't believe it!

I ran around to the entrance to the Battalion CP bunker and yelled, "Jesus Christ, who the hell is calling in artillery?"

"Oh, don't worry about it," Matt Caulfield replied, "It's being called in by One-Nine, from out at the Rock Quarry. Their FO thinks he sees some people moving up on our wire, but it's too close for air."

"Goddamn, 'close' is right! Are you sure they're observing?"

"Yes," Matt smiled. "Don't sweat it. It's observed fire."

So I calmed down and climbed back up to the top of the bunker, where I began struggling to get my gear packed. *Swish . . . Boom.* Another impact, and this time two Marines inside the wire were hit by shrapnel. I stalked off the top of the bunker and pushed my way inside. "Goddamn it! Two Marines were just hit by One-Nine's goddamn observed fire. Get on the goddamn radio and tell those SOBs they just got two confirmed WIAs. Tell them Captain Camp says, 'Good shooting.' "

Our senior FO indeed barged into the net and got the shooting turned off. When I knew it was safe, I retrieved my gear from topside, finished packing, and walked straight across the combat base toward the Regimental CP. I neglected to put on my flak jacket because it was filthy and would have dirtied my clean utility blouse, but I had it ready. As always, I had my helmet under my arm so I could hear the sound of incoming. My variation on the Khe Sanh Shuffle was guided by my supreme effort to step around the many muddy places.

I finally reached the Landing Support Agency, which regulated egress from the combat base, and I asked the first Marine I found, "Hey, where's the manifesting place? Where do you go to get the hell out of there?" He pointed to a nearby bunker and I walked over and looked in. Right inside the door was a hole that seemed to be thirty feet deep. A Marine was down there, working at a little desk. "Hey," I called down, "I got orders to get out of here."

The Marine looked up and his voice echoed back, "Okay, here's your ticket."

I climbed down the stairway, certain it might lead to the seventh level of Hell. When I got to the bottom of the pit, I saw that a pretty big bunker stretched out behind the desk. The bunker was wall-to-wall with bored-looking Marines.

I grabbed the piece of paper the Marine behind the desk was offering me. It had a number on it—255.

"What the hell's 'two-fifty-five,' " I asked.

"Sir, that's your number to get out of here."

It took a full five seconds for that to sink through my stupefaction. "What the hell! You mean I have to wait down here until two hundred and fifty-four Marines have gone ahead of me?"

"Yessir," the clerk replied as his eyes clouded over. Clearly, he had had this conversation before.

"So, what happens when my number comes up?"

"Well, you go topside, sir, and wait behind the blast wall. You grab whatever comes in, a helo or a C-123. Just run out and jump aboard after it unloads and before it takes off. The crew chief will let you know if it's full up."

"You mean, even if there's incoming?"

The Marine grinned. "Yessir, *especially* if there's incoming. We never get anything in here that doesn't draw incoming, sir."

"Corporal, is there any way to speed things up?"

"Oh, yessir, sure is. You could go on down to Charlie-Med and volunteer to help carry a litter aboard a helo or a plane. Casualties get top priority, then we start filling up planes from here. You help with a litter, you almost always get out on the same bird."

I turned on my heel, climbed out of the bunker, and hustled straight down to the big Charlie-Med triage bunker, which was beside the helo pad. I collared the first corpsman who ran across my path. "Doc, what's the score? You got any casualties going out?"

The doc looked me up and down, saw my willy-pete bag, knew right off I wanted out of Khe Sanh, and said, "Goddamn, sir, you just missed one! Why don't you wait over in the doctors' bunker? We'll call you first thing." I asked for directions and he led me next door, to where the surgeons lived. If anything, that bunker was fifty feet underground and roofed and sandbagged like it was meant to last a thousand years. I must have walked down fifty steps just to get inside. The doctors were sitting along one bulkhead, all decked out in surgical gowns, waiting for a call to action from the squawk box hooked up to the triage bunker. The doctors welcomed me and offered me a cup of coffee.

I had been waiting down there for about forty-five minutes when, all of a sudden, the corpsman from the triage bunker yelled down, "Hey, Skipper, come on over quick. We got an emergency medevac and there's a chopper inbound." I grabbed all my gear and flew out of there. When I staggered to the distant surface, I got my bearings and ran straight over to the triage bunker, where a pair of corpsmen were kneeling beside an ARVN Ranger who had an abdominal wound serious enough to rate an emergency medevac, the highest life-or-death priority.

Quickly, seven other Marines materialized. Two were sporting bandages, but they appeared to be ambulatory. To four of us, one of the corpsman brusquely ordered, "Okay, you guys grab the stretcher and get below this blast wall," indicating a little sandbag wall, about four feet high.

We grabbed the stretcher, pulled it behind the blast wall, and hunkered down beside it. Quickly, a seriously wounded Marine on another stretcher materialized from the triage bunker, and the other four Marines from my group pulled him over behind the blast wall. They were no sooner done than a CH-46 helicopter set down.

I believe we set the Olympic record for stretcher hauling. I was aboard the helo before I knew I was on my feet.

As soon as the crew chief had lashed the stretchers to the deck, I jumped down in a seat right behind the flight deck. I was ready to get out of there, but the chopper just sat there and sat there—and sat there and sat there. The longer it sat there, the more nervous I became. By the time it finally took off, I thought it might be the twenty-first century. By then, I had my helmet right down around my ankles.

After we lifted off, as I pushed stale air from my lungs, I realized that instead of heading right down the valley back toward Dong Ha, the goddamn helicopter was circling. I stood up and looked over the pilot's shoulder to see what was what. I was stunned speechless when I saw that we were circling right over the parachute-resupply drop zone between Lima Company and 1/9's position out at the Rock Quarry.

I knew damn well that the NVA had the zone covered by at least one .51-caliber machine gun, and I knew they opened fire every time anyone flew over. I couldn't stand it. I hit the pilot on the shoulder, screamed in his ear, "Machine gun! Machine gun," and pointed down through his windshield. He was startled, but he finally got the message. It was like being on an elevator racing to the top of the world's tallest building. I was pushed right down into my seat as we went straight up to what seemed like the two thousandth floor.

Then—I couldn't believe it—we landed back at Khe Sanh. By the time we settled to the ground, I was a nervous wreck. The rear ramp went down and the crew chief motioned for the five uninjured enlisted Marines to get out. I tried to make myself inconspicuous. I was going to be next; I just knew it. Then, from out of nowhere, five full body bags appeared on the deck. The five Marines who had loaded the bodies climbed back aboard, the ramp closed, the engines ran up to take-off power, and we leaped back into the sky. This time, we angled down, away from the Khe Sanh plateau, straight into Dong Ha.

As soon as I wobbled off the helo, I asked my way to the 3rd Marine Division Forward CP and reported in at the G-1's office. I told the colonel what I was in for and he told me I needed to catch a helo down to Phu Bai, which is where the general who needed an aide was conducting interviews. I was bending down to grab my gear, but the colonel said, "We can't get you a flight until tomorrow morning, but you're welcome to stay right here overnight. If you want, you can join me in the Commanding General's Mess for dinner." Less than an hour out of Khe Sanh and I was already facing impossible choices. "What the hell, Colonel, I guess I can make it." He briefly gave me a strange look but joined in my belated chuckle.

Late that afternoon I presented myself at a larger-than-usual SEA hut, a truly impressive structure with a Stateside-quality paint job. The starched and pressed old gunny who was guarding the door checked my name on a clipboard, scrunched up his nose in disapproval at my dress or my rank or both, and reluctantly motioned that I was free to enter.

I walked inside and my mouth dropped open at the sight of a huge table—it was thirty feet long—surrounded by thirty carved wooden chairs, each with a Marine Corps emblem on the back. There was china on the table, and glassware, and linen napkins—and cut flowers!

I was absolutely flabbergasted. The room was packed with starched and pressed officers. Except for the commanding general's aide, also a captain, I was the lowest rank in the room. There were more colonels than I had ever seen in one place, and hordes of lieutenant colonels and majors. I immediately found a little place off to the side, where I hoped nobody would see me. When we sat down for dinner, I plunked myself in a chair at the far end of the table, between two mere majors. The steak the steward set in front of me was almost bigger than the plate, the first real food I had seen since Hawaii.

So there I was, on my first evening out of Khe Sanh, a nondescript and, I hoped, unnoticed guest, but one who nonetheless was being wined and dined at the Commanding General's Mess. As I got up the nerve to look around the table, I inadvertently made eye contact with a really tough-looking colonel who, I found out later, was Colonel William Dick, the 3rd Marine Division chief of staff. He looked so tough he half scared me to death. As our eyes connected, he called, "Come here, Captain."

I walked over and sat down, as instructed by a wave of his arm, in the empty chair beside him. "What are you down here for?" I told him. "Oh"—he seemed surprised—"Well, how much longer have you got to do in-country?"

"Oh," I gulped, "About four months, Colonel."

"Well, you're going to have to extend."

"Sir," I admitted, "I'm really not that big on the idea of extending."

"Well, then," he said in a low tone tinged with an edge of dismissal, "there's no way you're gonna be the aide. You better think it over because you're gonna be asked officially to extend."

I felt my shoulders drop, but I decided to be truthful. "Sir, I just don't think I'm going to do it."

Colonel Dick looked at me with a sidelong glance and said, "Well, you'll be given the opportunity to change your mind."

Next morning, I flew on down to Phu Bai and, as instructed, found my way to the huge building with three wings that housed what was then called Provisional Corps, Vietnam. The PCV, as it was known, was being established because at least two Army divisions were being moved into the I Corps region and a structure thus was needed to stand between MACV, in Saigon, the Marine-run III Marine Amphibious Force. The PCV commander was an Army lieutenant general and the newly appointed deputy commander was a Marine major general. I was being considered for the position of aide to the Marine general, Major General Raymond Davis.

I found the PCV G-1, an Army colonel, and told him why I was there. He said, "Roger," and motioned me out of his office. I waited in the passageway for quite awhile, until the colonel came out, pointed to a closed door up the passageway, and said, "Okay, go right on into General Davis's office for the interview."

I had only a vague awareness then of who Major General Ray Davis was. I vaguely recalled that he was considered a Marine's Marine and had earned the Medal of Honor in the Korean War. As I soon found out, Raymond Gilbert Davis had been commissioned as an artilleryman in 1938 and, as a captain, had commanded a special weapons (antitank) battery at Guadalcanal. By late 1944, he was a major commanding an infantry battalion at Peleliu and, in 1950, he was a lieutenant colonel commanding an infantry battalion in the drive from Inchon to Seoul. In late November and early December 1950, Lieutenant Colonel Ray Davis led his battalion on an independent march to rescue an isolated, surrounded, and snowbound Marine infantry company and thus secure a vital hill overlooking the main supply route for more than half of the embattled and retreating 1st Marine Division. His leadership in the march and the attack was so extraordinary that he was awarded a Medal of Honor.

Before I entered General Davis's office for the interview, I had never met or even seen him, and I knew none of the details of his remarkable career.

I walked through the door and stood at attention. A short, burly

Marine major general was seated behind a desk piled high with papers and maps. The general looked up, smiled pleasantly, and pointed to a chair beside my left leg. I sat down but held my body at attention. His eyes were locked on my eyes.

I sat there and he threw questions at me—left, right, left right—like body blows. He seemed to be a scrappy character, very self-assured, but very pleasant. He had a southern drawl, but not too pronounced. He seemed genuinely interested in me—not just in my answers, in my performance, but in me.

He got into my background—into my recon work and my tour at Marine Barracks, Washington. I told him I had been an infantry-company commander for six months and was the 3-Alpha of an infantry battalion. General Davis asked, "Where did you operate," and I re-plied, "All over the Third Division area, sir, from Khe Sanh to Con Thien to Leatherneck Square. The whole shooting match, sir."

The whole interview couldn't have lasted twenty minutes. He said, "Okay, Captain, that's all," and I walked out of there. I had no idea whether it had gone good, bad, or indifferent. He had told me before dismissing me that he had another candidate coming in from the 1st Marine Division. He said he would interview him as soon as he arrived and that he would make an immediate decision.

My first thought on the way back to the G-1's office was, "Where the hell can I ambush the guy from First Division?" But, lo and behold, the other captain never showed up. Sometime that afternoon, the general told the G-1, "Bring Captain Camp in." When we arrived in front of General Davis's desk, he said, "I think you got the job. Do you want it?"

"Yessir!"

"Very well then. It's yours." He never asked me to extend.

As I walked out of General Davis's office, it occurred to me that I had no idea what the hell an aide did. I didn't even know where I was supposed to work. I didn't know where I was supposed to live. I didn't know where my seabag was. I didn't know what I was supposed to wear. I didn't know what weapons I was supposed to carry.

I didn't know a damn thing about my new job, but I knew one thing—I didn't have to go back to Khe Sanh.

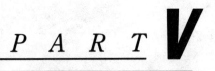

PART V

EPILOGUE

*G*eneral Davis served as the deputy commander of the Provisional Corps, Vietnam, and its successor, XXIV Army Corps, for two months in the early spring of 1968. During that time, I traveled everywhere in I Corps with him, often in the thick of battles undertaken by the 1st and 3rd Marine divisions and the Army's elite 1st Cavalry (Airmobile) and 101st Airborne divisions. In May 1968, General Davis assumed command of the 3rd Marine Division and from then until I rotated home, on schedule, I accompanied him on daily tours of all the regiments and most of the battalions under his command. We spent most nights in the field, so, though I never gave up hope, the general and I ate very few meals in the beautifully appointed 3rd Marine Division Commanding General's Mess. Ray Davis wasn't the type.

Throughout the remainder of my tour, I was privileged and awed to be a step away from one of the sharpest minds and bravest leaders I have ever seen in action.

The Siege of Khe Sanh ended with a sort of a whimper during the first week of April 1968, a few weeks after I started working for General Davis. The Marines claimed they broke the siege by attacking NVA positions outside the base and the Army's 1st Cavalry Division claims it broke the siege by throwing numerous aggressive airmobile assaults into the hills overlooking the combat base. In reality, the NVA broke the siege by leaving.

Ray Davis spent all his time as a deputy corps commander learning the way things were in I Corps. It was obvious to me when he assumed command of the 3rd Marine Division that he had absorbed an enormous amount of information and, more important, had drawn conclusions compatible with his incredible fighting spirit. The entire time I served at his side in 3rd Marine Division—I regret today that it was not longer—I saw a transformation in the unit I can still hardly believe. Previously "maneuver" battalions in name only, the twelve infantry battalions comprising the reinforced division virtually abandoned the support bases and lived and worked and killed NVA and VC in the field. Heads rolled. Oh my, how they rolled. Fire eaters of the Korean War—men who had earned their spurs as lieutenants and captains at Pusan, Inchon, and the Chosin Reservoir—found themselves relieved of their battalion and regimental commands because they had become afraid of the fire or merely complacent. The quality of the division rose and real progress in our area of operations became obvious. Morale was so high it almost deserved a new rating system.

It was an inspiring period of my life, perhaps the most inspiring behind my tour as a Marine combat infantry-company commander.

Major Joe Loughran, a wonderful human being and truly a good friend, was killed by a booby trap in May 1968 while on a patrol with the battalion. Word was that Joe opened his flak jacket because of the heat and, when he set off the booby trap, shrapnel penetrated his chest. I felt Joe's death deeply at the time and I feel it deeply now.

I left Vietnam exactly on schedule, whole and uplifted—and very, very happy to be out of there. To my utter amazement and profound pleasure, I sat next to Little John Prince during the entire arduous flight from Danang to California. For no reason either of us could fathom, for it was against the rules, Little John had served every day of his tour, except the first few and last few, as the commander of Lima Company's 2nd Platoon. During the long flight, we exchanged stories about many of our close calls, but we reveled in the fact that neither of us had been harmed beyond a few shrapnel scratches.

I last met up with Little John at Sergeant Ric Bender's wedding in Chicago several years after we all left Vietnam, and I have occasionally run into Lima Company Marines over the years, for many stayed in the Marine Corps. I am sad to report that, after they left Vietnam, I never again saw or even heard of Jaak Aulik, Dan Frazer, Larry Bratton, David Johnson, Donald Vogt, Tom Biondo, or Marvin Bailey. I know they all survived, so it is my fervent prayer that they—and all my Marines and corpsmen—have lived prosperous and happy lives.

Of the many officers of 3/26 who stayed in the Marine Corps after the war, many did very well. As of this writing, Carl Mundy is a lieutenant general on active duty and Matt Caulfield is a major general. Andy DeBona stayed in but was medically retired as a lieutenant colonel following a bout with cancer. Andy was expected to succumb quickly to the cancer, but years later he is still roving the United States in a motor home, visiting old friends and fishing in all the best places.

*T*hanks in part to my association with General Davis, whose path I crossed from time to time over the years, I was afforded the opportunity to attend some of the Marine Corps' best professional courses and, indeed, to teach new lieutenants at the Basic School. I commanded two other infantry companies during my years as a captain, but I never again served in combat.

As a young major, I served as the head of a regional recruiting station, the precursor of many recruiting assignments during the second half of my career. In the late 1970s, I served as an infantry-battalion executive officer on a peacetime cruise in the Mediterranean and on a Joint Chiefs of Staff team in Iran shortly before the overthrow of the Shah. As a lieutenant colonel, I commanded a Marine Corps recruit training battalion in the mid 1980s, and, as a colonel, I served as the director of a Marine Corps recruiting district and as the operations officer of the entire Marine Corps recruiting effort.

I retired from the Marine Corps as a colonel in July 1988, following more than twenty-six years of continuous active service. In all those years, no position I held was as vital or as rewarding as my half-year command of Lima Company, 3rd Battalion, 26th Marines—and nothing any fellow Marine has ever called me means more than "Lima-6."

B I B L I O G R A P H Y

Hammel, Eric. *Khe Sanh: Siege in the Clouds, an Oral History.* New York: Crown Publishers, 1989.

Shore, Captain Moyers S. *The Battle for Khe Sanh.* Washington, D.C.: Marine Corps Historical Division, 1963.

Telfer, Major Gary, Lieutenant Colonel Lane Rogers, and V. Keith Fleming. *U.S. Marines in Vietnam: Fighting the North Vietnamese, 1967.* Washington, D.C.: Marine Corps Historical Division, 1984.

Official documents consulted include the Command Chronologies of the 3rd Battalion, 26th Marines, for the months of June 1967 through March 1968, inclusive, and the 3rd Battalion, 26th Marines, Unit Diary for the month of September 1967.

I N D E X